FAMILY WEALTH

*Being Strategic About
Your Family Legacy*

TONY JEARY - The RESULTS Guy™
&
JOSEPH J. JANICZEK, MSFS, ChFC

Clovercroft Publishing

Family Wealth

©2017 by Tony Jeary and Joseph J. Janiczek

Published by Clovercroft Publishing, Franklin, Tennessee.

Scriptures taken from the Holy Bible, New International Version®, NIV®. Copyright © 1973, 1978, 1984, 2011 by Biblica, Inc.™ Used by permission of Zondervan. All rights reserved worldwide. www.zondervan.com The "NIV" and "New International Version" are trademarks registered in the United States Patent and Trademark Office by Biblica, Inc.™

Cover Design by Brooke Hawkins

Interior Design by Suzanne Lawing

Edited by Nonie Jobe

Printed in the United States of America

978-1-945507-37-3

Contents

Foreword

PAIGE JEARY (AGE 20)

I am very thankful for my dad, Tony Jeary, who helped guide me in decisions and direction in my life. He did a great job at pouring a great amount of knowledge into my life. He is very knowledgeable and always there to answer a question or suggest that we Google to find the answer. For example, a few weeks ago I had a question on taxes and he sat me down and summed up taxes in about thirty minutes.

One of my favorite things that he did was show me the world. Our family has traveled all around the United States and to other countries such as Australia, Costa Rica, Puerto Rico, Mexico, France, Greece, Italy, and many more. This exposed me to multiple cultures that I really appreciate now. I think it is very important to see the world from others' perspective, and traveling was a great way to do that. He encourages me to continue to travel throughout my life.

I feel blessed to have received a good education. My dad paid for me to attend a Christian college preparatory school, Liberty Christian, from pre-school through my senior year. Then, he paid for me to attend Baylor University. The mission trips I went on to Guatemala, El Salvador, and Panama were paid in full by my parents. These trips and schools helped transform and strengthen my walk with the Lord.

Connections were a theme that my dad taught me. A quote my dad said that stuck with me is, "It's not about the grades you make, but the number of hands you shake." I have learned the power of personal connections. He has helped one of my best friends from college line up an internship with a large international company. When we travel he always gives away free books that he has personally signed to the managers or concierges. Each year, my dad helps me set goals for the next year to help me improve each year.

Growing up in a Christian home built a strong foundation for my life. I knew my parents always had my back and the best intentions in mind. I have learned a plethora of things from my parents throughout the years.

Love,
Paige Jeary

JOHN J. JANICZEK AND MARGARET L. HANNUM

Our parents never helped us with homework. Then again, we never asked! From our parent's example, which we were able to observe from the periphery, we both had a strong sense of what it meant to be doing our own work, taking pride in it, learning on our own, and taking advantage of our time in school from a very early age. We feel very grateful that our parents encouraged education, independence, and autonomy. The legacy our parents left us has supported us in forging our own path!

While most of our early memories of dad's financial advisory business are literally sugar-coated (we have very fond early memories of his bringing home treats from seminars he put on while building up his business), we were also able to benefit from what he learned helping hundreds of families he encountered in a financial capacity. Through hearing about his work throughout the years, we think some financial lessons were just naturally transferred over to us (for example, both of us have successfully avoided any form of credit card debt).

Overall, there has been a respect on both sides of the person each of us in our family has become, as well as encouragement on the pieces we are still figuring out. It hasn't been perfect, of course—no family is—but developing open communication with our parents has been an essential and treasured part of our lives, and we will be happy to carry on their legacy of hard work, kindness, generosity, and love.

After all, there is something about family that is spectacular. Our mother's extended family, including second-cousins-twice-removed, get together every so often for an event known as "McNerneyfest." We look back at our family gatherings, impressed that so many people who see each other once every two years can feel so comfortable together as to have a talent show of singing, dancing, and even circus tricks.

We hope this book will help the readers think about the things they care most about and open some wonderful conversations with their own families to help them grow closer.

John J. Janiczek
Margaret L. Hannum
Children of Joseph & Mary Janiczek

Introduction

We all have a legacy, and yet many of us fail to intentionally and strategically plan what our legacy will be, especially as it pertains to our families. Is your legacy important to you? Do you know what you will be passing down in terms of legacy to your children, your grandchildren, and even beyond? Are you taking the steps now to ensure your legacy plays out the way you want?

Making an indelible, positive mark on your loved ones, an impact so profound that it naturally lives on, is an honorable goal and the laser-focused subject of this book. We want everything you've done—building a successful life and meaningful fortune, persevering through great challenges and opportunities, and making the world a better place—to continue when you're gone from this world, and you probably do as well.

We want this book to be a tool that will open your mind to the idea of being strategic about how you want to pass on your wealth to the following generations. It's about much more than money. Wealth, under our definition, includes:

- Monetary items, such as:
  - Investments
  - Companies
  - Interests

- Non-monetary items, such as:
  - Wisdom (including thinking, principles, and standards)
  - Reputation/brand
  - Contacts (business contacts and your "Life Team")

- Intellectual property
- Philanthropy
- Methodology
- Capabilities (including skills, knowledge, processes, and systems)
- Spiritual understanding and formation
- Mindsets
- Values
- Work ethics
- Beliefs

• Other desirable advantages, such as:
- High levels of confidence
- Trust
- Self-esteem
- Humility
- Connections
- Commitments
- Habits

Families who see financial resources as only one part of an abundant life are more likely to pinpoint and transmit essential, life-enhancing values and wisdom over time and successfully pass down their all-encompassing wealth.

In this book we'll be talking specifically about the family aspect of legacy, which we've defined as a gift handed down to your family that could include all the things we listed above.

Legacy can certainly be looked at in a much broader way than family. In addition to your family legacy, you may in fact make an indelible mark in your community, industry, profession, church, or even world. Steve Jobs, famed founder of Apple and Pixar, for example, made profound, long-lasting marks in computers, smartphones, apps, animated movies, and the music industry. In this book, we decided to purposely isolate the topic to family legacy so you can concentrate on this very important and often-neglected dimension of legacy building.

At this point, you may be wondering why you should listen to us about how to build your family legacy. First, we would not be able to offer you advice on how to build a legacy for your family if we had not lived out what we are saying. We asked our children to write the Foreword for this book so they could share their perspective of how the truths and techniques we present in this book have been passed down from us to them. Second, we want you to know that we've both dedicated a large part of our lives to helping people be better, influencing their lives, and sharpening their thinking, including thinking strategically about their family legacies. We've both been in the trenches with people for decades; and when you're in the trenches as an advisor, you're in a very honorable position where people share their most intimate life situations and problems and goals and achievements. We've been there with them through the different stages within the timeline of the family—births, childhood, college, adulthood, marriage, early career, mid/late career, early-retirement, long-retired, assisted living, end of life, and everything in between. Our goal with this book is to help you be better positioned to make strategic legacy decisions at each of these stages.

BACKGROUNDS

Tony grew up in an entrepreneurial family, and as a young man he began establishing and operating a number of extremely profitable entrepreneurial ventures. He actually beat his goal of becoming a millionaire by the age of twenty-five by two years. Then when the market changed and he lost it all, he stepped back and asked, *What do I truly want to do with my life?* As he explored the various possibilities and continued to challenge his own thinking, he realized that he actually wanted to be an advisor to impact people and help them be more successful, using as a launching pad the experiences and lessons he had learned. That's when he started on his life's journey of studying, accumulating, and learning best practices.

Years of focus from his early-adult experience enabled Tony to become a highly successful executive coach, public speaker, and author of over forty-five books, including several best sellers. After he started coaching the president of Walmart, others began saying, "He must be good!" Tony's clients include the presidents of Walmart, Sam's Club, Samsung, Ford, Firestone, and TGI Fridays, and even people from the

Forbes Richest 400, as well as the Sergeant-at-Arms of the US Senate.

Today, top performers and their teams from around the globe fly to Tony's headquarters in Dallas, Texas, to be coached. Tony helps them shape their visions and develop focus so they can more efficiently execute. His signature book, *Strategic Acceleration* (Perseus 2009), is the best-selling book that teaches how to get accelerated results through his proven formula: Clarity, Focus, and Execution. Another of his books, *Life is a Series of Presentations* (Simon and Schuster 2004), was recently recommended by Daymond John from *Shark Tank*. From John's perspective, Tony's book ranks right up there with *Think and Grow Rich* and *Who Moved My Cheese*.

In many respects, Joseph's life has paralleled Tony's. He, too, was very interested in business success from a very young age, wondering in particular why some people were more successful than others. Like Tony, he pursued opportunities ambitiously. He had not one, but three, paper routes at a time as a child. He founded an oil company when he was seventeen, and in his early twenties he invented the first conventional motor oil with high-endurance features, designed for annual oil changes. In his mid-twenties he went on to found and lead (to this day) a wealth management company that has been named multiple times among the top, best, and most exclusive wealth advisors and managers in the nation.[1] Janiczek Wealth Management, headquartered in Denver, Colorado, serves high net-worth investors

---

[1] Ranked/Named among Top, Best and Most Exclusive Advisors sources: Barron's March 2017, 2016, 2015, 2014; Advisory HQ March 2016; Financial Times June 2015; Five Star Professional November 2015, 2013, 2012,2011, 2010, 2009; Mutual Funds Magazine January 2001; NABCAP September 2010, 2011, 2013; Worth Magazine July 2002, January 2004, October 2004, October 2008; Wealth & Finance International, October 2014. Rankings and/or recognition by unaffiliated rating services and/or publications should not be construed by a client or prospective client as a guarantee that he/she will experience a certain level of results if Janiczek & Company, Ltd. is engaged, or continues to be engaged, to provide investment advisory services, nor should it be construed as a current or past endorsement of Janiczek & Company, Ltd. by any of its clients. Rankings published by magazines, and others, generally base their selections exclusively on information prepared and/or submitted by the recognized adviser. A copy of the Janiczek & Company, Ltd. written disclosure statement discussing our advisory services and fees is available upon request. Go to www.janiczek.com for more details or call 303-721-7000.

(those with $2 million to $20 million portfolios) and ultra-high net-worth investors (those with $20 million-plus porttfolios) across the country and remains Joseph's ever-growing enterprise, of which he remains as the CEO and majority shareholder.

An avid inventor, Joseph holds the patent on Systems and Methods for Optimizing Wealth and has many trademarked and copyrighted tools, techniques, and processes for mastering wealth. He is the award-winning author of *Absolute Financial Freedom* (Prosperity Press 2001), and he also authored *Investing from a Position of Strength* (Prosperity Press 2010). He is a pioneer in the disciplines of Strength-Based Wealth Management and Evidence-Based Investing and a long advocate for individual investors, dedicating his firm to the high standard of fee-only, fiduciary advice.

When Joseph and Tony connected, both realized that their individual visions and life work shared much common ground, especially when it came to helping other people build a legacy for their families. This book is the result of their collaboration.

WHO THIS BOOK IS FOR

We want to be crystal clear from the beginning about who this book is tailored toward. As we collaborated in the formative stages, we came to the realization that the ideal candidate for reading and gaining the most out of this book has eight mindsets and/or life circumstances that happen to match our own:

1. You have a strong, noticeably unquenchable desire and sense of duty to help others—first and foremost the next generations of your family.

2. You have decent, open, honest, and respectful relationships with all or most of your children.

3. You feel pretty strongly that your perseverance, hard work, lessons learned, and life experiences resulted in some uncommon knowledge and wisdom that you would hate to see lost (not passed on for the benefit of your loved ones).

4. You've built some excess financial resources, contacts, and

knowledge that you want to utilize in your lifetime to strategically help your kids and grandkids without spoiling them or taking them away from their own life ambition and healthy struggle.

5. When you and your spouse pass on, you would like for your heirs to be optimally prepared and equipped to be good, resourceful stewards of the wealth and other assets you pass down to them.

6. You feel outright horrible when you see a family member battling with things you have acquired some life lessons and wisdom around, and you seek to better share such learning with them so they need not waste time and resources finding every solution on their own.

7. You recognize your mortality (you will not live forever), and you seek to make a long-lasting, indelible mark on your loved ones' lives.

8. You have a faith life and seek to integrate this in with all of the above. Note: We both have deep Christian faith beliefs, and in this book we unabashedly and openly share how we integrate this component into our family legacy activities.

MENTORING

In Tony's book *Advice Matters,* he talks about the wisdom of listening to people who have successfully gone where you want to go and are willing to share their advice and counsel with you. We have both intentionally sought out mentors and coaches over the years who have guided us and helped us do life and business better. Through this book, we want to mentor you, if you will, by sharing the concepts and principles we've developed over the years that will help you devise the best plan to pass on to your family the things that are important to you.

Tony teaches that his *Strategic Acceleration* formula—Clarity, Focus and Execution—are the three legs of the stool of getting the right results you want faster. It certainly applies here. You must be clear on the outcomes you want. You must focus on the things that matter, and of course you must take executable actions accordingly. Being clear and focused about what you want for your family will help you execute the specific things you could or should do that we talk about in Part Two of the book.

Joseph's wealth of knowledge and experience in helping clients build optimal levels of financial strength and security can also be applied to *living* from the position of strength and passing that strength down to your family. Similarly, becoming "unleashed from the complexity of wealth so you can flourish with your good fortune" is a desirable outcome for the family patriarch and matriarch and each generation beyond. He will teach you how to harness and utilize wealth in the right ways—to fuel your family legacy—and how to guide your kids to be super-resourceful stewards of what they have, whether that's a small, mid-sized, or large amount. Equally as important, you'll learn how to do this in a way that doesn't take all of your time and effort. We are both proponents of finding what Tony has coined as *Elegant Solutions* (and what Joseph calls the Essential 15%), achieving multiple objectives with the least amount of effort.

As we live life, we learn and we course-correct; and as we course-correct, we get more definition and intentional commitment. Then we continue refining, because the world, our lives, and our family stages are constantly changing. Because we've both been around this for so many decades, it is our hope that putting this book together as a tool for you to use in building your family legacy will make a significant impact on you and your heirs. Your biggest obstacle to building the legacy you've always wanted is simply not being aware of what it takes to do so.

COMMON MISTAKES/EXCUSES FOR NOT STRATEGICALLY BUILDING A FAMILY LEGACY

As critically important as it is for families to successfully preserve all aspects of their wealth for future generations, there are some who don't understand the significance of building a family legacy and who offer up mistaken ideas or excuses why it can't or shouldn't be done. Maybe that's where you are. As you read this list, you may say, "Yes, these are legitimate objections that have stopped me or held me back," or "Yes, these really hit home; they're some of the same things I'm concerned about."

General Excuses:
- Our parents didn't focus on this, and we all turned out fine.
- I believe our children need to learn how to solve problems on their own, and any help from us just makes them weaker and/or more dependent on us.
- I don't have a clue about how to go about this.
- I don't have enough wealth to really worry about this. Family legacy matters are for the ultra-high net-worth.

Excuses during your kids' childhood:
- I think parents who try too hard to impose their beliefs on their children end up raising either rebellious kids or brainwashed kids, and neither are desirable to me.
- Between church, school, activities, and family time, we cover quite a bit of our values, religion, and work ethic. This is plenty; I don't see why we should go any further.

Excuses when kids are adults and out of the house:
- I did all I could during their childhood, and that was enough.
- Our adult kids are so busy with their own jobs, careers, kids, etc. that they have no real time or interest to learn from or listen to us.
- They are married adults living their own lives now. It's not my place to impose.
- Any financial help I have sent their way has been quickly blown. I'm quite concerned that they are not resourceful with gifts of money—or knowledge.
- They have left our church, joined the exact opposite political party, and think we are off base in all we do. We don't see the opportunity to gain traction in building a family legacy with them.
- I simply don't have the ear or respect of my kids anymore.

If we're articulating some of the things you've felt, then take heart. With the book you have in your hands, we'll help you not only get excited about the beautiful legacy you can build (or further shape) for your family, but we'll also give you specific steps you can take to make it happen.

HOW THIS BOOK IS ORGANIZED

The book is divided into three parts. Part One is the "What and the Why." As we delve into the concept of family legacy and how you can build a meaningful and lasting legacy for your family, we encourage you begin with the end in mind and start thinking about that golden nugget you want to pass down to your heirs.

Part Two, Best Practices for Creating a Great Family Legacy (The How), has five chapters. Chapter One will highlight the strategic impact of proactive communication within a family. Communication is truly a cornerstone of family legacy. High-level, thought-filled communication is the foundation of trusting relationships. Communication leads to collaboration, and collaboration leads to new ideas and better preparation for the impending wealth transfer to the next generation. We'll discuss the powerful influence that family mission statements can have on your legacy, especially when they are intentionally and strategically discussed and lived out on a daily basis. Tony will personally share how he and his wife built a family mission statement when his kids were four and seven, and how that's had such a positive impact that you may want to consider modeling it.

In Chapter Two we address the people aspect of your family legacy. We'll talk about the importance of having the right people in your lives. We also discuss the wisdom of building a life team to support you and your family, and the power of passing along to your kids the contacts and relationships you've spent a lifetime nourishing and developing. Also, we will address the nuances of expanding your legacy to new additions to your family, such as inlaws (the spouses of your kids) and, of course, grandchildren.

Chapter Three will cover the intellectual capital you can pass on to your children as you define, model, and pass on your values; create and implement strong family standards; find your family's rhythm of success through traditions and rituals; and capitalize on truisms and models that can impact your family.

In Chapter Four, we'll cover the all-important financial aspect of family legacy. Here you will learn more on how to best utilize your financial resources to support and fuel your family legacy mission. We will share simple dos, don'ts, dead ends, and fast tracks. You'll discover how financial wealth is the equivalent to powerful, stored-up, highly transferable, and explosive energy and capability. When harnessed and utilized in the right way, it can inspire, cultivate, and ignite greatness. When not, it can create mass destruction and actually negate all other goods and efforts. We will candidly explore the "shirt-sleeves to shirt-sleeves" threat (how the advantages of wealth are commonly squandered in three generations or less) and how to avoid this tragedy. We'll discuss how to master money at all levels, and we'll cover highly refined tools like the Stages of Financial Freedom, the 35 Essential Strengths, and the Family Financial Manifesto, all of which provide the system of success needed to effectively transfer financial resources and wisdom to best serve your family and others.

And finally, in Chapter Five, we'll talk about the importance of passing along your deepest and most important beliefs (spiritual and otherwise) to bring purpose of life, tradition, and unity to your family. We'll look at the impact you can have by modeling lifelong learning, creating positive habits, and using the talents you've been blessed with to live an effective and efficient life. Then we'll take an indepth look at the Four Levels of Happiness, properly ordering the things we desire and pursue by their pervasiveness, endurance, and depth.

In Part Three, the Conclusion, we're going to filter down everything we shared and give you a review of the main points of the book that you can use to rate yourself as you go forward.

By the time you finish the book, we hope you have not only crystalized your thoughts and ideas, but that you have also intentionally and strategically formulated your plan and started acting on it to instantly begin benefiting you and your family.

Graphic Overview

Beliefs	Financial	Intellectual Capital	People	Communication
Be a Lifelong Learner	Understand and Master the Stages of Financial Freedom	Define Model, and Pass on Your Values	Build the Right Communities; Choose the Right Friends	Five Stages of Relationships
Discover and Share Your Greatest Gifts and Talents	Master and Model the 35 Essential Strengths	Create and Implement Strong Family Standards	Build a Great Life Team to Share	Meet Your Family Members Where They Are
Reinforce Meaningful Goals with Powerful Habits	Document and Declare Your Family Financial Manifesto	Find Your Family's Rhythm of Success through Traditions/Rituals	Open Doors with Your Contacts (Rolodex)	Remain Communication Ready to Combat Outside Influences
Recognize and Pursue all Four Levels of Happiness	Support it All with a Complete Legacy Solution	Capitalize on Truisms and Models	Integrate Inlaws and Grandkids into the Legacy	Create Proactive Communication

PART ONE:
The Family Legacy (The What and Why)

The Family Legacy
(The What and Why)

Our legacy is basically the indelible footprint we leave on the earth with those we were able to touch and influence in a certain way—our family members (immediate and extended), friends, co-workers, customers/clients, community, and church.

In this book we will focus specifically on that footprint we leave on our families. As parents, we want the best for our children and their children, and on down the line. We want them to be successful and resourceful in all aspects of their lives. We want them to make good choices. We want them to be good citizens. We want them to be happy and to lead their families in a way that will nurture happiness and success. We want them to benefit from the best of what we learned, grew, stood for, inherited, accumulated, stewarded, and built, and we want them to responsibly steward, build upon, and transfer it to the next generations themselves. And in the process, we would also like for them to make meaningful contributions to the family, to their communities, and to our world, making it a better place for all.

Any discussion on legacy must begin with the end in mind. It's critical to know what you're after as you plan your legacy—what that golden nugget is that you want your legacy to be and how you want it to impact your family members. Consider this, for example: If you could only pass on selected assets, would you choose any of these? If so, why and in what order?

- Money
- Values
- Wisdom
- Connections

What other treasures would you like to pass down to your heirs? Exactly what would you like for your family legacy to be?

As we got together to talk about and put a strategy in place for this book, this is how we described our "golden nugget" for what we want to convey: When you're passing on a strong legacy, you're essentially passing on all of the advantages, all of the hard work, all of the short-cuts, and all of the wisdom that have helped you live a meaningful and successful life, through thick and thin. You're passing all of that on so that the next generation can leverage it and grow from it. It's like the old saying, "Give a man a fish, and you feed him for a day. Teach a man to fish, and you feed him for a lifetime." You want to teach your children and future heirs how to fish rather than just give them the fish; you want to help teach them

> When you're passing on a strong legacy, you're essentially passing on all of the advantages, all of the hard work, all of the short-cuts, and all of the wisdom that have helped you live a meaningful and successful life.

how to operate in life by knowing how to pursue opportunities and solve problems, and how to course-correct quickly when they need to. They need to know how to change and grow and learn and transform across life domains. And it's not just about teaching them what transformation does and how we got there in our own lives; it's also about modeling to our children, grandchildren, and maybe even great-grandchildren, how to powerfully grow and transform throughout life so they intuitively know how to do so themselves. We must do all of this, not in any forced, coerced way; rather, we must do it in a way they willingly seek, embody, and live. We've done it right when they very naturally take our best work, combine it with their own education and life experiences, and go much further with it all than we have.

As you start with the end in mind and consider the golden nugget you want to achieve in building your family legacy, here are a few important questions that we hope will challenge you to strategically think about your legacy on a higher plane:

- Do you have clarity on what you are really pursuing?
- Is lifelong, even eternal, happiness a part of your goals and belief system?
- How do wealth, values, capabilities, and advantages, financial and otherwise, fit into your desired end for your family?
- Can your desired end be obtained by focusing on happiness, achievement, or money alone?

Buckminster Fuller (1895-1983), an American philosopher, architect, humanitarian, visionary, inventor, and author, conceived the idea of the universal Law of Precession, which says that when we pursue a goal, the real reason is in the peripheral (ninety degrees from the target). In other words, there are always side effects at a ninety-degree angle from your actions, which produce results equal to or greater than your original action. Thus, a honey bee goes through life pursuing nectar and making honey, when in fact its true higher purpose is cross pollination.

If you looked at your family legacy in this way, would your thinking be transformed in a way that might lead you to a higher degree of purpose? What if you saw it as though it were intended for a greater good? What would you then want to pass down to your heirs that would both achieve your objectives for your family *and* benefit mankind? Would that alter the choices you make in building your legacy with your family?

We both think beyond worldly success (and even think worldly success, if put in the wrong perspective, could take away from eternal success). What we're saying here is that we all must get crystal clear about our priorities as a part of the process so we don't fall short. And when we do so, beautiful (and yes, unexpected) by-products will materialize in our families and in our world in unanticipated ways. This is one of the fascinating mysteries of a well-lived life and legacy.

Part Two of the book gives specific "how to's" in five different areas that we believe will help you be more effective in building your family legacy. You may already be doing some of them, and there will be others that you may not have considered. There may be some suggestions that are not a fit for you and your family, and that's okay. We hope you will take those that do fit and put them to work to make a great family legacy that becomes the culmination of a life well-lived.

VIPS

- Any discussion on legacy must begin with the end in mind. It's critical to know what you're after as you plan your legacy—what that golden nugget is that you want your legacy to be and how you want it to impact your family members.

- When you're passing on a strong legacy, you're essentially passing on all of the advantages, all of the hard work, all of the short-cuts, and all of the wisdom that have helped you live a meaningful and successful life.

- It's not just about teaching your children and future heirs what transformation does and how we got there in our own lives; it's also about modeling to them how to grow and transform throughout life so they intuitively know how to do so themselves.

- Looking at your family legacy as though it were intended for a greater good could impact what you would want to pass down to your heirs—things that would both achieve your objectives for your family and benefit mankind. (See much more on this in Chapter Five: Beliefs.)

PART TWO:
Best Practices for Creating a Great Family Legacy (The How)

CHAPTER ONE

Communication

Success comes from being specific and proactive; failure often comes from being vague and reactive. That bit of wisdom applies to all pursuits of success, of course, and it's especially true when you're building a family legacy. Communication truly is a cornerstone of family legacy. Being proactive, strategic, and intentional about communicating those things you want to pass down to the generations below you will enhance your chances of success.

FIVE STAGES OF RELATIONSHIPS

Your family environment is constantly adjusting and changing, which obviously creates new opportunities and challenges for communication. There are potentially five stages of relationship with your children, and each stage requires adjustments in the way you communicate:

- When they are living in your home under your parenthood
- When they are transitioning into adulthood
- When they are adults, taking full ownership of their own lives
- When you have grandchildren and are grand-parenting the next generation
- When you start declining in your own ability to manage things

and your children take over and start supporting you

Tony: When my kids were growing up, we looked at driving them to school as a great fifteen-minute opportunity to talk one-on-one about whatever subjects were appropriate at the time, and we also found that there was great power in just listening during those one-on-one experiences. As the relationship changed when they went off to college, we kept the lines of communication wide open, and we trusted that they would be guided by the legacy we had already poured into them. By this time we had lived out our family mission statement (which we will talk about later in this chapter) for over a dozen years in their lives, and we were grateful that they turned out to be exceptional young women.

When my oldest daughter got married, she and her husband borrowed money from our family bank to buy their first house. When we went to the closing company, the closer wanted to seat me in front of the table so he could explain the documents to me, and he was just going to bring up chairs for my daughter and son-in-law. I said to my daughter, "No, you two are buying the house. You sit here in front of the closer, and I'll sit over here." Then I asked the closer to just involve me if they had a question. My daughter was now an adult, and I wanted the communication here to be directed to her and her husband. I was transferring ownership to them, both literally and figuratively.

A few years ago I was with one of my mentors who had been advising me for years on how to raise my daughters, and I asked if he had any advice to share as his two daughters were getting older and having kids. He shared with me that one of the big mistakes he had made for years was running over and hugging his grandkids first when they would come into his presence, and skipping much communication with his daughter. He said that was a *Blind Spot* for him; and he urged me not to make that mistake, because our children still want and need that love and connection, even at that stage when they have their own families. I thought that was a pretty powerful communication *Blind Spot* that many people may be missing, and I was grateful for the reminder.

Joseph: When the environment you're operating in as a family is adjusting and changing, which essentially is always, it creates new challenges and opportunities to make subtle and not so subtle changes in approach. For instance, my wife Mary and I noticed our need to adjust our approach as our children advanced through grade school, then high school, then college, then gainful employment, then marriage, then parenthood, and so on. Each transition point required delicate adjustments in our approach and style as they accepted and demanded greater and greater levels of personal responsibility, ownership, independence, and consequence.

As an example, early on in their college years, we made the decision to immerse our kids in the real-world ways of being responsible and resourceful. They—not us—were the ones who had college tuition due; so even though they had the advantage of college funds already set aside, we engaged them fully in the payment and management process by having them write the checks to the university. It worked so well in a small way with our first child Margie, that with John, our second child, we literally transferred an account with thousands of dollars in it fully under his control and told him, "This is your money; use it as you wish for room and board expenses and so on. If you have a remainder after you graduate, it's yours to keep as a cushion to get started on your own. If you spend it all, you'll have less as you begin your career."

Making subtle adjustments in our approach, as early as we could fully engage them, has played a major role in our good fortune of having personally and financially independent children. We now see how it has equipped them, right from their very first jobs through graduate school, to be highly responsible, skilled, and frugal stewards of their time, talent, and treasure. As they advance their careers and education, marry, and begin their own families, we see this ongoing need to modify our approach. We also see the opportunity to strategically contribute to their lives in various ways, such as funding special experiences or trips that they may otherwise not be able to afford early in their careers or family life.

MEET YOUR FAMILY MEMBERS WHERE THEY ARE

As your family evolves through those five stages and your family members are growing, learning, and adapting to prevailing life and economic circumstances, it's important to meet them where they are in life—and to be sure to keep the focus on building and nurturing a rock-solid relationship full of unconditional love, radically honest communication, and mutual respect.

Joseph: I was contacted by a client whose father had built a very successful company worth over $50 million. His father had already nailed first-generation to second-generation family legacy goals that most would love to replicate. He had taught him how to run a very successful business, and they had had great continued business success, now two generations strong.

However, when our new client's father passed away and he took over running the family business, he began noticing that he had great difficulty engaging his own children (the third generation) in life the same way his father had engaged him. He suspected the sheer complexity of his wealth, which now included a rapidly growing liquid portfolio worth $20 million, was taking its toll on his time and relationships.

We dove into the case; the easy part was diagnosing what was missing and putting in place

> The moral of the story is this: Do whatever it takes to build and nurture a rock-solid relationship with each family member you want to be a part of your family legacy. Great communication begins with trusting and loving relationships that meet them where they are in life.

the proper systems, structure, support, and disciplines to optimally manage his liquid wealth in a fraction of the time it formerly required. This elimination of time-consuming complexity was low-hanging fruit. But as in all of our most favorite cases, the most rewarding part was when we saw the light go on in our client's eyes when he realized that new possibilities were on the horizon for his relationships with his children. Nothing was as important to him; and, in this case, all he needed in order to focus on these precious relationships was to eliminate a nagging time-consuming distraction and complexity.

The moral of the story is this: Do whatever it takes to build and nurture a rock-solid relationship with each family member you want to be a part of your family legacy. Great communication begins with trusting and loving relationships that meet them where they are in life.

Tony: Here's another example of meeting your family members where they are. My youngest daughter loves sports. She started out playing basketball, and then she switched over to volleyball. We supported that, and we built a sand volleyball court on our property. She was tracking to do exceptionally well in volleyball. When she was a freshman in high school, she was even selected as one of the top fourteen-year-old girls to train at the US Olympic volleyball training center in Chula Vista, California. Then the next year she wanted to switch to track. In fact, throughout her high school years, she bounced around among the different sports. We were okay with that. We could have said, "No, we've spent all that money on a volleyball court, so you have to play volleyball and get a college scholarship." We didn't; instead, we said, "We want you to discover where your talent and your passion meet. We're here to support your happiness and to help you become a successful adult."

REMAIN *COMMUNICATION READY* TO COMBAT OUTSIDE INFLUENCES

In today's society, there are many outside barriers that combat our efforts to build strong families. Authentic, intentional, and ongoing communication often creates a durable bond that can help shield your family members from those outside influences.

When you maintain a mindset of strategically building your family legacy, you're able to be more intentional about communicating at the moment events happen in your family, in life, and in the world around you. Immense benefit can be gained when you're able to be *Communication Ready* to respond and course-correct in real time when events happen, as opposed to reacting to the circumstances. We can't always protect our family members from random happenings; however, we can use those happenings as opportunities to communicate the valuable lessons we want to help them learn. During those times, the proper communication is not only specific, proactive, and intentional; it also has to loop back to what's relevant in life and work and in our families.

We both have stories to share from our own families that demonstrate the value of being *Communication Ready* when life events happen:

Joseph: The very week before my son John graduated from college with an Electrical Engineering degree, he applied for a full-time position with a prestigious spacecraft organization he had worked for part-time during college. The stars were aligned, as he had done a fine job for the same organization for two years working part time, had the support and testimonial of his boss (during the part-time position), and had what he felt were good interviews. He was called in by his supportive boss, and he thought he was about to get the nod for the new role, in a new department. Instead, his boss informed him that he did not get the new full-time position. It was a heart-breaking first rejection (though it was probably harder on us, as his parents, to see our son get rejected), but a perfect time to remain cool, calm, and collected.

We chatted with him about what had transpired, shared our own experiences of being rejected numerous times in our lives (identifying how natural and normal it is when stretching for rare gems), and listened. He had already gone through the process of reviewing the interview in his head so he could learn from the experience, and he began explaining that his supportive part-time job boss was more committed than ever to getting him a great new full-time role at the same organization, with all the compensation and benefit bells and whistles. Long story short, a few days later he was interviewed by three other departments; and all three offered him a position. He went on to formally accept one of the positions, turning the series of events into a perfect example of cool-headed persistence in the face of adversity.

John was well prepared to handle all of this on his own; and, in fact, he did. For years, he has attended workshops we've put on in our company, like Pacific Institute's "Thought Patterns for High Performance" and other workshops that covered personal discovery and growth topics. Those workshops provided him and us with the perfect avenue to talk about the best way to respond to challenges and opportunities. We were there to chat with him, adult to adult, at his discretion, and to help him remember one of our family values: maintain exemplary persistence in the face of challenge and obstacles.

When it came time to accept the offer and select benefits, John asked for our wealth management team's guidance in helping him select the right retirement plan options and begin aggressively saving to buy a home. Frugality, living under his means, and saving (three other family values) have been some of John's traits since early on. This is how legacies are built—interacting with current events and threading them back with lessons learned, expert team members, and best practices.

Tony: When my daughter Brooke was about 16, she backed her new car into the steps of our auto court. While everyone around me was saying, "That's terrible," my response to the accident was, "That's terrific!" My thinking was that, for just a few hundred dollars for a repair bill, a lesson had been forever embedded in her mind that she needed to be more safe and aware. I was *Communication Ready* and took advantage of the situation to pass on to my kids the idea of thinking ahead, being safe, and being smart. If you step back and look at circumstances when they happen, you may be able to see a good teaching experience when others only see it as being negative.

About six months ago that same daughter, who has now graduated from college, is married, and has her own graphics company, asked me to coach her on asking for a raise with her primary client. I walked her through how her client probably thought about things and how she could present it in a way that he wouldn't feel backed into a corner. I didn't just address the immediate situation; I gave her some really nice kernels of advice about communication that I thought she could use for the rest of her life. About a month ago, she had another client that she wanted to ask for a bump in her rate, and I suggested that the timing wasn't right. I said the business was really flowing from that client; it was working very nicely, and I thought she needed to have a longer run with the client before she asked for an increase in her rate. In both instances, I was *Communication Ready*—not just with advice for the situation she was facing, but with wisdom I wanted to pass down to her for the years to come. In the second situation, she was able to course-correct and avoid something that could have put her in a losing position.

CREATE A FAMILY MISSION STATEMENT

One excellent way to combat outside influences from infringing on your legacy is to involve your entire family early on in creating a family mission statement, and then strategically and intentionally communicate it and live it out over the years so that it becomes a part of who you are as a family.

Tony: When my daughters were four and seven years old, I read an article that talked about developing a family mission statement. It pointed out that most of us spend time creating and living by vision and mission statements for our businesses, and yet very few of us take the time to create and live by a mission statement for our families. That really resonated with me.

Soon after that, my wife and I involved our two young daughters in creating a mission statement for our family, and it's had a powerful impact on our success as a family. After careful thought, prayer, and discussion among the four of us, this is what we came up with:

As a family, we will always support each other as a team. We commit to doing together these five things as much as possible: playing and having fun, worshipping God, teaching one another, walking (exercise), and helping others. We will show everyone, including ourselves, these five qualities all the time: sharing, supporting, love, being thankful, being nice.

We posted our mission statement on our refrigerator, we put it on our vision (results) board, and we laminated it on business cards that we could carry with us. All through our girls' lives, we have focused on it, discussed it, and lived it. As we've lived out our mission statement, it has truly helped our family become a tight-knit team, and it's been very instrumental in helping us build our family legacy.

I strongly urge you to create one with your family, and then live by it. Post it in a prominent place in your home, and then read and reinforce it over and over again, so that it becomes a mission that everyone in the family is working toward together. It's a powerful way to help you keep the negative outside influences at bay while you're building your family legacy.

THE ROLE OF TRUST IN BUILDING A FAMILY LEGACY

Another great tool for minimizing negative outside influence is building trusting relationships with your family over the years that are open, giving, and loving. That's what facilitates good communication; ego-oriented relationships simply shut down communication. Nothing is gained from taking the stance of the "all-knowing, successful parent" who demands the attention and respect of the child. Rather, the legacy you want to build with your family flows naturally from relationships that are based on open communication and trust. Maintaining a foundation of trust and openness helps you to be real with your children, and that's the sweet spot that will carry you through the tough times and build the bona fide legacy you want.

Tony: I got a call from the vice-principal of our school several years ago, and he said my daughter, who was sixteen at the time, was in trouble for doing something she shouldn't have done. When he told me what she was accused of doing, I said, "No, she didn't do that. I know my daughter." He continued to assert her guilt and asked me to come to the school to discuss it. When I got to the school, I discovered that he had failed to get her side of the story. Sure enough, she really had not done what he thought, and upon our request he apologized to her. Through that whole learning experience, my daughter saw that I was always going to support her because I trusted her explicitly. She knew I had her back, and she knew that my (and my wife's) first reaction would be to trust her rather than immediately thinking the worst when the vice-principal accused her of doing something wrong. A large part of our family legacy is that we have a mutual trust among our family members. That kind of trust within a family is very powerful.

Along the same lines of openness and trust, one of my daughters called me on the carpet a few years ago when we were at a restaurant in California and I was too sharp with our waitress. I knew she was right, so I called the waitress over and apologized. Besides the fact that that was the right thing to do, I wanted to reinforce to my daughter that she has an open line of communication with me that allows her to bring up anything she sees me do that doesn't line up with our values.

And here's how that legacy of trust works on the other side of the generations, as we get older and must start depending on our children to manage things for us. A strong level of trust had been built over the years between me and my parents. My dad passed away a few months ago, and my mom was getting to the point where it was no longer appropriate for her to write checks. My wife and I drove over to her home recently to discuss the issue. Before we could even broach the subject, she surprised us by saying, basically, "You know what? I don't need to write checks anymore. Here's my checkbook. If you don't mind, I'm just going to turn all of my finances over to you. I trust you to handle it all. Just bring me some cash every now and then." Tammy and I walked out of there elated that we had not even had to bring it up. Through the years she had poured into us, and we had enjoyed that relationship of open communication and trust. Now she had enough trust in us to ask us to handle everything in her estate.

CREATE PROACTIVE COMMUNICATION

As you're raising your family, there are many opportunities to proactively communicate with your children. We encourage you to be creative in finding those opportunities in everyday life. Here are some tips that we've found to be particularly helpful:

- Take advantage of holidays and events to create proactive communication and promote legacy with your children. Holidays and special events like birthdays, award days, and milestone achievements are built-in opportunities for communicating your love and appreciation in a special way through cards, letters, notes, or meaningful gifts.

Tony: My daughter Paige is a photographer. A few years ago I spent months selecting her best pictures, naming them, and building a photograph book similar to one a famous photographer would have. On the first page was a picture I had taken of her photographing something, and throughout the book I told the story of how she is carrying out our family legacy of art and creativity. Then I presented it to her on Father's Day and told her that one of the greatest gifts a father can have is an incredible daughter like her. She was very moved, and it was a special time of bonding between the two of us that we will always remember.

- Create fun and exciting life experiences with your family members that allow you to communicate at a higher level. Commemorate those experiences with videos and albums that can be enjoyed and passed down through the years.

Joseph: A few years ago, I created a special three-generation experience when I took my son and my dad, along with one of my brothers, on a fishing trip to Canada, nine hundred miles north of the US border. On one memorable day, we were eating our lunch when a bear came out of the bushes. Needless to say, we quickly abandoned our lunch and hopped on the boat! The whole trip was an extraordinary experience, as it enabled bonding and communication at a deeper level than ever before. My son saw how my eighty-six-year-old dad was able to handle camping and fishing out in the middle of nowhere—bears, bad weather, and all—and it really strengthened our family legacy.

As I help my clients set goals to create experiences with their kids and grandkids, we're mindful that events like these are what all generations of the family really crave. It's not so much about "things" anymore—buying them a car or giving them expensive gadgets. It's more about having profound experiences where you can encounter and communicate at a deeper level.

- Engage with your children in an authentic way in things that interest them (such as sports, cooking, music, etc.), and create *Reverse Experiences* in which they are simultaneously teaching you and building legacy. Nothing creates bonding and communication more than allowing the next generation to get you involved in something they are excited about. There's something about flipping roles—when they become the teacher and you the student—that intensifies their enthusiasm and creates prime experiences.

Joseph: My son John recently got me into mountain biking. Even though I grew up riding bikes, I had not been on a bike for decades. Suddenly I found myself researching mountain bikes and then buying one. The first time I put on those biking shoes with clips, I had them so tight I couldn't get my feet off of the pedals! Biking with my son has already created many fun memories and perfect opportunities for bonding and communication.

I've also had a wonderful opportunity recently to further bond with my daughter Margie. She is an exceptional writer, and I mentioned to her my goal to create an abridged version of my book *Absolute Financial Freedom* and a new edition of my book *Investing from a Position of Strength*. Margie, who is now in graduate school studying biostatistics, said she would love to help out with those projects and earn some extra money on the side, and she took them on with great vigor. Working together has been an absolutely amazing win-win father/daughter experience. In the process, she has come to know details about my work and how to master money that she otherwise would not have been privy to. I, on the other hand, have learned so much from her and about her as we collaborated, and it has been an amazing, rich experience for me. In my mind, it has been a perfect family legacy project— co-creating value together while also exchanging wisdom.

• Formal or informal family meetings (or both) can be a significant tool in communicating with your family and creating legacy.

Tony: Over the years we've occasionally had what I call "staff meetings" with our family, where we would plan vacations or talk about what's coming up in the next stage of life. In fact, I had such a meeting with our kids in Jamaica just this past Christmas. My new son-in-law was with us, of course, and I used that opportunity to talk about things that were related to the family trust and other family issues. I had even prepared a short PowerPoint in which I laid out the information I wanted to talk about. Then after we talked, we went out and enjoyed our three or four days together. (That's an example of the *Elegant Solutions* we talked about in the Introduction—with that family vacation we achieve multiple objectives.)

Joseph: Facilitating family meetings is part of the Complete Legacy Solution, which is a multigenerational experience we provide for our clients. In our experience, we've found that there are certain points in time that are ripe for a family meeting, based on what is happening within the family. It could be triggered by an event that has happened or by the occasion to plan an event like a family vacation. Family meetings are a great tool for proactively communicating and interacting within the family. They can be formal or informal; and, depending on your family's needs, you can choose whether to involve an outside consultant—like a financial advisor, a psychologist, or a coach, for example, for a part of the meeting. You have many options available to you, and you can choose the right ones at the right time for your family.

In Chapter Four I outline the Stages of Financial Freedom, the 35 Essential Strengths, and the Family Financial Manifesto. These are three great topics for a family meeting, because every single family member can relate to how these concepts apply to them. Without going into confidential details, family members can openly speak about successes and struggles while pursuing these items. This is a perfect way to help family members avoid dead-ends, overcome obstacles, and learn elegant best-practices.

Though no two families are alike, we all have the same opportunities to utilize communication to our best advantage in building a legacy for our families. It's never too late to start, even if your kids are grown and have families of their own. In fact, grand-parenting brings built-in opportunities for starting and building family legacies. Whether you're new parents or grandparents or somewhere in between, right now is an ideal time to start being proactive, strategic, and intentional about communicating those things you want to pass down to your heirs.

VIPS

- Success comes from being specific and proactive; failure often comes from being vague and reactive. That bit of wisdom applies to all pursuits of success, of course, and it's especially true when you're building a family legacy.

- Your family environment is constantly adjusting and changing, which creates new opportunities and challenges for communication. There are potentially five stages of relationship with your children—from when they are small and living in your home to when they help you manage your affairs in your declining years—and each stage requires adjustments in the way you communicate:

- If you want to be successful in building an outstanding family legacy, meet your family members where they are in life as they grow and learn and explore their own places.

- Immense benefit can be gained when you're able to be *Communication Ready* to respond and course-correct in real time when events happen, as opposed to reacting to the circumstances.

- One excellent way to combat outside influences from infringing on your legacy is to involve your entire family early on in creating a family mission statement, and then strategically and intentionally communicate it and live it out over the years so that it becomes a part of who you are as a family.

- Building trusting relationships with your family over the years that are open, giving, and loving facilitates good communication; ego-oriented relationships simply shut down communication.

- Take advantage of holidays and events to create proactive communication and promote legacy with your children.

- Create fun and exciting life experiences with your family members that allow you to communicate at a higher level.

CHAPTER TWO

People

Your family legacy is determined by how you guide and encourage your children (and ultimately your grandchildren) from early childhood, through their teenage years, into early adulthood, and even through their thirties, forties, and beyond. The impact you make on your family (your legacy footprint) is so affected by people—the friends you hang with; the people on your team; the relationships and contacts you choose to pass along; and the integration of your legacy efforts with spouses, grandchildren, and great-grandchildren. So let's explore each of these four areas.

BUILD THE RIGHT COMMUNITIES; CHOOSE THE RIGHT FRIENDS

We all build communities in life—those various groups of like-minded people we choose to invest our time with—that have a powerful impact on who we become, and ultimately on the legacy we leave. We build those communities with people who embody the different areas we share in life, and it's from those groups of people that we choose the close friends we hang with. The communities we build, and ultimately the friends we choose from those communities, probably have more influence on us and our families than anything else in life.

Joseph: I have an extremely deep and wide faith community that continually encourages and nourishes my faith formation; I have a talented business community that continually challenges and informs my vocation and enterprise; I have a brilliant market intelligence community that provides me (and my organization) with quality perspectives on dangers, opportunities, and strengths across the globe; I have an inspiring intellectual capital community that keeps me updated in the latest best practices in creating, packaging, and distributing innovations; I have a super-talented productivity community that feeds me with constant best practices on being more orderly, effective, and efficient; and, in a smaller way, I seek out affinity groups when pursuing personal interests like travel, exercise, technology, and so on. Within each of these groups are people of great influence and insight who can connect me to the right people when I'm pursuing a big new goal that requires knowledge and capabilities I do not yet have.

The simple truth is, who you spend time with, you become. Ideally, the friends we and our children hang with will closely mirror our family values, because peer pressure—no matter what the age—can have either a positive or negative impact on the paths of our lives. If you truly desire to go to another level in being strategic about your family legacy, it's important that you understand this, that your kids understand it, and that you model it and guide them accordingly.

Think for a moment about who you hang around with—those you invest the most time with. Do they share your values? Is their influence positive or negative?

Tony: This is something my wife and I thought about the entire time we were raising our kids. For example, we found a private school for them that would not only provide the best teachers and learning experiences, but that would also have the kind of students enrolled that would be the best influence for our kids. We carefully guided them through the process of selecting the right kinds of friends; we talked about it constantly, and they took ownership of this principle early on. We helped them think about the type of friends they invited to parties at our home, those we invited to travel with us, and those who would be at places we encouraged our kids to go (like mission trips, track meets, cheer events, etc.). Of course none of us can shelter our kids all the time from being around the wrong type of people.

What I'm saying, though, is that as parents we can choose options for our kids that give them the greatest chances of being surrounded by people who encourage and influence them positively. And, by the way, that includes neighbors. I recommend that you choose your neighborhood carefully, as well as teachers (to the extent you can), coaches, and even the church you choose to attend. We even went so far as to purposefully spend time with families who had children a tad older than ours so they could model the right things for our kids and serve as their mentors. All of this matters if you want the right people having an impact on your kids.

Joseph: The communities that my wife Mary and I have built over the years have been solid, and it has been quite natural to see how they continue to benefit our children. But let me share a key tip we learned from a wonderful Iranian family we became great friends with through Rotary almost three decades ago. We went to their home for a business-type cocktail party and were quite impressed that they had their children, ages nine to nineteen at the time, fully participate in the party, including conversations. In short, it taught us to fully engage our children from an early age with all of our groups, and this has been an absolute game-changer. They learned very early in life how to interact with adults and professionals in interesting ways. This has served them well.

Beyond community involvement, we have also been fortunate to have opportunities to select private schools, church traditions and activities, piano and voice teachers, foreign exchange students (living with us for periods of time), and personal growth and travel experiences that contributed to the community surrounding our children. Frankly, we carefully co-selected activities with our children to avoid being overcommitted. We had no interest in being so busy with activities that there was no time for church or good old free time.

BUILD A GREAT *LIFE TEAM* TO SHARE

The ideal legacy mindset includes building an expert, trusted team around you that will support you and your family, as well as support the next generation's success. We call this your Life Team.

Tony: I have intentionally formed my *Life Team* over the years, and

Tony recently completed filming, in partnership with SUCCESS Academy, a sister division of *Success Magazine*, a seven-module, twenty-one-lesson on-line video course entitled *RESULTS Faster!* A compilation of his life's work and teaching, the course gives valuable advice when applied to living a masterful life, which, of course, includes leaving a great legacy. Consider signing up for the course at www.tonyjeary.com/resultsfaster.

I recommend you do the same. Today, mine consists of more than sixty people I have purposefully placed around me who can execute and/or advise me and my family, on either an as-needed or regular basis, in all the different areas of my life. Some of those people are doers, like the handyman who takes care of my home. Others are advisors, like the wealth managers who manage my overall estate strategy. These are people I trust, who can help me and my family on an ongoing basis. We have people who take care of our property, our estate, our vehicles, our health, our legal issues, and all the other different segments of our lives. And some of these people, like one of our CPAs, have been with us for over two decades. Part of the wealth I began passing on to my children years ago is the connectivity I have to many of these *Life Team* members.

We've listed below the top people who we believe are absolutely essential to have on your *Life Team*. As you look at this list, you may want to ask yourself these question:

- Are you aware of your need for these people?
- What are the characteristics of the right ones for your team?
- Do you have the right people in place?
- Have you started transferring these relationships to your family at the right time?

1. Financial Advisors:
    - Wealth Manager

- Investment Advisor

Note: These are broad categories; sometimes these functions can be provided by one person, and other times it takes multiple people.

2. Certified Public Accountant(s)

3. Banker(s)

4. Attorneys:
   - Trust attorney
   - Family Attorney
   - Deal Attorney
   - Business Attorney

5. Insurance Agents:
   - Property and Casualty
   - Life
   - Health

6. Bookkeeper/Bill Payer

Let me give you some examples of the importance of having long-term relationships with your *Life Team* members, and how those relationships can be passed down to the next generation. Our CPA, who has been on my *Life Team* for twenty-five years, has been doing my daughter's tax returns since she was twelve years old. She has now been married for a year and has decided to handle her own tax returns, using TurboTax. I obviously didn't want to force my whole system on her, so I told her I would be happy to make my CPA available to her, at my expense, to make the transition easier for her. She and her husband have their independence, and they also know they have a trusted family CPA as support and backup.

Here's another example of the value of having a *Life Team*. Last week our CPA was completing a transaction in my dad's estate; and in order to do that, he needed a quit-claim deed for one piece of property that was still in a trust that we had collapsed. Because of my relationships with certain *Life Team* members, I was able to basically send one email and get back a verified document showing that the quit-claim deed had been already filed, all with burning very little energy. All the right *Life Team* members came together for the benefit of the family, with just a couple of clicks of an email.

You may make an occasional misstep in choosing the right people for your *Life Team*. (The likelihood of that diminishes if you inherit a proven team like I did from my dad, which I'm also passing on to my kids.) If you do choose the wrong person, step back, course-correct, and move forward on the right track.

Joseph: My wife Mary and I have a comprehensive *Life Team* across every aspect of our personal and business life. Because I am in the wealth management field and have clientele across the country, and because one of our services is to help high- and ultra-high-net-worth clients build quality teams, this team is quite large and consists of many specialists.

It's been a joy to engage our *Life Team* with our children. For starters, they know they can contact us for any financial, legal, tax, investment, or transaction-type need, and we will instantly give them access to the appropriate expertise. They understand that our team is their team (if they want it) and is available to help them with any need. Our hope is that they learn to collaborate with experts in an effective way, from small needs to large, getting the most value from every transaction.

Beyond financially-oriented *Life Team* members, we regularly share tips, articles, and resources from *Life Team* member organizations. Our aim is to model the process of identifying and utilizing experts across all aspects of life, whether it's a pro to help us build our wardrobe, maintain our home, or improve our presentation skills. Mary and I realize that we are in the financial position to have a larger team than our kids can afford this early in their careers, but we see how sharing tips can be beneficial. For instance, I receive a short weekly tip from one of my *Life Team* members that is so helpful that I frequently pass it along, and I often set the context of how I use the tip/technique myself. My aim is to continually model how I use such *Life Team* members and, of course, encourage them to utilize the same ones or find and build their own when the need arises. Tony's book

Advice Matters explains the benefit of having a broad network of pros and mentors.

Beyond my *Life Team* list, I think it is also important to share with my family how I lead and manage *Life Team* members for the greatest value. For instance, I have modeled numerous times how I have established success criteria for *Life Team* members and how I engage in check-ins from time to time to optimize our teamwork. My children also know I am not bashful about speaking up to improve teamwork, craftsmanship, or efficiencies with team members. I model this so they can learn to be active in gaining the greatest benefit out of such relationships. In short, it's no place to be passive or aggressive; the sweet spot is optimally collaborative and respectful.

Of course, it is necessary to keep certain team members informed of important information, ideally as easily as possible so that you do not get bogged down with paperwork. For example, as part of our legacy advising at my company, we give our clients tools for maximizing the collaboration of *Life Team* members. One such tool provides *Life Team* members a one-page concise summary of the client's circumstances, values, goals, key relationships, and so on. Our online client portal then allows clients to give *Life Team* members select access to up-to-date information and documents to facilitate collaboration. For instance, a client's CPA can see up-to-the-second realized capital gain, interest, and dividend income data (needed for tax planning and compliance), and the client's estate attorney can see accurate snapshots of who owns what in the estate (needed for estate optimization). Streamlined *Life Team* collaboration is essential, and today's modern technology supports such collaboration at a high level.

Beyond your trusted *Life Team,* you want to have systems in place that document where assets and data are custodied. Your family must have access to the wealth you will be transferring, so you want to surround yourself with people you trust who know what you have. If this information isn't communicated right, it can turn into a long and difficult legal battle. As a financial advisor, I often see people left with enormous estates who don't have any idea where everything is. In the opposite extreme, I've seen clients create elaborate notebooks or electronic vaults that document what they have and where their assets are located. The more this information is documented and communicated, the easier it is to transfer your wealth in the proper manner and timing.

I designed a first-class digital vault system for my family, and I also have a manual backup. Everyone assumes the electricity and the internet will always be around or available when needed, and yet it's very easy to lose digital data, even with backup. So even if a digital cloud storage device was somehow corrupted, I (or my heirs, or people on my *Life Team*) would be able to find a manual backup of key documents in my safe.

I believe it's also important to map access to all this information. For example, I sent my kids very specific instructions showing where these digital and manual items are kept. It's literally a document that maps out exactly where everything is, including photographs of the safe and its location, to make it very simple for them to find.

I might add that it's important for the purpose of legacy to talk to your kids about who you have in what role on your *Life Team,* why that role is important, why you chose that particular person to fill that role, and what the best practices of that role may include. Since people retire, die, and leave their practices for other reasons, passing on to your heirs the name of a person isn't enough. Share with them the criteria to look for if they need to replace someone in that role, including the kind of best practices that person needs to employ. In estate planning, for example, there is an organization made up of elite estate attorneys (ACTEC) who really are the cream of the crop. If they choose any estate attorney who is part of that fellowship, they are assured of finding one of the best.

OPEN DOORS WITH YOUR CONTACTS (ROLODEX)

Today, everyone has a Rolodex; you may call it your phone list, your connections, or your list of contacts. With today's technology you have the electronic means to capture as many contacts as you want, and most successful people have thousands. Think of all the names you have on your lists, whether they are in a software on your computer, on your phone, or on your Facebook and other social media lists. Your contact list can be considered one of the most valuable assets you have; and that's why we believe it's important to strategically set up and pass on that element of your wealth to your heirs. Even from an early age, your kids can benefit from many of the different relationships you have.

Tony: One of the best wealth components my family passed on to me—and one that allowed me to win big at a young age—was both my father's and my grandfather's list of contacts and relationships that they had built for decades. They both transferred to me the trust and credibility they had with their many contacts, which opened doors for me and allowed me to do things that most people couldn't do. Now, I certainly had to go out and do the work behind those doors; I realized, however, that my family's contacts afforded me advantages that most others didn't have. My dad had a system he passed on to me, as well. Back then, before computers, he kept stacks and stacks of business cards bound by rubber bands, and he could find someone to advise him or get something done in just about any area he needed. It's fun for me to look back now and remember his looking for and finding just the card he needed within a matter of seconds. I can just see him smiling after he found it and then dialing that old rotary phone to make things happen.

I've now invested over four decades of my life building relationships and adding on to what my parents and grandparents handed over to me. My contact list today is in the tens of thousands. Each time I make a new contact, my team logs it into our database and catalogs it with details. I know not everyone has a team and will take it to the level I do; however, I believe most everyone can be more intentional about transferring contacts and relationships to their kids as part of the wealth legacy puzzle. It's really

> With each new contact, my team and I ask, "How can we nourish that relationship? How can we give this person something of value? How can we do more than is expected to help him or her win?" I'm a big fan of doing *Favors in Advance.*

important to me.

While we're on the subject, let me share another way I use my Rolodex. I also use it to identify people who can help me with specific issues. When I have a particular need, I call someone from my contact list who has the knowledge, expertise, or connections that can fill that need. Conversely, I am always ready to help them win in any way I can. In fact, we take it even further. With each new contact, my team and I ask, "How can we nourish that relationship? How can we give this person something of value? How can we do more than is expected to help him or her win?" I'm a big fan of doing *Favors in Advance* (FIAs), because you never know when you—or your kids—might need a favor in return. Because I enjoy great reciprocal relationships with almost every one of my contacts, I know I can call just about any one of them for help when I need their expertise, and they know the same about me. What a great asset to pass on to my kids, and I've been extremely intentional about doing that since they were very young! (While I'm writing this very paragraph, I'm in Waco, Texas, with my wife, both daughters, and my son-in-law. As we were going to my daughter's dorm room this afternoon to give her roommates a gift I bought them, I enjoyed watching my daughter putting to practice what I taught her about the importance of building relationships. She walked across campus hugging, shaking hands, and taking pictures with dozens of people. And now, as I'm getting ready to go to bed, I'm discussing with my son-in-law Bret an email connection I just made for him with a former CEO in the retail industry. The CEO just emailed back that he will be happy to help Bret with his Keep Exploring business [wekeepexploring.com].)

As you can see, perhaps more clearly after reading this chapter, there are many people involved in all our lives at so many levels. Being smart about opening doors for your kids and grandkids by sharing your relationships and connecting them with your contacts can truly pay big dividends and add to the wealth of your family.

INTEGRATE INLAWS AND GRANDKIDS INTO THE LEGACY

In our role as parents, it's important to guide and encourage our kids in the choice of a mate. When Tony's daughters were young, he bought a bride-and-groom picture frame. On the bride side, he put a picture of his two girls; on the groom side he framed a list, compiled by his girls with the help of their parents, of the twelve characteristics they wanted to find in a future spouse.

They had many discussions about this list over the years, and they prayed about it together often. It was not something that was forced on them; in fact, just the opposite—it was just made a natural part of their everyday lives. Tony and his wife wanted to help their girls envision with clarity, from an early age, who they wanted to become and therefore what kind of person they wanted to attract. If it turned out that someone Tony's daughters dated for the first time did not meet the standards they had established together early on, his girls politely  moved apart from any future dating relationship. When his oldest daughter got married, her husband possessed virtually every characteristic listed in the frame.

Tony has taught this to many of his clients and audience members over the years, and with great response. Many have been intrigued and impressed by the idea. Tony teaches that, in order to help your kids attract an exceptional spouse, they themselves needed to become exceptional men or women. This prepares them for dating.

Tony: The person who will likely have the most influence on your life, other than your parents, is your spouse. We taught our kids that when you marry, you marry into a family. We taught them to look at the parents and family of the people they date, to envision the impact they will have when they are merged with our family. We are so fortunate that our kids selected wisely the young men they dated, and that our oldest daughter married an incredible man with an incredible family. We all enjoy attending events together and even worshiping together. We held their wedding in our home. With hundreds of people moving around and multiple tasks to tend to, there was not one conflict with her new in-laws. Everyone was respectful and pitched in to help. We love and appreciate his family and feel blessed in joining our family with theirs.

As your family grows as a result of marriage and birth, its is going to be equally important to lovingly make your mark on the lives of your children's spouses, kids, and grandkids. When you can state that you successfully bonded with in-laws and grandkids and are able to contribute to their lives toward the ends defined in this book, that is when you have truly advanced to another level of legacy mastery.

All of your efforts to help your children grow, including modeling a loving marriage and family life, will have played a key role up to this point. Now, as you embrace spouses and grandchildren and form quality relationships, your efforts will need to be repeated to listen, accept, connect, and assist them all in the same way, albeit in less time, as you had with your children when they were growing up.

As with anything in life, we cannot force our beliefs, values, or assistance on anyone else. Clearly, when your children marry, they are adults of their own free-will and absolutely will decide for themselves how they will live their lives. This said, you will continue to have a relationship with them and can continue to make a mark on their lives via your contact and continued, yet evolving, relationship.

The key point is that the topics in this book continue to apply; you simply filter your efforts in respect of their personal freedom as adults living their own lives and building their own families. You want to lovingly support their development and advancement, and as they interact with you and benefit by your efforts and relationship, your legacy continues to expand.

Finally, it's important to recognize that your legacy and your life benefit greatly by the contributions your children, inlaws, and grandchildren add to your life. While most of this book is about making your mark on them, it is important to recognize and appreciate the profound mark they leave upon you. Yes, legacy is viral and flows in all directions, not just north to south.

VIPS

- The impact you make on your family (your legacy footprint) is so affected by people—the friends you hang with; the people on your team; the relationships and contacts you choose to pass along; and the integration of your legacy efforts with spouses, grandchildren, and great-grandchildren.

- Who you spend time with, you become. If you truly desire to go to another level in being strategic about your family legacy, it's important that you understand this, that your kids understand it, and that you model it and guide them accordingly.

- Clearly identify the top five to ten *Life Team* members who support your family legacy, and ensure that those external *Life Team* members have clarity about and are aligned with the actions to take in the transfer of your wealth when the time comes.

- Ensure that your children and grandchildren (or other heirs) have an understanding of who your *Life Team* members are and what their roles are, and how they can win by using their expertise in the transfer of your wealth.

- Passing on a name is not enough. Discuss with your heirs why you have those people in those roles and the best practices to look for if they need to replace that person.

- Be extremely intentional about transferring your connections and relationships to your heirs.

- Talk about and model how you look for ways to help others win so your contacts are more than just a list; they are reciprocal relationships that can and will be a great asset to your heirs.

- Expand your legacy-building efforts to in-laws and grandchildren, when the time comes. Legacy is viral and flows in all directions, not just north to south.

CHAPTER THREE

Intellectual Capital

A few years ago, when Tony's daughter was nineteen years old and home for the summer after one year of college, she and Tony had lunch together in downtown Dallas. During their conversation, she said, "One thing I learned during my first year of college, Dad, is that college isn't going to teach me how the world works. People in the world pay you to show them how it works; so I'd like you to take the next three years of my college, and, as time permits, show me how the world works." What she was asking for was intellectual capital.

The intellectual capital you have invested a lifetime capturing and practicing—within your family, in your chosen career, and in your life experiences—is a significant component of your legacy. We'll focus in this chapter on passing down intellectual capital to your family through the use of family values, daily standards, traditions and rituals, and truisms and models.

DEFINE, MODEL, AND PASS ON YOUR FAMILY VALUES

So much of what we pass down to our kids, and consequently to the generations below them, is imparted during the formative and fertile years of our children's lives. The values we instill in our children play a substantial role in teaching them to be successful in life and in passing down family legacy.

Over the years, Tony has coached his clients about values and the significant role they play in success, and he has developed a special deck of cards that helps them identify the values that are important to them. Each card shows a different value, and he has them pull out the ten that are most important to them. Tony and his wife played that out personally early on to help them be very intentional and definitive about their values as parents, and they communicated those values to their kids in various ways while they were young. Then once their kids got to be ten or twelve years old, they had them start using the deck to identify what they, as individuals, valued the most.

We've included a list of values in Appendix A in the back of this book. If you have not already defined your values, we encourage you to choose from the list those that are important to you; then prioritize them and start communicating them to your family and aligning your goals and your life with those values. We suggest that you then consistently lead your children and ultimately your grandchildren (from mid-childhood into adulthood) through the same exercise from time to time. As you continue to intentionally and strategically communicate to your children that values are a component of being successful in life, and as they mature and get to the point of choosing their professions and their spouses, it's more likely that their choices will align with their values.

Since each individual is unique, it's unlikely that everything your children value will exactly match yours, as parents; ideally, though, their values will closely align with the family values in the things that really matter. Tony's daughter, Paige, for example, aspires to be a teacher. She has a gift for teaching, and she teaches at church and on mission trips, and even volunteers each summer to teach at a camp for special-needs kids. Although Tony values altruism and loves teaching, his life's aim and gifts do not involve teaching special needs students. That's not who he is, and yet that's who Paige is. In fact, both of Tony's daughters have a heart for special-needs kids, and Tony is very proud of both of them for their contributions through volunteerism. Obviously, their family legacy of altruism and service was passed on to his girls. Sadly, many people live half of their lives or more before they align their lives with their core values—and some never do—because no one has ever communicated to them the power of strategically thinking about what they really value and then setting their goals and living their lives accordingly.

We both take our values from God's plan for our lives. We strongly believe that our commitment to God and living in His will come first. Then our families come next, and then our vocations. Many people live their lives in reverse; they put their careers first, then their families, and then they give what time and effort and regard they have left, if any, to God. To us, loving God and loving others are very important values. And we believe that marriage, in God's plan, is a total giving of yourself to your spouse. Other values that are definitely intertwined in our spiritual beliefs are those of honesty, hard work, and value-added delivery to others.

Joseph: The easiest way for me to explain my search for and prioritization of values to pursue in my life and my family's legacy is this: *to earnestly seek and live the truth.* I don't limit my search to my own limited abilities; I seek out and learn from some of the greatest thinkers of all time, as well as those who have synthesized, interpreted, and explained such deep thinking into laymen's terms that I may be better able to understand and apply. As I do so, I can often relate to the insights and see if and where I have gone wrong (where I was unaligned with the truth), and this then serves as guidance to take corrective action to the best of my ability.

There is so much available in this realm that I can only scratch the surface. However, for the purposes of this book, I'll share one. A document I hold in high regard is a handbook called *Vocation of the Business Leader,* which was put together by business leaders, university professors, and experts from various disciplines that encourages business leaders to, "engage with the contemporary economic and financial world in light of the principles of human dignity and the common good."[2] Here's how the document's executive summary describes the challenge:

---

2 Vocation of the Business Leader: A Reflection, Pontifical Council for Justice and Peace, Vatican City, and John A. Ryan Institute for Catholic Social Thought, St. Thomas, MN, 2014, Pg. 1.

Obstacles to serving the common good come in many forms—corruption, absence of rule of law, tendencies towards greed, poor stewardship of resources—but the most significant for a business leader on a personal level is leading a divided life. This split between faith and daily business practice can lead to imbalances and misplaced devotion to worldly success. The alternative path of faith-based "servant leadership" provides business leaders with a larger perspective and helps them to balance the demands of the business world with those of ethical social principles, illuminated for Christians by the Gospel.[3]

A couple of years ago, we hosted Monsignor James P. Shea, president of the University of Mary in Bismarck, North Dakota, to make a presentation to a group at our office about *The Vocation of a Business Leader*. Monsignor Shea proposed that all beauty, including beautiful lives, is made up of three components—wholeness, harmony, and radiance. The idea here is that if we seek wholeness and harmony in life, rather than balance, the result will be a beautiful (radiant) life. In seeking wholeness and harmony, we have to look at how work and leisure interact to give us meaning and purpose to life.

All of us see work on one of three different levels, and each level integrates with leisure in a different way, as shown in the following matrix.

WORK	LEISURE	INTEGRATION
Vocation (Giving)	Contemplation (Receiving)	Integrity (Being)
Career (Taking)	Functional (Using)	Achievement (Doing)
Job (Getting)	Amusement (Escaping)	Gratification (Having)

Matrix taken from PowerPoint supplied by Michael Naughton, Director of the Center of Catholic Studies, Koch Chair in Catholic Studies.

3 Ibid, Pg. 2.

In the lowest level, we see work as only a job—an essential function for making money in order to live life; and in our leisure time we seek amusement (entertainment) in order to find "relief" from the day-to-day burden of our jobs. We embrace the idea that leisure is where real life takes place, because work is just a job. The resulting integration is gratification, which is steeped in consumerism, where "having" takes precedence over "being."

In the next level, we see work as a career, a noble pursuit that produces self-esteem and personal satisfaction. I admittedly was in this space for many years of my life, not being aware of a higher truth. This does not mean it was bad—just that it was incomplete. In this level, we're goal oriented and focus on the thrill of accomplishment. We put the emphasis on ourselves, rather than the needs of the world around us. Leisure, in this view, is functional. We see it as though it were a tool to make us more productive. Seeing work as a career and leisure as functional integrates into achievement ("doing" over "being"). The problem at this level is that when we are no longer achieving, life often loses its purpose.

In the American culture, we predominantly see the first two views. In actuality, though, our work is not about what we achieve; it is about who we become. In the third level, then, we view work as a vocation, in the sense that it is a calling to give of ourselves. We will only find purpose and meaning once we realize that our lives are about exercising our gifts in serving others. In this view, leisure is seen as contemplation—a time when we can consider our gifts and what we have to offer. The integration of work as a vocation and leisure as contemplation is integrity, or wholeness of life ("being"). Our work is meaningful, as we are offering ourselves to society.[4]

The hope, of course, is that as we teach our children to live by our family values—informed by such wisdom—and model them every day in all aspects of our lives, including our lives as business leaders, they will adopt similar values in their adult lives. This is one rich

---

4 Taken from a presentation by Monsignor James P. Shea on "The Vocation of the Business Leader," Janiczek Wealth Management headquarters, March 2015.

source of my values. I encourage you to find a rich source that speaks to you and use it as your inspiration, updating it as you discover higher truths.

CREATE AND IMPLEMENT STRONG FAMILY STANDARDS

Daily performance standards are things we do every day that set the stage for minimal distractions and allow us to focus on the activities that will bring the best results we actually want out of each day. These performance standard activities provide clarity, direction, and inspiration for our days and serve as our touch point for the things that are important to us. In Tony's SUCCESS on-line *RESULTS Faster!* course, he shares his own personal way of writing down his twelve selected daily standards that help him guide his own day. He teaches people to use the simple formula of typing them into their phone and occasionally reviewing them until they become second nature. We want to make you aware of this concept, because it is an incredible tool that can be part of the wealth you pass on to your family. By creating and adhering to daily performance standards for yourself, teaching the concept to your family, and encouraging them to create and live by their own standards, you can help them live each day happier and healthier.

Tony: These are the twelve standards that I've carved out for myself to work on daily. If I do these twelve things well, then I lived a good day.

1. Ask in prayer for smartness, Holy Spirit support, and alignment with God's will

2. Do team huddles and stimulate huddles

3. Glance at pipeline each morning to have actions fresh in mind

4. Determine VIPs for the day (from master list)

5. Touch team members inspirationally

6. Communicate appreciation to all those around me (personal and professional)

7. Strength, flex, and breathe with confidence, and think gratitude

8. Organize (rationalize) so more good things can come in

9. Visualize with further clarity our goals, direction, vision, and refinement

10. Model exceptional behavior, including enjoying life

11. Eat healthy

12. Do favors and help advance my clients' success

We also recommend that you create performance standards at work. One of the things we have as a standard at Tony Jeary International is to do things quickly. Our oldest daughter, Brooke, is now an independent graphic artist, and I often see her do things in lightning speed time. I'm so grateful that she bought into the fact that the world appreciates speed (as part of the intellectual capital I've passed down to her), and that she operates her business that way.

Joseph: I regularly reflect on and then attempt to succinctly write down what helps me live my life in a better way. Though it's taken a while to really zero in on those standards, their remarkable impact makes it worthwhile to capture them, get them down on paper, live them out daily, and pass them on. The one thing we don't want to do is just put them down into a stagnant document. What makes them come alive is regular implementation—personally and with our families. To me, this is what truly builds a legacy—living your standards, demonstrating them, reflecting on them, and talking about them.

In my role as a financial advisor, I have diligently worked toward identifying pithy guiding principles and standards of excellence that make it much easier for our clients to master money in a fraction of the time otherwise required. I have included in Appendix B summaries of the 35 Essential Strengths and Five Guiding Principles, which are examples of this technique.

FIND YOUR FAMILY'S RHYTHM OF SUCCESS THROUGH TRADITIONS AND RITUALS

Every family has a unique rhythm of success, which includes family rituals and traditions as well as all the distinctions we've already talked about in this book—like shared values and trust, special family events and experiences, family meetings, *Reverse Experiences,* and being *Communication Ready.* Just as we create a rhythm of success in business, it's also important to intentionally create a unique rhythm of success for your family.

Family rituals are great tools for passing on a rich family legacy. Rituals can include anything from how you communicate at a Christmas dinner (or any dinner, for that matter) to serving the needy at Thanksgiving, to the way you celebrate birthdays or other special events as a family. Some families have special rituals in the way they say good night or how they pray together as a family.

Tony: One of the rituals we have as a family is what we call the branding or appreciation exercise. From time to time we go around the dinner table and talk about what we most appreciate about each other. We like to do those kinds of rituals that stimulate appreciation and support for each other. They bind us together as a family, and they build self-esteem as we hear how our family members see us.

Joseph: One informal tradition we share in our family is a thread of emails and texts in which we share articles and give insights about what we are reading and learning. Sometimes the messages contain bits of wisdom, and some are about interesting innovations that stretch our minds and thinking in a fun way. Because we all like learning, it's a great way to stay in contact.

CAPITALIZE ON TRUISMS AND MODELS

There are certain truisms that we all apply to our lives; they're not values, and they're different from standards. They are simply things that are so intuitively true that they need no evidence. For example, do you live by the truism, "You are what you eat"? How about, "A penny saved is a penny earned"? Sometimes a truism is so powerful and meaningful to us that we latch onto it, pattern our behavior around it, and teach our children to do the same. Such truisms are a rich part of the legacy we can pass down to our families.

Tony: One of the truisms I've taught my kids is, "Everyone loves to win." That's an indisputable fact. And because everyone loves to win, we need to help ensure that everyone does win in whatever we're doing—whether it's in a marriage or in a sorority, or whether we're meeting new people or participating in sports. We need to do our best to look at the other person's situation and see how we can help that person win. Even when we're involved in something that will improve our own life positions, we want to make sure that we're advancing other people's lives, as well.

Models—concepts that have been proven to work well—are also great tools to pass down to your children. For example, Tony has taught his daughters since they were very young how to use the DiSC personalality assessment effectively, to help them understand and relate to people according to their personality styles. Another model that we both endorse is the book by Gary Chapman called *The Five Love Languages*—a great transformational resource that helps you understand the different ways people show and receive love.

> "A penny saved is a penny earned.* A penny earned and prudently invested is a good fortune. A good fortune elegantly stewarded and generously shared is a great legacy."
> —Joseph J. Janiczek

One thing we want to note is that you cannot and should not force your intellectual capital on your kids or grandkids. An effective transfer takes place when the intellectual capital is modeled and when they seek you out and ask questions about it, just as Tony's daughter did after her first year of college. We both love it when our kids ask challenging questions about any of these things or even provide different input. Discussion is healthy; just ensure that the conversation is deep enough to be effec-

---

*This maxim is often attributed to Benjamin Franklin. However, Franklin's actual 1737 statement was "a penny saved is two pence clear." Then in 1758, his famous almanac noted "a penny saved is a penny got." More on this is available at www. forbes.com/ sites/realspin/2014/08/18/a-penny-saved-was-never-a-penny-earned/.

tive. The whole cycle of communication—when we're living it, reflecting on it, writing it down, speaking about it regularly, and getting input and feedback—is what helps get our intellectual capital ingrained in our kids to the point that it's intuitive. Writing it down in a flat document captures it and helps you retain it, to be sure. However, the constant back-and-forth communication about it is where the real legacy handoff takes place.

Joseph: I like to say: "A penny saved is a penny earned.* A penny saved and prudently invested is a good fortune. A good fortune elegantly stewarded and generously shared is a great legacy."

---

*This maxim is often attributed to Benjamin Franklin. However, Franklin's actual 1737 statement was "a penny saved is two pence clear." Then in 1758, his famous almanac noted "a penny saved is a penny got." More on this is available at www. forbes.com/sites/realspin/2014/08/18/a-penny-saved-was-never-a-penny-earned/.

VIPS

- The values we instill in our children play a substantial role in teaching them to be successful in life and in passing down family legacy.

- Encourage each family member to develop standards that reflect the way they want to live each day, and pass that concept on as part of the wealth you transfer to your family.

- Every family has a unique rhythm of success, which includes family rituals and traditions, as well as distinctions like shared values and trust, special family events and experiences, family meetings, *Reverse Experiences,* and being *Communication Ready.* Just as we create a rhythm of success in business, it's also important to intentionally create a unique rhythm of success for your family.

- Sometimes a truism is so powerful and meaningful to us that we latch onto it, pattern our behavior around it, and teach our children to do the same. Such truisms are a rich part of the legacy we can pass down to our families.

- Models, like the DiSC personality assessment or the book *The Five Love Languages,* are great tools to pass down to your children to help them understand and relate to people effectively.

- You shouldn't force your intellectual capital on your kids or grandkids. An effective transfer takes place when the intellectual capital is modeled and when they seek you out and ask questions about it. Discussion is healthy; just ensure that the conversation is deep enough to be effective.

CHAPTER FOUR

Financial

"Shirtsleeves to shirtsleeves in three generations."
— PROVERB

What good is a book on legacy and family wealth if we do not address one of the most commonly observed, experienced, and quoted cycles about family legacies and wealth: "Shirtsleeves to shirtsleeves in three generations"? This proverb speaks to the worldwide phenomenon of a humble, uneducated first generation working very hard, breaking through barriers, and creating wealth while maintaining a frugal lifestyle. Then the second generation attends quality schools, becomes somewhat sophisticated professionals, and lives quite a high standard of living on the heels of the first. Then a third generation, who perhaps grew up in luxury, struggles with ambition and does little productive work, consumes wealth, and sets the stage for the fourth generation to go back to conditions very similar to where the first generation began.

Joseph: Having devoted decades in the trenches with multiple generations of wealthy families, I am here to tell you this wealth consumption cycle is real but can absolutely be avoided. Because it is my specialty and passion, Tony and I agreed that I would take the lead in this chapter.

My aim is to help you see how financial wealth is the equivalent of powerful, stored-up, highly transferable, and explosive energy and capability. When harnessed and utilized in the right way, it can inspire, cultivate, and ignite greatness in your family. When not, it can create mass destruction and negate other strengths and advantages.

Financially related legacy goals are quite common. I know; I've personally interviewed and served hundreds of family patriarchs and matriarchs, their adult children, and their adult grandchildren; and in some cases, even great-grandchildren have entered the picture. In this chapter, I'm going to show you how to pass on valuable financial wisdom, judgement, habits, and resources. These are the raw materials of how each generation can be resourceful, responsible, and highly effective stewards of time, talent, and treasure. I'm going to challenge you to lead by example and to engage the next generations as early as you can in the same journey.

ONE AIM, THREE GOALS

I think it's always healthy to begin with the end in mind. As succinctly as I can, I will convey the one aim and three aligned goals I want to encourage and challenge you to pursue related to your financial legacy:

Aim: Unleash yourself from the complexity of wealth so you and your family can flourish with good fortune.

Goal 1: Be a depletion-resistant wealth steward and encourage and teach each adult child and grandchild to be the same.

Goal 2: Be a penalty-resistant investor and encourage and teach each adult child and grandchild to be the same.

Goal 3: Be a stagnation-resistant individual and encourage and teach each adult child and grandchild to be the same.

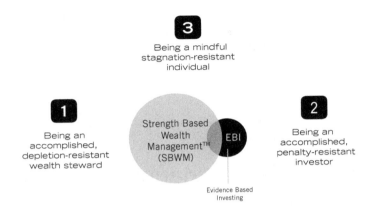

3 Milestones for Becoming Unleashed from the Complexities of Wealth
(So you can soar with your good fortune)

While it is beyond the scope of this book to dive into every detail of what it takes to achieve these outcomes, I do think it is very possible to point you in the right direction and get you solidly started with four indisputable fundamentals that took me a quarter of a century to pinpoint and develop with family matriarchs and patriarchs and the generations of their families:

1. Understand and master the Stages of Financial Freedom

2. Master and model the 35 Essential Strengths

3. Document and declare your Family Financial Manifesto

4. Support it all with a Complete Legacy Solution

UNDERSTAND AND MASTER THE STAGES OF FINANCIAL FREEDOM

The Stages of Financial Freedom (the Stages) is a simple concept that illustrates the ideal and not so ideal possibilities everyone has with money. Regardless of your age, or the age of your children or grandchildren, or the level of income or financial resources, the Stages provides a glimpse of each family member's financial past, present, and future. It's powerful because every single person in your family will be able to instantly pinpoint where they are, where they want to go, and where they are excelling or stagnating. In this way it opens up communication lines between spouses and the family as a whole about what it genuinely takes to navigate through each stage and achieve the aim and goals defined above.

As illustrated, there are five stages to be considered:

The Stages of Financial Freedom®

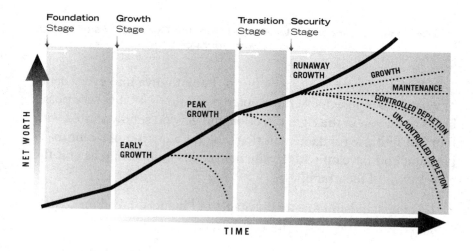

1. **The Foundation Stage**: The beginning point, typically in our early adulthood, where we focus on acquiring the basic necessities of life (employment, housing, furnishings, transportation, and other items) to establish a stable lifestyle upon which to build.

2. **The Growth Stage**: The typically long period of time when we grow our net worth and standard of living to the point where we accumulate the critical mass of assets needed to sustain a desired standard of living in the future with little or no dependence on earned income. This period is further divided into the Early Growth Stage (the first and second quartile) and the Peak Growth Stage (the third and fourth quartile). Notice how it is absolutely possible to stagnate or

even deplete wealth in the growth stage—an occurrence every family member will want to avoid.

3. **The Transition Stage**: The three-year period before and after retirement when we transition from earned income to retirement income. This is a period of economic and life adjustment, where numerous tax, investment, lifestyle, and estate planning modifications and decisions are made.

4. **The Security Stage**: The time in our lives when we need or choose to primarily live off of what we have built and accumulated. As illustrated, there are five potential directions our finances can go during the security stage: the maintenance, growth, or runaway growth distribution modes or the controlled depletion or uncontrolled depletion distribution modes. Since people are living longer and longer and extended periods of flat, low-return, or even waterfall-decline economic periods are possible, maximum levels of financial strength, agility, flexibility, and endurance (SAFE) need to be built, with room to spare, in order to avoid a higher probability of depletion than advisable in the security stage.

5. **The Distribution Stage**: The time when we use the last financial acts we control, through wills, trusts, and other estate planning tools, to distribute our estate to the next generation(s). This is when we make our final impact on our loved ones and the world. Those who succeed in preparing their estates and heirs for this eventuality, so the threat of depletion is mitigated for the next generations, succeed in navigating the Stages and avoid the shirtsleeves to shirtsleeves in three generations (or less) cycle.

Much can be said about optimally navigating the Stages. This is the financial task you must model first and foremost, via your legacy efforts, so you can help your children, and ultimately your grandchildren, be highly informed and master these stages themselves. Some generations will have it easier than others, simply because of the economic conditions that exist during their adulthood. Success is achieved when each generation avoids long stints of stagnation or outright depletion (see illustration below).

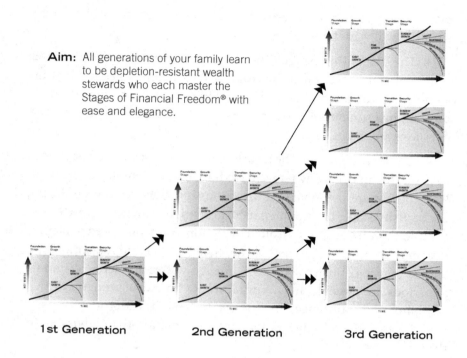

Aim: All generations of your family learn to be depletion-resistant wealth stewards who each master the Stages of Financial Freedom® with ease and elegance.

1st Generation   **2nd Generation**   **3rd Generation**

For now, simply begin by bringing this tool into your lives. A detailed discussion of the Stages, Habits, and Seeds of Financial Freedom can be obtained in my book, *Absolute Financial Freedom*. Also, I created a video presentation and workbook called "The Big Financial Breakthrough," which is available at www.janiczek.com/tbfb. I encourage you to watch it and then send it along to your adult children and grandchildren.

MASTER AND MODEL THE 35 ESSENTIAL STRENGTHS

I have dedicated three decades of my life and counting in the trenches with hundreds of families navigating the Stages of Financial Freedom. As I did this, it became quite clear to me that one financial advantage trumps all the others: operating from a position of optimal financial strength. This led me to develop and patent the Systems and Methods for Optimizing Wealth (United States Patent #8,903,739).

A key part of the patent is the 35 Essential Strengths I carefully researched, pinpointed, and fine-tuned. Your mission for your legacy should be to lead by example and make every single one an absolute strength in your personal finances. When you are well on your way, your mission will be to encourage and help each family member in the generation to follow to master and gain all thirty-five strengths.

In the introduction of this chapter, I mentioned one aim and three goals: **Aim**: Unleash yourself from the complexity of wealth so you and your family can flourish with good fortune. **Goal 1**: Be a depletion-resistant wealth steward and encourage and teach each adult child and grandchild to be the same. **Goal 2**: Be a penalty-resistant investor and encourage and teach each adult child and grandchild to be the same. (Go to www.janiczek.com/ebi for details on the merits of evidence-based investing.) **Goal 3**: Be a stagnation-resistant individual and encourage and teach each adult child and grandchild to be the same. The 35 Essential Strengths will take you far down this path; and in the process, they will best equip you and you next generations to successfully navigate the Stages through the ups, downs, and plateaus of life.

Appendix B outlines the 35 Essential Strengths and provides you with a glimpse of what a not-so-healthy and a healthy Wealth Optimization Dashboard looks like. Use this material to begin familiarizing yourself with the concept.

DOCUMENT AND DECLARE YOUR FAMILY FINANCIAL MANIFESTO

In working with many financially successful families, it has become quite clear to me that through time family members can easily forget what values, standards of excellence, and strategies got them to where they are and what values, standards of excellence, and strategies the family wants to formally declare and adopt going forward. In short, I began seeing the need to prepare a fairly formal document the family matriarch and patriarch can utilize themselves and then selectively share with the rest of the family over time. This document turned into the Family Financial Manifesto, and I encourage you to develop one for your family once you are far enough along in the Peak Growth Stage (fourth quartile and beyond). An abbreviated example of a Family Financial Manifesto is provided in Appendix C. Here's a brief overview of what one should contain:

1. An introductory statement that describes the purpose of the manifesto (to establish specific standards of excellence) and who is to utilize it (family, trustees, advisors)

2. A crystal clear declaration of how your assets should be proportioned to achieve preservation, lifestyle protection, and continued wealth creation goals. This should include the purpose of safety, market, and aspirational assets within your net worth

3. A clear declaration of investment standards you strongly believe in and want followed at all times such as diversification, cost efficiency, and simplicity

4. A clear declaration regarding the aim of all generations becoming accomplished, depletion-resistant wealth stewards

5. Standards related to the overall qualities of your balance sheet, cash flow, and portfolio

6. An explicit list of don't's/shall nots (from lessons learned from past mistakes made by you or others)

7. A listing of overall standards regarding wealth management

8. A listing of important financially related values the family is to follow

SUPPORT IT ALL WITH A COMPLETE LEGACY SOLUTION

As you get a glimpse of what it takes to successfully navigate the Stages, what it takes to master the 35 Essential Strengths, and the great need to document and educate family members on the standards of excellence you established through your Family Financial Manifesto, it should become abundantly clear to you how much sense it makes to have the proper systems, structure, support, and disciplines in place to achieve your family financial legacy goals. Putting all of these resources and techniques together in a cohesive solution for you and each generation of your family is what we call the Complete Legacy Solution. I advise you to select a professional advisor of your choice to authentically put these capabilities in place in a systematic way, along with the ongoing support needed to help each generation, beginning with yours, to achieve the overall aim and the three goals outlined at the beginning of this chapter. They will firmly put you and your family on the path of financial mastery.

Lastly, I repeat the truism I shared in Chapter Three to wrap this brief but useful chapter on finances with a bow: "A penny saved is a penny earned.* A penny saved and prudently invested is a good fortune. A good fortune elegantly stewarded and generously shared is a great legacy."

---

*This maxim is often attributed to Benjamin Franklin. However, Franklin's actual 1737 statement was "a penny saved is two pence clear." Then in 1758, his famous almanac noted "a penny saved is a penny got." More on this is available at www. forbes.com/sites/realspin/2014/08/18/a-penny-saved-was-never-a-penny-earned/.

VIPS

- Make it perfectly clear to your loved ones what success as a resourceful steward of wealth (no matter how little or much they have) looks like with the Stages of Financial Freedom.

- Share stories of success, failure, and course corrections. Zero in on wisdom learned from what worked and what did not.

- Acknowledge how external economic and creative destruction factors impact trajectories, and challenge each family member to learn how to successfully adapt to such conditions. (Conditions will differ between generations, and the best equipped families expect such change.)

- Utilize the 35 Essential Strengths, your own Family Financial Manifesto, and your own complete legacy solution (with advisors of your choosing) to formally establish standards of excellence and support that can greatly aid yourself and family members in mastering money.

- Tie in how items addressed in Chapter Five (be a lifelong learner, discover and share your greatest gifts and talents, reinforce meaningful goals with powerful habits, and recognize and pursue all four levels of happiness) influence your path on the Stages of Financial Freedom.

CHAPTER FIVE

Beliefs

"Give a man a fish and you feed him for a day.
Teach him to fish and you feed him for a lifetime."
— Proverb

As you read this book, you may come to recognize that making your indelible mark on the next generations comes from deep, loving relationships aimed at helping each family member confidently embrace life, truth, wisdom, challenge, and opportunity with dignity and fortitude. As much as you can and should share ways of thinking, acting, and being that have served you well in your own journey (as well as those that have not—so as to help family members avoid repeating the same mistakes), you come to a point of realizing that there are some basic, super-charged beliefs at the root of your being that gave you the ambition, perseverance, values, and course-correcting capability that led to all else. These super-charged beliefs are the most important to pass on, as they do not just feed the family for a day, a year, a decade, or a century; rather, they will feed them for their lifetime and eternity.

We encourage you to dig deep to identify these core beliefs that have served you and boldly make them the foundation of all of your legacy-building efforts. You will likely find that they are quite aligned with most or all of your other valuable tips and techniques. Frankly, if and when your family members embrace these root beliefs, they will be equipped to rapidly discover or create all the rest. It's also likely true that if they do not embrace these core beliefs, all the other tips and techniques may be beneficial to them but will in some way be hollow and vulnerable. What root beliefs are so critically important to you and your success that they meet all of this criteria and thus are the most important for you to pass on?

We put our heads together and zeroed in on four root beliefs that are on the top of both our lists. We humbly share them with you here. Feel free to embrace them if they ring true to you. Some or all may match yours, or you may want to start from scratch to identify your own. The key is to genuinely drill into the core beliefs that help you continually grow, help you make good decisions from the start, help you make timely course corrections when you err, and, simply put, are the root beliefs that serve you best and point you to an ultimate level of happiness. It is likely that the root of the highest transcendent order of things, such as love, beauty, justice, truth, peace, freedom, wisdom, and knowledge, are in some way connected to your super-beliefs. Once you document them, you will want to continually model and share them with each generation of your family so they can either consciously or subconsciously adopt them, very naturally and with full personal freedom of choice.

Here are our four:

1. Be a lifelong learner

2. Discover and share your greatest gifts and talents

3. Reinforce meaningful goals with powerful habits

4. Recognize and pursue all four levels of happiness (the fourth being the most important and enduring)

Here's an explanation of each of our core beliefs:

BE A LIFELONG LEARNER

Both of us enjoy an unquenchable hunger and thirst for the truth, and this appetite has helped us both to become quite intense lifelong learners. When we sat down to reflect on what root characteristics, beliefs, and values helped us the most, and which we would most want our children and grandchildren to embrace, being a lifelong learner made the top-four list.

Joseph: My wife Mary and I have modeled life-long learning so much that I believe it has naturally become quite ingrained in our family and legacy. It's been interesting to see how learning in our family manifests in different forms tailored to each family member by the type of structure that works best for each.

- I excel in experiential learning environments and in immersed self-study (books or recordings) that is quickly applied in real life situations.
- Our daughter Margie enjoys learning in the more formal structure of an academic setting or professional setting (self-teaching new skills when needed).
- Mary (who certainly had her full share of formal education all the way through to an MBA) now tends to excel by learning through groups (active group learning structure) and having an active reading regimen.
- John, an electrical engineer in an aerospace laboratory, seems to like the combination of formal and informal structures; and since he is so relationship oriented, he tends to go to those he respects and admires and asks for advice (the structure of informal mentoring).

The point is, with life-long learning as a strong belief, I think it is important to pursue the structure of learning that best fits each family member (and not force on them a structure that doesn't work).

In my research over the years, I have learned a lot from the work of Fred Kofman, a philosopher, author of *Conscious Business: How to Build Value through Values,* and now a vice president at LinkedIn. Among the jewels I found in his work, through a conference I attended, are the nine Enemies of Learning that I outlined with permission in my first book, Absolute Financial Freedom (Prosperity Press, 70–73). The first step to becoming a perpetual learner is to recognize and thwart the Enemies of Learning, which are essentially ill-conceived attitudes about the process of learning.

THE ENEMIES OF LEARNING

- "I already know this." Often at the root of this behavior is an insecure ego frightened of exposing an "expert's" ignorance. The person who says this may quickly discount valid information to support current beliefs.

- "I don't need to know this." This narrow focus is often a way of avoiding personal responsibility.

- "I don't want to know this." People say this who may be too impatient to learn, who believe that new information will threaten a strong belief, or who fear learning will reveal ignorance and make them look bad.

- "I can't learn this." This attitude often characterizes those who suffer from low self-esteem and insecurity, and who believe they are unable to comprehend a topic.

- "I won't give you permission to teach me this." People who say this automatically discount an author's competence or the relevance of the information.

- "I want to have it clear all the time." Many people don't enjoy the confusion that comes with learning and growing—often uncertainty and a required leap of faith on the front end and a sense of excitement, motivation, and clarity on the back end.

- "I want to be progressing all the time." The learning process involves plateaus where learning is still going on but not as obviously as some would like. Enjoying both the plateaus and the breakthroughs can be powerful and fulfilling.

- "I want to be entertained." Entertainment can lead to the debilitating instant-gratification attitude of, "If it's not fun, I don't want to do it." In the end, learning will provide more value and enjoyment.

- "Just answer my questions." Limiting yourself to specific, narrow questions stems from a posture of presumption. When you enter a new domain, this stand is usually ineffective.

When you recognize these Enemies of Learning and see them coming, step back, realize they are not consistent with your long-term objectives—for your success and for your legacy—and move forward with a healthy learner's attitude.

It's important that you clarify your own thinking about learning and what it means for you and your family to be lifelong seekers of truth. Include in your thought processes the purpose for such learning resources as college, workshops, reading, YouTube, the world today, and electronic options for learning.

Tony: Most people at the time of this publishing believe it's smart to get a college degree; and if that's your belief, you certainly need to pass that along to your kids. I happen to believe that college isn't for everyone and that *real-life learning* trumps getting a college degree. Of course, if someone wants to go into a career that requires a degree or a specific discipline of learning, then college is for sure the best path of learning for them. However, if a person wants to learn skill sets about how to be successful in life, there are faster and more efficient ways to learn than college.

> My belief is that learning and developing real-life concepts in your late teens and early twenties can give you a great jump on life.

When my kids went to college, I told them, "I really don't care about your grades; what I care about is your learning how to be successful in life. I want you to spend the most energy learning the things that you can really use." When my oldest daughter asked me after her first year of college to teach her how the world works, she was basically saying, "I'm not getting from college everything I need to know about how to be successful in this world, so I would like for you to teach me that." Like me, she has an insatiable hunger for truth, and she really got the fact that I didn't even care if she went to college to find it. However, since the college experience can be fun and it's a place to gain maturity, I wanted her to have that experience if that's what she desired. Your belief about learning may be similar to mine or you may have different beliefs; just know that it's important be clear on what you do believe so you can pass that along.

As a side note, when I hired coaches for my kids as they were growing up, I asked the college prep coach not to teach my kids using the word "jobs"; I asked the coach to teach them about careers. You may remember in Chapter Three that Joseph talked about how our lives are affected by the way we look at work—as a job, as a career, or as a vocation. I love his distinction, and it has transformed my thinking. Now what I want for my kids is for them to pursue a vocation rather than a career or a job.

> Continually expanding your knowledge can enhance your results infinitely into the future.

It's important to understand that learning is a verb, not a noun. It's more than just acquiring head knowledge; it's applying what you've learned to your life. You haven't truly learned anything until you've acted on it. A perpetual learner maintains a constant state of wonder (curiosity) and a hunger and thirst for learning—a skill increasingly important with today's rapid changes. Continually expanding your knowledge can enhance your results infinitely into the future. Perpetual learning helps you consistently learn things that you're not seeing (your *Blind Spots*) and course-correct to adapt to the most absolute truth.

DISCOVER AND SHARE YOUR GREATEST GIFTS AND TALENTS

Upon reflection, we both recognized that discovering and focusing on developing our greatest gifts and talents fairly early in life had had a deep impact on our success. In fact, we would both say our life journey has been a continual process of discovering our gifts and talents and finding the best ways to avoid being held back by our weaknesses. We both agreed that the more we can help our children grasp and live this concept, the more certain we can be that our kids are well suited to live a life of meaning, adventure, and mastery, rather than mediocrity.

Joseph: It's a little easier for me to see what worked in my life, now that I can reflectively weave together what I've read in great books, what I've learned from coaching, and what I've gleaned from a whole lot of experience (in our family and in many client families). What I discovered was that assessing and focusing on your natural talents, abilities, and competencies (not passions) is a very crucial, yet somewhat controversial, step in the process.

An important point is made in a book that came out several years ago called *So Good They Can't Ignore You: Why Skills Trump Passion in the Quest for Work You Love*, written by Cal Newport. The story behind the book is that Cal discovered a flaw in the conventional wisdom that so many profess: follow your passion. He made his case in the book and declared that approach to be outright wrong and dangerous.

In the book, Cal lays out a set of rules for focusing on craftsmanship and mastery (those areas where you have great talent and ability) and explains how passion is actually a byproduct of mastery. He got the idea while watching an interview of comedian Steve Martin on the Charlie Rose show, where Martin was talking about the advice he gives beginning actors and comedians when they ask him about career success. Martin said, "Nobody ever takes note (of my advice), because it's not the answer they want to hear. What they want to hear is 'Here's how you get an agent, here's how you write a script...' but what I always say is, 'Be so good they can't ignore you.'"

> "Be so good they can't ignore you."
> —Steve Martin

It's important to accept the fact that you and your children were born with many talents—just not in every domain of life. You excel in some areas and struggle in others. The secret to your success—and the success of your children—is to soar with the talents in which you very naturally and elegantly excel, and be so good with them that you can't be ignored.

It is actually very liberating to know you can let go of the areas where you struggle and embrace the ones in which you are gifted. Here's an exercise I first wrote about in my book *Absolute Financial Freedom* (246–252) that you can do for yourself and then encourage your young adult and adult children to complete on their own and then openly discuss with you if they feel comfortable:

Here's the process: Take out a sheet of paper and draw one line down the middle vertically and one across the middle horizontally.

In the upper left quadrant, write, "Extraordinary Ability, Results and Talent (EART)." These are the areas in which you absolutely demonstrate great promise and profound natural skill and ability, and in which you consistently achieve superior results when compared to all others. When these extraordinary capabilities are developed and combined with great skill, craftsmanship, and persistence, true passion, genius, innovation, and creativity will emerge and it will be clear that this is a valid talent to apply and pursue.

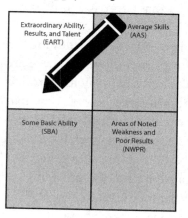

Your job with your children when they are young, when they are in the very formative early adulthood period, and when they go out on their own is to help them discover, challenge, and hone this extraordinary talent. It is here where you want to invest time, talent, and treasure the most to support and encourage, with everything from formal and informal education to helping them meet and regularly collaborate with others with similar and dissimilar EART (yes, amazing things happen when EARTs collide). Your goal is to provide a fruitful environment where they can learn to overcome obstacles, make course corrections, develop disciplines, and strategically think and act in ways that will maximize the EART opportunity at hand.

Now go to the bottom right quadrant and write: "Areas of Noted Weakness and Poor Results (NWPR)." I believe we all have weaknesses and should be open and honest about them so we can learn how to eliminate or mitigate them. A long time entrepreneurial coach of mine, Dan Sullivan, says, "All progress begins with the truth," and I know this to be true. Simply make a list of what weaknesses show up from time-to-time and where you very consistently experience poor results.

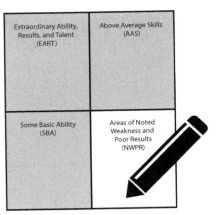

Your job with your children is neither to ignore weaknesses nor to over-emphasize them. It is mostly about helping them face and learn to creatively mitigate or eliminate such weaknesses. *We all have them!* Sharing your own stories and stories of how others have successfully overcome weaknesses is a great way to model this success skill. Using strategic thinking, you will want to help them learn how to consider items in this category as they make important life decisions about such things as college, profession, trade, and ultimately vocation focus. Of course, the items discovered in the EART category will need to be the dominant lead, and items in the NWPR will need to be confidently and thoughtfully neutralized.

Now move to the upper right quadrant and write "Above Average Skill (AAS)." List here the skills you're very good at, but not at the same level of extraordinary ability and results as those in the EART category. Frankly, it is this category that will help you separate very good from exceptional. The best way to distinguish between the two categories is the level of creativity, innovation, and elegance involved in achieving results. EART items not only achieve exceptional results; creativity, innovation, and elegance are undeniably demonstrated in the process, as well. AAS-category items achieve above-average results and stop just short of the rest.

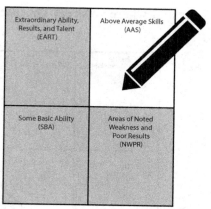

Your job with your children regarding AAS-category items is to acknowledge them and then support and develop them in a strong secondary capacity. Since opportunities will open up here, the more challenging part will be to help your child focus on the EART-category items and avoid pursuing AAS at the expense of EART. Simply put, be the parent/mentor that lovingly encourages them to pursue their EART and trust that they will naturally find the way. As for AAS, knowing they are above average in such talents will be an asset and will build their confidence. It's simply about not over-playing the AAS category and under-playing the EART.

Finally, in the bottom left quadrant, write: "Some Basic Ability (SBA)." In this quadrant list items where a basic level of competency exists—no less, no more. You might categorize these items as being in the mediocre level of skill and ability. Certainly any obstacle, challenge, or time constraint would greatly impact results (cause them to "fail"), and above-average results and creativity are out of the question with these items.

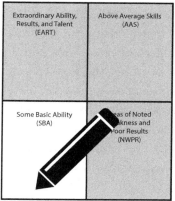

Your task here as a parent and mentor is very similar to your charge in the NWPR category above. There is only one exception: There may be an area in which some proper training would move the item into the AAS category. Either way, some effort needs to be expended here to mitigate the item, as SBA is a category to avoid.

We all have things in all four categories. If you asked me to fix a car or physically build something, I'd likely break things, I'd be frustrated, I'd hate it, and I would avoid doing it. That's in my "Areas of Noted Weakness and Poor Results" zone. However, financial advisory is part of my unique ability. I'm able to capture the essence of what it takes to get the Essential 15% of things to succeed at the highest level. (The

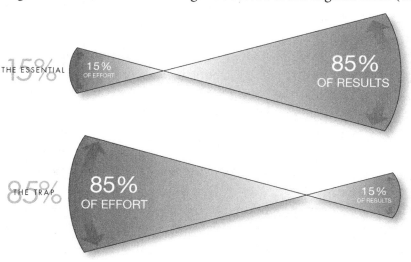

Essential 15% approach, similar to Tony's *High Leverage Activities,* was inspired by systems and statistical expert W. Edwards Deming, who statistically proved that focusing on the first 15 percent of anything and getting that right gives you 85 percent of the results you want. In contrast, when any of us get the first 15 percent wrong [such as selecting the wrong strategy or approach], we doom ourselves to what I coined as the 85 Percent Trap. The 85 Percent Trap is akin to spinning your wheels in conditions where you only have the possibility to influence a maximum of 15 percent of results [see graphic]. The goal is to teach our kids to be effective and efficient. Effective is doing the right thing; and that, to me, is the Essential 15%. Efficiency is doing things right, which is basically the Essential 15% squared.)

When we help our kids discover where they truly have unique talents, skills, and abilities, it will help them create such a hunger and thirst and interest that they will go into that alpha state of their brain that erases time when they're working in those areas. Many of my days and even weeks and months have nothing to do with time whatsoever, because I'm working in this alpha state. It's where I have my greatest breakthroughs, and I would love for my kids to be able to enjoy the same advantage and privilege.

Of course, how you work with your kids to help them discover their gifts and talents will differ, depending on your stage of life—whether you're still parenting younger kids, they're coming into adulthood, they're out on their own, or they're newly in the workforce or long in the workforce.

I think it's important that we address here the negative pressure that our kids may get from high school or college counselors to choose a degree path under the wrong approach (follow passion instead of follow gifted talents). I believe our kids would be better served if guidance counselors would break away from current conventional wisdom and instead route them toward exceptional craftsmanship by working with them and their parents to assess their talents and incompetencies.

Most of us want our children to be effective (do the right things) and efficient (do things right) in life. By uncovering, observing, assessing, nourishing, and guiding their talents during each stage of their lives, we can help them not only pursue the things that contribute to their happiness, but also support the best use of their natural talents to be both effective and efficient in the process.

Each individual is born with a unique DNA and personality; and a powerful thing you can do as a parent is to identify any of your kids' talents that might come as a result of your family's DNA, as well as those that are built into their unique personalities. Looking for early signs of talent and then nourishing those talents could help them discover their pathway to happiness and success.

Tony: As an example, we noticed when she was four that Brooke, our oldest daughter, would go into her closet and organize her shoes, and then she would organize her clothes. So, even though she was only four years old, I had a business card made for her that said, "Brooke Jeary, Organizer." I nourished that talent for years while she was young, and then I saw that organization morph into creativity. Then I began nourishing and highlighting that talent by finding ways to post and/or frame her paintings and drawings. Her passion and her gifting eventually led her to become a very talented and organized graphic artist.

As they grew older, I put my kids through different talent assessments and personality profiles so they could understand where their strengths were and so I could better route them accordingly. My youngest daughter, Paige, has a very special eye for photography, so I have encouraged and reinforced that talent for years, as well. I explained to both girls that those gifts and talents seemed to be passed down from my mother and grandmother, who were artistically gifted and who started a highly successful arts and crafts show (Affair of the Heart) ten years before my girls were even born that has grown over the last thirty-plus years into one of the largest and oldest in the world. I was happy to see them flourish in the talents that had been passed down through our family legacy.

We believe it's important, though, to allow your kids to follow their own path to happiness by pursuing the talents of their own choosing, rather than the talents you selectively point out or choose for them. I've seen several successful and wealthy parents who push their kids to take over their business, rather than letting their kids choose their own pathway. Both of our daughters are leaders and have the perfect personalities to take over my business, and yet they currently have no interest in doing so. I realize that my life's work may not live on like it could if my girls had an interest in taking on the platform and connections related to my agency, and I'm really okay with that. My daughters won't find happiness doing something I might want them to do; they will only find happiness doing what they want to do.

REINFORCE MEANINGFUL GOALS WITH POWERFUL HABITS

As we thought about other super-beliefs that have served us well and also helped our children be successful in life, we knew that habits had to be the third belief we would recommend for you to model and teach to your own family members. We have both dedicated an enormous amount of time to developing powerful habits around meaningful goals in our lives, and we're convinced we would not be anywhere nearly as successful without this root capability. Both of us have also invested decades into developing a great body of work around habits.

Simply put, the results we get in our lives can be directly attributed to the habits we form. You can change your life to be anything you want it to be by changing your habits. Tony made habits the last foundational lesson of his SUCCESS course and book (RESULTS Faster!), because they are so important to success—period! Habits are a huge part of the legacy puzzle; they are powerful forces in your life that represent the combination of action and behaviors you execute on a conscious and subconscious basis daily. Developing good habits allows you to master the things in life that are important to you and helps you weed out bad habits. The bottom line is, good habits make you more productive and set you up to better succeed. So by developing, modeling, and then passing good habits along to your children, you give them many lifelong benefits.

It's important to model for your children that any of us can achieve mastery in any area of our lives if we're truly willing to commit our habits to it entirely. We continue in our habits because we crave and reward the outcomes. Think about it. How often do you keep a bad habit because you crave what it gives you? Here's a profound truth:

You have to strategically lift up and see the big picture, and then make whatever changes are necessary to improve your habits. If you're intentional about developing good habits, you will eventually replace the bad habits. It's like growing grass. If you grow grass, it chokes out the weeds. If you put good habits in, you can choke out your bad habits.

The truth is, habits are so powerful that you are 100 percent disciplined to them, good or bad. Whatever your habit, you execute it with great consistency—over and over into the future. For example, people with poor eating habits often remain loyal to them even when they know they will likely lead to weight or health problems.

You have habits both by design and by default. Your habits by design are those you purposefully implant to align your consistent behavior with your goals. If your goal is to have healthy teeth and fresh breath, for instance, your habit of brushing your teeth multiple times a day is a habit by design. On the other hand, you form habits by default out of chance and environment—like washing your hands before each meal because your parents ingrained that habit in you. By creating an awareness of which habits you formed by design and by default, you will be empowered to discover how to develop habits by choice.

The good news is, the enormous power of developing good habits can actually be considered a shortcut to success. You can program yourself for success by selecting and mastering desirable habits at will. There is actually no such thing as "successful" or "unsuccessful" people. Rather, there are people with successful habits and people with unsuccessful habits. The key is aligning your habits with your goals, your values, and the natural forces in life to create your desired outcomes.

By modeling and teaching your children to align their habits and goals with their values, you will help them have a much more congruent and masterful life. Think back to Chapter Three when we were talking about values, and we asked you to identify the values that are most important to you. If you'll pull out that list right now, we'll show you how to connect habits to each one of them.

Tony: In my 2017 book *RESULTS Faster!* I shared my top ten values to show the reader the power of correlating your habits with your values. I'll share a sampling of that exercise here so you can really grasp what we're talking about and model this exercise for yourself and your children.

1. One of my top values is personal faith. One of my habits, then, is to constantly pray throughout the day.

2. Another of my top values is altruism. One of my ongoing habits is to look for ways to be of value to others, and I have strategically built my life-long value arsenal that helps me do that.

3. Good health is another of my top values. I apply my strategic health habit by training virtually every day and eating healthy (approximately every ninety minutes). I'm even strategic about my snacking. Another habit is to go to bed early and sleep eight hours a night. All of these are habits that lead to my good health.

4. My family is obviously one of my top values, so I developed the habit of scheduling activities of interest, fun, and learning with my family members. Another habit I developed is carefully asking questions and listening to my kids. My daughter often says to me, "Dad, I love it that you listen to me." If you're around your kids and you're not listening, maybe that's a habit you need to pick up. Another habit is that I give sincere compliments to my kids, encouraging them and building up their self-esteem.

I think you get the picture. Now, using the values and habits I shared as a model, you can go through the same exercise and identify the habits that will support your top values. Then make those values and matching habits part of your legacy to help your children be the best they can be.

Joseph: The best way I like to put it is that I love putting things on automatic. In fact, once I learn how to do something that is extremely effective (doing the right thing) and efficient (doing it right) I immediately begin looking for ways to put the success on automatic via powerful habits.

I dedicated a good portion of my book *Absolute Financial Freedom* to the power of habits, and I talked about the Habits of Financial Freedom I've identified in my work. In short, I discovered three categories of financial habits that, when mastered, put a person on the path to financial mastery:

1. The Control Habits
   a. The Point of Reference Habit
   b. The Saving Habit
   c. The Short-term Security Habit
   d. The Debt Habit
   e. The Spending Habit
   f. The Giving Habit

2. The Optimization Habits
   a. The Income Optimization Habit
   b. The Balance Sheet Optimization Habit
   c. The Investment Optimization Habit
   d. The Estate Optimization Habit

3. The Integration Habits
   a. The Financial Freedom Habit
   b. The Unified Goal Habit

I recognize that when someone looks at the quantity of these habits, they may think, *I'm just not that interested in money matters.* Here's my response to that, as surprising as it may sound (coming from a financial advisor): I am not that interested in money, either. The reality is that my interest is in unleashing people from the complexities of money so they can flourish with good and great fortunes. My interest comes from absolutely hating to see people struggle with money (money mastering them instead of vice versa). The Habits of Financial Freedom are really about ways to make money mastery automated and less time-consuming so you can dedicate your time to much more important pursuits.

My work on the Habits of Financial Freedom led to an even more elegant way to put these habits on automatic via the 35 Essential Strengths and the Wealth Optimization Dashboard that is a part of the system I patented. (See Appendix B for an example.)

Both Tony and I strongly believe that you need to consciously focus on the action leading to a habit for a long enough period that it becomes automatic—both consciously and subconsciously. This requires focus, because until the new habit is burned in, any drifting outside of the focus goes straight back to old habits, sabotaging your success in implanting new desired habits. In my book *Absolute Financial Freedom* (118-127), I list seven rules to follow that are crucial for your success in developing new habits. See Appendix D for a listing of the seven rules.

RECOGNIZE AND PURSUE ALL FOUR LEVELS OF HAPPINESS (THE FOURTH BEING THE MOST IMPORTANT AND ENDURING).

Okay, we deliberately saved what we both believe to be the most important belief for last. No, not because it is last on our minds (actually, its first and foremost on both of our minds), but mainly due to the fact that it gives very natural order to the other three, as well as everything else in the book. Yes, this fourth belief can be considered the super-belief of super-beliefs because it ties in basic human desires with the transcendent desires (love, beauty, justice, truth, eternal life, and God). Nothing is as important to us as passing this wisdom on to our family members (and, of course, others).

Joseph: I first learned about the Aristotilian four levels of happiness from Fr. Robert Spitzer, SJ, Ph.D., who has written and spoken extensively about them. Fr. Spitzer points out that throughout the centuries philosophers (and later psychologists) have written extensively about four major kinds of desire and happiness (discussed below), so a tremendous body of work exists in support of this material.

Here is my paraphrased and borrowed (with permission) explanation of the four levels, organized on the basis of their pervasiveness, endurance, and depth:

1. **Level One: Immediate Gratification (External Pleasure).** These are bursts of mostly pleasure-inducing pursuits that are connected with biological instincts for survival and propagation (food, drink,

shelter, physical stimulus, procreation, and safety). While not bad, in and of themselves; they are shallow and relatively short-lived. If we over indulge or fixate on these pursuits, they will lead to a crisis and unhappiness (over eating, addiction, etc.). Most move to the second kind of happiness, and then to the third and hopefully to the fourth.

2. **Level Two: Achievement (Ego-Comparative Desires).** Because we are human and have the ability to be aware of ourselves and the outer world, it doesn't take long for us to become competitive. The competition goes beyond winning and losing, and we begin to seek advantage in anything from achievement to popularity, status, beauty, intelligence, control, power, and every other form of honor or prestige. It's the desire for happiness at this level that leads us to make money, have a nice house, achieve fame and fortune, win over someone else, gain a new degree, etc. Yes, these quests can create longer enduring happiness and pleasure than the pursuits in Level One; however, if you pursue comparative achievement as an end, once you look harder, you soon discover that someone else has more, is smarter, is more popular, healthier, younger, stronger, etc., and an existential crisis will be created. Again, there's nothing wrong with pursuing achievement goals; it just becomes an issue when our search for desire and happiness artificially ends here. Most of us learn that we can apply our self-awareness in a new way that is less about us (and our achievement) and more about others, giving rise to the third level of desire/happiness.

3. **Level Three: Giving/Charity (Contributive-Empathetic).** Once we recognize we have the ability to enhance the outer world—even to the point of self-sacrifice—and make others' lives better, we enter this third level. Since you're reading this book and interested in making an indelible positive mark on the lives of your family members, it's probably safe to say your motivation comes from this empathetic desire. Both Tony's and my motivation for writing this book is strongly tied to this third level of happiness (and yes, no doubt there are Level Two elements at play as well). Empathy (a radical openness to the goodness of another) moves us from the self-centeredness and competition of Level Two and opens the way to sympathy (caring about and caring for others), which is the source of charity. Giving to someone evokes great feelings of joy and happiness; and whether it's giving to our kids,

to our friends, or to the poor or sick, it's seen as a pursuit of the common good. Great thinkers throughout the ages have recognized that we each have a conscience that manifests in an attraction to and love of goodness-justice and an inner shunning and fear of evil-injustice. It is our conscience that leads us to adhere to the silver rule—do not do a harm to others that you do not want done to you—which is the foundation for human civility, common law, and social order. Empathy and conscience can not only prevent us from doing something negative; they can also move us toward great heights of good and give us a sense of purpose. Living a life of significance is related to this desire. However, as great as giving is, and as much as it makes the world a better place, if you stop here you hit a crisis point, because Level Three does not deal with transcendental desires (see below) and the yearning for the sacred that is inherent in all of us.

4. **Level Four: Transcendental Happiness (perfect love, truth, goodness, beauty, home, and the sacred—God).** According to a 2012 study by the Pew Center,[5] 84 percent of the world's population identifies with a religious group that worships some sort of "divine other." Some religions refer to this "divine other" as a personal God, some as a universal creative power, and some as a supreme consciousness that is both within us and beyond us. It's all related to the cosmic struggle between good and evil and our human desire for perfect truth, perfect love, perfect goodness, perfect beauty and perfect home. If these perfect things are not to be found in this finite world, then our nature must be transcendent (beyond the limits of ordinary experience) and our destiny beyond this world. If we want to live our lives to the fullest degree possible here on this earth, we will live it in earnest pursuit of this most enduring and pervasive level, with its highest rewards gained after we leave this life.[6]

While beyond the scope of this book to explore at length, Tony and I both profess the good news of Jesus in the sacred Christian Gospels

---

5 "The Global Religious Landscape," Pew Research Center, December 18, 2012, http://www.pewforum.org/2012/12/18/global-religious-landscape-exec/ (accessed 1/23/17).
6 Information in this section taken from "The Four Levels of Happiness" by Robert J. Spitzer, May 2014, Magis Center of Reason and Faith.

as the truth, the light, and the way (to Transcendental Level Four Happiness). We believe these Gospels and the Holy Bible (Old and New Testaments) reveal the truth of creation, the source of evil (twisted truth to be overcome), and the redemptive truth (salvation through following Jesus Christ) and earnestly seek to pass on this good news to our children and grandchildren so our happiness can be enjoyed, by the grace of God, for all of eternity together.

We believe ordering our lives centered on love of God and neighbor, which Jesus said are the two greatest commandments (Matthew 22:37-39), helps us to be humble and avoid being prideful (the root of evil). We further believe that God's plan for happiness is set out in the eight "beatitudes" found in Matthew 5:3-10 in the Bible. The first beatitude, "Blessed are the poor in spirit, for theirs is the kingdom of heaven (Matthew 5:3, NIV)," can basically be interpreted as a promise of happiness (being "blessed") for those who have a hunger and thirst for truth (are "poor in spirit"). The highest order of this truth is transcendental truth. Other beatitudes are about disconnecting to worldly things, which relates to not putting Levels One, Two, and Three above Level Four. The highest and best aim we have for our legacy is to pass along our Christian faith to our children and grandchildren and ecourage their lifelong hunger and thirst for this truth.

Given that we believe that the most important thing we can do as parents is to guide our children on a path that will lead them to heaven, we want to share with you some great truths we discovered in the book *Families and Faith: How Religion is Passed Down across Generations*, by Vern Bengtson. The author points out that, "For religious mothers and fathers, transmitting faith to offspring is an important part of that [socialization] preparation. Their efforts at religious socialization in most cases are reinforced and amplified through religious organizations, most of which have extensive programs and activities directed toward training children and youth in practices and beliefs. *Still, parents are the key to religious socialization*" (emphasis ours).[7] He went on to say, "In studying religious transmission, we wanted to examine

---

7 Vern Bengtson, *Families and Faith: How Religion is Passed Down across Generations,* (New York, Oxford University Press, 2013), 72.

differences between children who feel close to their parents compared to those who do not. In each wave of the study, we asked questions assessing intergenerational solidarity of both parents and children... *Close parent-child bonds are more conducive to religious socialization, and in the absence of close parent-child bonds, this transmission is less likely to occur"* (emphasis ours).[8]

Whatever your beliefs are, it's important to understand that the pursuit of perfect truth, perfect love, perfect beauty, perfect justice and perfect home is the most significant thing you can do to find happiness. You can debate many different things, and yet most everyone can agree that absolute truth exists and must be pursued if we are to find the truly meaningful life. We suggest you think about what's really important to your happiness and constantly filter your activities accordingly. Then pass along that understanding to your children and watch them flourish!

---

8 Ibid, 73-74.

VIPS

- There are some basic, super-charged beliefs at the root of your being that gave you the direction, ambition, virtues, perseverance, values, and course-correcting capability that led to all else. These super-charged beliefs are the most important to pass on, as they do not just feed the family for a day, a year, a decade, or a century; rather, they will feed them for their lifetime and eternity.

- Clarify your own thinking about learning and what it means for you and your family to be lifelong seekers of truth. Include in your thought processes the purpose for such learning resources as college, workshops, reading, YouTube, the world today, and electronic options for learning. Be sure to pursue the structure of learning that best fits each family member and not force on them a structure that doesn't work.

- Learning is a verb, not a noun. It's more than just acquiring head knowledge; it's applying what you've learned to your life. You haven't truly learned anything until you've acted on it.

- We all want our children to be effective (do the right things) and efficient (do things right) in life. By uncovering, observing, assessing, nourishing, and guiding their talents during each stage of their lives, we can help them not only pursue the things that make them happy, but also support the best use of their natural talents to be both effective and efficient in the process.

- Strategically allow your kids to follow their own path to happiness by pursuing the talents of their own choosing, rather than the talents and/or career paths you choose for them.

- The results we get in our lives can be directly attributed to the habits we form. Developing good habits, modeling them, and then passing them along to your children gives them many lifelong benefits and can put otherwise complex components of success on automatic.

- Model for your children that any of us can achieve mastery in any area of our lives if we're truly willing to commit our habits to it entirely.

- By teaching your children to align their habits with their values, you will help them have a much more congruent and masterful life.

- The Four Levels of Happiness provide context, order, and priority to various life pursuits and explain the crisis you can or will experience if stopping short of Level Four (Transcendental Happiness).

- Whatever your beliefs presently are, it's important to understand that your and your family's pursuit of perfect truth, perfect love, perfect beauty, perfect justice, and perfect home is the most significant thing you all can do to experience eternal joy and happiness together.

PART THREE:

Conclusion: Ensuring You Have the Right Team and Tools

Conclusion: Ensuring You Have the Right Team and Tools

To get the optimal results from any endeavor, it's best to think of form before function. After you get really clear on what you want to achieve, look at the form that's there to support you before you go on to execution.

When you started reading this book you signed up to expand your thinking about family legacy; and to help you do that we've given you some of our best thinking in five different areas: Communication, People, Intellectual Capital, Financial, and Beliefs. When you have the right team and tools in place (the form), you have the infrastructure to function masterfully in each of those areas, and the stars will align to increase your chances of success. The right team and tools are the key forms that will help you make the greatest progress.

In Chapter Two we talked about having the right team members in place to not only support our individual success but to also support our ability to transfer a big part of who we are to our heirs. And throughout the book we talked about a variety of tools that we have used personally and with our clients. Now it's up to you. If you really want to ensure that your legacy plays out the way you want, then you must be diligent in putting your personal team together and making the best use of the tools we've suggested.

THE ESSENCE OF THE BOOK

This book is about being more strategic in creating the legacy you want for your family, and we've given you our best ideas on how that can be done. We realize that we've shared a great deal of information, and we know it can be overwhelming. One of the things we both do when we read a book and expand our own thinking is filter it down and really get the essence of it. So in order to make it easier for you, we decided to give you a review of the main points of the book that you can use to rate yourself as you go forward. If we've impacted you as a reader, you may want to take this little summary and make it your action plan.

PART ONE: THE FAMILY LEGACY (THE WHAT AND WHY)

- As you plan your legacy, know what that golden nugget is and how you want it to impact your family members.
- Strategically think about your legacy on a higher plane.

PART TWO: BEST PRACTICES FOR CREATING A GREAT FAMILY LEGACY (THE HOW)

Chapter One: Communication

- There are potentially five stages of relationship with your children, and each stage requires adjustments in the way you communicate.
- Meet your family members where they are in life as they grow and learn and explore their own places.
- Be *Communication Ready* to respond and course-correct in real time when events happen.
- Take advantage of holidays and events to create proactive communication and promote legacy with your children.

Chapter Two: People

- Who you spend time with, you become. Model this for your kids and make sure they understand it and live it.

- Build a great Life Team and share it with your heirs.

- Open doors for your children by transferring your connections and relationships.

- Expand your legacy-building efforts to in-laws and grandchildren, when the time comes. Legacy is viral and flows in all directions, not just north to south.

Chapter Three: Intellectual Capital

- The values we instill in our children play a substantial role in teaching them to be successful in life and in passing down family legacy.

- Encourage each family member to develop standards that reflect the way they want to live each day.

- Find your family's rhythm of success through rituals and traditions.

- You shouldn't force your intellectual capital on your kids or grandkids. An effective transfer takes place when the intellectual capital is modeled and when they seek you out and ask questions about it.

Chapter Four: Financial

- Make it perfectly clear to your loved-ones what success as a resourceful steward of wealth (no matter how little or much they have) looks like with the Stages of Financial Freedom.

- Share stories of success, failure, and course corrections. Zero in on wisdom learned from what worked and what did not.

- Acknowledge how external economic and creative destruction factors impact trajectories, and challenge each family member to learn how to successfully adapt to such conditions. (Conditions will differ between generations and the best-equipped families expect such change.)

- Utilize the 35 Essential Strengths, your own Family Financial Manifesto and your own complete legacy solution (with advisors of your choosing) to formally establish standards of excellence and support that can greatly aid yourself and family members in mastering money.

Chapter Five: Beliefs

- There are some basic, super-charged beliefs at the root of your being that gave you the direction, ambition, virtues, perseverance, values, and course-correcting capability that led to all else. It is these super-charged beliefs that are the most important to pass on, as they do not just feed the family for a day, a year, a decade, or a century; rather, they will feed them for their lifetime and eternity.

- Learning is a verb, not a noun. It's more than just acquiring head knowledge; it's applying what you've learned to your life. You haven't truly learned anything until you've acted on it.

- We all want our children to be effective (do the right things) and efficient (do things right) in life. By uncovering, observing, assessing, nourishing, and guiding their talents during each stage of their lives, we can help them not only pursue the things that make them happy, but also support the best use of their natural talents to be both effective and efficient in the process.

- The results we get in our lives can be directly attributed to the habits we form. Developing good habits, modeling them, and then passing them along to your children gives them many lifelong benefits and can put otherwise complex components of success on automatic. Model for your children that any of us can achieve mastery in any area of our lives if we're truly willing to commit our habits to it entirely. By teaching your children to align their habits with their values, you will help them have a much more congruent and masterful life.

- The Four Levels of Happiness provide context, order, and priority to various life pursuits and explain the crisis you can or will experience if stopping short of Level Four (Transcendental

Graphic Overview

Communication	People	Intellectual Capital	Financial	Beliefs
Five Stages of Relationships	Build the Right Communities; Choose the Right Friends	Define Model, and Pass on Your Values	Understand and Master the Stages of Financial Freedom	Be a Lifelong Learner
Meet Your Family Members Where They Are	Build a Great Life Team to Share	Create and Implement Strong Family Standards	Master and Model the 35 Essential Strengths	Discover and Share Your Greatest Gifts and Talents
Remain Communication Ready to Combat Outside Influences	Open Doors with Your Contacts (Rolodex)	Find Your Family's Rhythm of Success through Traditions/Rituals	Document and Declare Your Family Financial Manifesto	Reinforce Meaningful Goals with Powerful Habits
Create Proactive Communication	Integrate Inlaws and Grandkids into the Legacy	Capitalize on Truisms and Models	Support it All with a Complete Legacy Solution	Recognize and Pursue all Four Levels of Happiness

Happiness). Whatever your beliefs presently are, it's important to understand that your and your family's pursuit of perfect truth, perfect love, perfect beauty, perfect justice, and perfect home is the most significant thing you all can do to experience eternal joy and happiness together.

We sincerely pray that you can use the ideas we've shared in this book to shape an incredible legacy for your family. If we've made that kind of impact on you, we hope you will pass along a copy of this book to each of your adult children and grandchildren and make it a part of your legacy.

About the Authors

Tony Jeary, known as The RESULTS Guy™, is a strategist, thought leader, and prolific author of over forty titles, multiple best sellers, and hundreds of courses.

Tony is unique and sought after by the world's best. His client list has now exceeded 1,000 organizations in over fifty countries. He truly is a special resource that delivers and is a "secret weapon" to many business savvy leaders.

For more than two decades, Tony has coached the world's top CEOs, entrepreneurs, and high achievers. He has personally advised the presidents of Walmart, SAM's Club, Ford, Shell, Samsung, New York Life, American Airlines, Texaco, TGI Fridays, and Firestone, as well as entrepreneurs from Forbes Richest 400 and even the US Senate's Sergeant of Arms.

His specialty is compressed time. He partners with selected clients to clarify their visions and ensure they stay focused so they execute with extreme accountability, resulting in carving years off most client's strategic visions. He delivers "Vision to Reality" in time frames many can't even believe.

Tony practices daily the business mantra his father taught him growing up, "Give Value... Do More Than is Expected."

Tony lives and works in DFW where, at his private RESULTS Center, he and his hand-picked team strategically assemble powerful game plans, inspire high performance, and encourage all those he touches, resulting in enhanced sales/profits, and raising companies' value. He has been happily married for over twenty-five years; and at the time of this publishing, he and his wife have three wonderful adult children—two daughters and a son-in-law.

Joseph J. Janiczek, ChFC, MSFS, is Founder and CEO of Denver, Colorado, headquartered Janiczek Wealth Management, which exclusively serves high net-worth ($2 million to $20 million portfolios) and ultra-high-net-worth ($20 million + portfolios) individuals and families across the country. He and his firm have been named among the top, best and most exclusive wealth advisors in the nation multiple times.* Go to www.janiczek.com for more information.

Joseph spent decades in the trenches with families experiencing life-changing liquidity events (such as selling a business, exercising highly appreciated stock options, etc.) and ultimately developed and patented Systems and Methods for Optimizing Wealth. He is a pioneer in the disciplines of Evidence-Based Investing (EBI) and Strength-Based Wealth Management (SBWM) and an award-winning author of *Absolute Financial Freedom* and *Investing from a Position of Strength.*

Joseph and his wife Mary reside in Colorado, where they raised their (now adult) children Margie and John. They both feel quite blessed to have grown up in loving, caring, and relationship-oriented families and attribute the roots of their resourcefulness, work ethic, and faith formation to their parents and their robust Catholic church and faith community.

*Ranked/Named among Top, Best and Most Exclusive Advisors sources: Barron's March 2017, 2016, 2015, 2014; Advisory HQ March 2016; Financial Times June 2015; Five Star Professional November 2015, 2013, 2012,2011, 2010, 2009; Mutual Funds Magazine January 2001; NABCAP September 2010, 2011, 2013; Worth Magazine July 2002, January 2004, October 2004, October 2008; Wealth & Finance International, October 2014. Rankings and/or recognition by unaffiliated rating services and/or publications should not be construed by a client or prospective client as a guarantee that he/she will experience a certain level of results if Janiczek & Company, Ltd. is engaged, or continues to be engaged, to provide investment advisory services, nor should it be construed as a current or past endorsement of Janiczek & Company, Ltd. by any of its clients. Rankings published by magazines, and others, generally base their selections exclusively on information prepared and/or submitted by the recognized adviser. A copy of the Janiczek & Company, Ltd. written disclosure statement discussing our advisory services and fees is available upon request. Go to www.janiczek.com for more details or call 303-721-7000.

Other Books and Resources

OTHER BOOKS BY TONY JEARY

1. Inspire Any Audience
2. Strategies for Business Peak Performance
3. Designing Your Own Life
4. Finding 100 Extra Minutes in a Day
5. Meeting Magic
6. We've Got to Stop Meeting Like This
7. Ice Breakers
8. Speaking Spice
9. A Good Sense Guide to Happiness
10. Success Acceleration
11. Happy Families
12. Fun Things to do as Kids
13. Persuade Any Audience
14. Presenting with Style
15. Building Your Dream Home
16. Too Many Emails
17. Winning Seminars
18. 136 Effective Presentation Tips
19. Complete Guide to Effective Facilitation
20. Training Others to Train
21. NLP Mastery
22. Neuro Linguistic Communication P.A.
23. 10 Essentials to Execution
24. One-on-One Presentations (Coaching)
25. Monday Morning Communications

26. Speaking from the Top
27. Nervous to Natural
28. Images of Beauty
29. Presentation Mastery for Realtors
30. Presenting Learning
31. Life Is A Series Of Presentations
32. Purpose Filled Presentations
33. Negotiation Mastery
34. The 180 Rules
35. Ultimate Health
36. Leadership 25
37. Strategic Acceleration
38. We've Got to Start Meeting and Emailing Like This
39. Thinking Pays!
40. Business Ground Rules
41. Strategic Parenting
42. Living in the Black
43. Leverage
44. Rich Relationships
45. Advice Matters
46. Strategic Selling
47. Change—It's All About Mindset
48. RESULTS Faster

Coming Soon:
49. Black Card Access
50. Strategic Network Marketing
51. Money Mastery
52. Money Kit
53. Strategic Learning

**Visit www.tonyjeary.com and watch Tony's free webinar
at www.tonyjeary.com/resultsfasterwebinar**

OTHER BOOKS AND RESOURCES BY JOSEPH J. JANICZEK

Investing from a Position of Strength

Many people fail to see and capitalize on the connection between optimal levels of financial strength, agility, flexibility, endurance, and investment success. This book identifies that the key to surviving and thriving in all economic and investment climates is financial strength. Joseph J. Janiczek, MSFS, ChFC, named among the top, best, and most exclusive wealth advisors in the nation multiple times,* pioneered optimal ways of measuring, building, and permanently maintaining financial strength; and he shares his many tools and techniques in this groundbreaking book.

Absolute Financial Freedom

This book was named Best Business/Finance book of the Year by CIPA when it was first released (in 2000). It's Mr. Janiczek's extensive look into the Stages of Financial Freedom® (a detailed financial road map, including commonly experienced dead-ends—and how to avoid them), the Habits of Financial Freedom® (over a dozen key habits to develop and put on automatic), and the Seeds of Financial Freedom® (key attitudes and beliefs most compatible with financial success and mastery). Written to demonstrate the complete path from poverty to priviledge, this book is designed to assist all generations of your family in learning to be exceptional, depletion-resistant stewards of financial resources (whether you have a small, medium, or large amount).

www.janiczek.com

Read timely blog posts written by Mr. Janiczek and other professionals at his highly specialized investment and wealth-management company. Keep up on the latest in Evidence-Based Investing (EBI) and Strength-Based Wealth Management® (SBWM).

Coming Soon:

1. 10 Major Things High Net Worth Investors Miss (and how to quickly pivot to gain them)

2. Leashed Unleashed: How to tame money when you have a little, a lot, or somewhere in between

Our Offerings and Services

TONY JEARY

Results Coaching

Advice Matters, if it's the right advice. Having coached the world's top CEOs, published over forty books and advised over one thousand clients, Tony has positioned himself with a unique track record to take serious high achievers to a whole new level of results.

Interactive Keynotes

Tony not only energizes, entertains and educates, he also has his team work strategically and smartly with the event team to make his part as well as the entire experience a super win. An hour with Tony often changes people's lives forever and impacts an organization's results immediately. He delivers value, a fun factor, and best practices people can really use.

Strategic Acceleration Facilitation Planning

Tony can do in a single day what takes many others days and even weeks to accomplish. He has refined a process so powerful the world travels to his private think tank (called the RESULTS Center) to experience clarity, focus, and the ability to synergistically execute. He provides at your fingertips two decades of best practices, processes, and tools for accelerating dramatic, sustained results in any organization.

Collaborative Relationships

We selectively partner with organizations in an annual collaborative engagement where we pour into an entire organization and help build a super-charging, motivated, and engaged *High-Performing Team*. We align with the C-Level management vision and become an extension of them.

See www.TonyJearyTheResultsGuy.com for five questions and answers every executive wants to know.

The bottom line is we help: CLARIFY Vision, FOCUS on What Matters Most—High Leverage Activities (HLAs)—so people EXECUTE and get the Right Results Faster!

www.tonyjeary.com

JOSEPH J. JANICZEK

www.janiczek.com
303-721-7000
cwegner@janiczek.com*

New client inquiries will be directed to our Director of New Client Engagement, Cathy Wegner, who will begin the conversation, assist you in answering any immediate questions and put you in touch with a Janiczek professional advisor when the time is right.

About Janiczek Wealth Management

Named among the top, best and most exclusive investment and wealth advisors and managers in the nation multiple times,* Janiczek Wealth Management is a pioneer in the disciplines of Evidence Based Investing and Strength Based Wealth Management. Headquartered in Denver, Colorado, the 27-year old enterprise serves high and ultra-high net worth clientele across the country with a concentration of clients in the Rocky Mountain region.

Who We Serve

We exclusively serve high net worth investors (those with portfolios of $2 million to $20 million) and ultra-high net worth investors (those with portfolios of $20 million+). We have specific specialization in assisting accomplished business leaders who have experienced or will experience a life-changing liquidity event (ideally beginning

3-years before, continuing right at and most significantly, continually after a business sale, stock option exercise, transaction, etc.). Given the multi-generational aspect of our clientele, our Complete Legacy Solution (see below) is a natural outcome of significant work and proprietary tools and processes aimed at assisting multi-generations of a family in mastering wealth.

Five Standards of Excellence

1. **Fiduciary.** Legally bound to do what is in client's best interest 100% of the time.
2. **Fee-only.** No selling of products or earning of commissions.
3. **Full Disclosure.** No undisclosed arrangements.
4. **Full Breadth.** No narrow scope limiting advisor's perspective. Our Evidence Based Investing and Strength Based Wealth Management is our full-breadth approach.
5. **Free Agency.** No proprietary products, we offer comprehensive access to broad offerings globally.

Service Packages

The Complete Wealth Solution

Investing with Strength, System, Structure, Support and Discipline

Our Complete Wealth Solution is or flagship service package. It provides the combination of Strength Based Wealth Management (SBWM) and Evidenced Based Investing (EBI) we find most needed by clientele seeking to be depletion-resistant wealth stewards and penalty-resistant investors. Think of it as a comprehensive investment management service integrated with our most popular financial, retirement and estate planning services and techniques. Central to this service are our Five Guiding Principles, Wealth Optimization Dashboard, 35 Essential Strengths and, of course, the Stages of Financial Freedom.

The Complete Legacy Solution

Investing with Strength, System, Structure, Support and Discipline...for Generations

If your goal is to master all the elements of the Complete Wealth Solution (see above) for yourself and you would like your adult children, and perhaps adult grandchildren to also engage in the process of learning to master money, this service package is for you. It includes the services of the Complete Wealth Solution for you and tailored services, including periodic family meetings (if desired) and coaching/advising of adult children and adult grandchildren. It is an ideal way to consider to make money mastery a part of your family legacy. Includes the Family Financial Manifesto and other tools, techniques and processes aimed at maximizing the opportunity at hand.

The Complete Investment Solution

Investing with System, Structure, Support and Discipline

Recognizing that in some cases, clients want to immediately engage our Evidence Based Investing (EBI) services, and turn on other components of our services later, this service package offers our investment management services only. It includes all our start-up and ongoing services related to building and managing an investment portfolio tailored to your time horizon, risk temperament, investment objectives, cash flow (expected portfolio distributions) and liquidity needs, as defined by you in our Investor Profile (IP) form. It includes the robust investment management components of our services but none of the financial, retirement, estate or legacy planning and advising services.

Discovery Session and Gap Analysis & Remedy Session Offer

The above is a summary of our service packages. We also have a variety of ala carte services that may be applicable in certain situations, such as business exit planning (services tailored to those who own a business and engage us before a liquidity event to prepare for such an event). *Call us at 303-721-7000 if you are interested in considering and evaluating where a match to work together may exist. We offer a Discovery Session and a Gap Analysis & Remedy Session to qualified prospective new clients as a great way to begin the conversation, evaluate needs and options, and determine if/where a best fit exists. Call us at 303-721-7000 to begin the conversation.*

See our ADV Part II disclosure brochure, available upon request and distributed to all clients, to see important disclosures about our fees, personnel and services, before selecting and engaging in any services.

For more information:
Janiczek Wealth Management
www.janiczek.com
303-721-7000

* Ranked/Named among Top, Best and Most Exclusive Advisors sources: Barron's March 2017, 2016, 2015, 2014; Advisory HQ March 2016; Financial Times June 2015; Five Star Professional November 2015, 2013, 2012, 2011, 2010, 2009; Mutual Funds Magazine January 2001; NABCAP September 2010, 2011, 2013; Worth Magazine July 2002, January 2004, October 2004, October 2008; Wealth & Finance International, October 2014. Rankings and/or recognition by unaffiliated rating services and/or publications should not be construed by a client or prospective client as a guarantee that he/she will experience a certain level of results if Janiczek & Company, Ltd. is engaged, or continues to be engaged, to provide investment advisory services, nor should it be construed as a current or past endorsement of Janiczek & Company, Ltd. by any of its clients. Rankings published by magazines, and others, generally base their selections exclusively on information prepared and/or submitted by the recognized adviser. A copy of the Janiczek & Company, Ltd. written disclosure statement discussing our advisory services and fees is available upon request. Go to www.janiczek.com for more details or call 303-721-7000.

Acknowledgments

We want to thank Nonie Jobe, Madison Walker, Morgan Collins, Marlo Haft, Brooke Hawkins, and the entire TJI team for helping us assemble, sort, and organize the content of this book. We also want to thank the Intellectual Capital Teams at Janiczek Wealth Management and Wealth with Ease, LLC., especially Margie Hannum and Monty Jorgensen. And we are both grateful for those who helped us write our individual books in the past, as well, for those books have provided much of the content we share here.

We want to thank our remarkable kids for allowing us to prove out what we've attempted to do in our own lives to date, and we encourage them and others to keep spreading the word about the value of building a great family legacy. Writing this book has certainly been a dual process with our wives, who have been so instrumental in helping us build an extraordinary legacy for our own families. And we want to express our appreciation to our parents and grandparents, who have had such an important hand in mentoring and teaching us and our children and modeling the value of leaving a wonderful legacy. We're grateful for our church families, as well, for expanding our understanding of the real value of legacy.

We also owe a great deal to the many client families we've worked with over the years, who have entrusted us to go deep into their lives, their families, their finances, and their goals, ambitions, and passions. Through them we've had the opportunity to grow and learn how to achieve the issues we talk about in this book.

Glossary of Terms

COINED PHRASES /TERMS CREATED AND/OR ADOPTED BY TONY JEARY AND JOSEPH JANICZEK

35 Essential Strengths®: Thirty-five key financial strengths, backed up by over one-hundred proprietary standards of excellence, that greatly impact the elastic limit wealth threshold (how much stress your finances can withstand before being irreparably damaged) of your wealth. A summary of these are provided in Appendix B. (Go to www.janiczek.com/sbwm for more details.)

3D Outline™: A powerful outline format that includes the What, Why, and How aspects of a presentation or meeting; used for shortening the planning process and to insure every minute is maximized. (Ask about TJI's 3-D Outline™ Builder Software.)

85% Trap™: The 85% of activities that only influence 15% of results. When you work hard and yet feel like you are only spinning your wheels, it could be a sign that you are in the 85% Trap. It is the opposite of the Essenitial 15%™, which are the 15% of powerful activities that influence 85% of results. It's best to seek to avoid the 85% Trap™ and identify and focus on Essential 15%™ activities.

Accelerator Matrix: A TJI tool that includes the overall objective and generally three columns that list: 1) five to ten HLAs, 2) acceleration actions related to each HLA, and 3) potential roadblocks related to each HLA to bust before they happen.

ADOME: An internal mnemonic for the defined type of client we want to attract and do business with: <u>A</u>ggressive and Appreciative, they want to <u>D</u>o business with TJI, <u>O</u>pen minded, <u>M</u>oney is to be made, and there is opportunity for an <u>E</u>quity play or success fee based on extraordinary results.

Aspirational Assets: Assets that have the great exaggerated potential to increase in value in multiples (2x, 10x, 100x, etc.) as opposed to more traditional investment market assets (stocks, bonds, mutual funds, ETFs) expected, in normal long-term economic expansion periods, to perform in the single to lower double digit return spectrum. Private companies/ventures, venture capital, angel investing, etc. can all fit into this speculative category.

Belief Window: A model of a filter through which you view the world and make decisions accordingly. It includes everything you believe to be true, false, correct, incorrect, appropriate, inappropriate, possible, and impossible.

Blind Spots: Things you miss and can't even see in terms of how things are, how they work, or what's even available.

Branding Matrix: A tool invented by TJI to help bring clarity to either your personal brand or your organization's brand.

Business Entertainment: Appropriate fun factor related to and inside a presentation or meeting. Includes the use of activities, games, role-playing, and even a video clip to counter a short attention span. Usually these activities are placed at five-to-seven-minute intervals.

Career Capital: Asking what worked and what didn't work with each step in your career development. It's also about making course corrections, decisions, commitments, and refinements based on the lessons, experiences, relationships, strengths, weaknesses, interests, and truly unique talents we discovered along the way.

Clarity: Defined understanding of your goals and/or your vision; in essence, clearly knowing what you want to achieve.

Elegant Solutions: Special activities that are created when you are so clear on what you want to accomplish that multiple objectives can be simultaneously met through a single action/activity.

Essential 15%™: The 15% of activities that influence 85% of results. Based upon the work of statistical expert W. Edwards Deming, who pioneered efforts in root cause analysis and quality engineering. The opposite of the Essential 15%™ is the 85% Trap™.

Evidence-Based Investing (EBI): A highly disciplined approach to investment management that seeks to filter through noise, information, hype, and emotion in order to make reasoned investment decisions void of as much investor behavior penalty as possible. (Go to www.janiczek.com/ebi for more details, including white papers, on this approach)

Execution: Action you take to get things done (ideally in strategic alignment with the vision).

Favors in Advance (FIA): Actions to benefit others. Instead of doing favors because you expect something in return, develop an attitude of paying it forward and giving value in advance.

Financial Manifesto™: A formal document, written and confidentially distributed to family members and trusted advisors, to specify standards, beliefs, and guidelines that can help keep the family in line with wealth preservation, mastery, and creation objectives. The document can also include explanations of what the family wants to avoid, such as becoming arrogant, spoiled, entitled, greedy, or fearful. (Go to www.janiczek.com for more information on the Complete Legacy Solution™ service package, which includes the formal creation and distribution of such a document for your family)

Focus: Opposite of distraction; concentrating on what really matters and filtering out what doesn't.

Force Multiplier: A factor (tool/activity/action) that dramatically increases (multiplies) the effectiveness of something someone is doing.

High Leverage Activities (HLAs): Actions that are most relevant to your strategic agenda, success, and achievement, and that most directly impact the results you need and want. The ability to identify and focus on these significant activities is the major factor in improving and accelerating results.

High-Performing Team (HPT): A team that focuses on being as effective as possible while continually reevaluating to work toward quality processes; each team member has a high level of investment in the outcome and is individually motivated.

Intentionally Strategic: Deliberate, planned, and intended use of overall thinking/planning.

Leadership: One who sets a clear vision and shares that vision with others so they can willingly focus their efforts to ensure execution of the vision with the right information, resources, and methods.

Life Team: A group of hand-picked individuals who help you make decisions and or execute (examples could include your executive assistant, coach, mentors, colleagues, readers, driver, lawyer, trainer, CPA, etc.).

Low Leverage Activities (LLAs): The things that consume your time that have the least amount of return. They are typically task-oriented in nature and often become distractions to what your true focus should be.

Market Asset: Investment assets that are higher risk/reward than safety assets (bank accounts) and lower risk/reward than aspirational assets (venture capital). These can includes stocks, bonds, mutual funds, and ETFs traded in traditional open public markets around the world.

Mastery: Performing at your top level.

Mastery Impact Curve: A model that demonstrates three basic levels: Good, Great, and Mastery; used to show that many stop at the Great level.

MOLO: A TJI tool to help an individual or organization identify what they need to eliminate so they can focus on what matters most; an evaluation of what should be done More Often and Less Often will ensure time is best invested on proactive, productive HLAs instead of on time-wasting, less effective tasks.

People of Influence (POI): Those individuals who are part of your life that can and do have a huge impact on your success

Planned Spontaneity: Being so prepared you can respond to an audience in impromptu fashion; the better prepared you are the more spontaneity you can bring to your meetings and presentations with confidence.

Preparation[2]: Preparing to the extreme.

Presentation Mastery™: Being at the highest level of presentation effectiveness.

Presentation Ready: Being in a state with the right tools to respond instantly to a request for a briefing or for insight on a particular subject or area of management.

Presentation Universe: All the presentation opportunities in your daily life, both personal and professional (i.e., staff meetings, speeches, and one-on–ones).

Production Before Perfection (PBP): A TJI principle that says you must not allow the fear of perfectionism to stop you from starting. You should most often start and perfect as you go.

Reticular Activating System (RAS): A set of nerves at the bottom of the brain that acts as a gatekeeper to allow or disallow information to come into your brain, based on what you care about or need.

Safety Assets: Assets which traditionally have the lowest probability of loss in value and greatest in terms of liquidity, even in times of extreme financial stress. This can include bank and money market accounts (with SIPC or FDIC protections), short-term, high quality US government or municipal bonds, insurance type assets (with guarantees by high rated insurers) or other liquid assets secured by organizations with very high credit ratings. See Market Assets and Aspirational Assets for an explantation of other asset categories.

Smart Reports: A TJI term that refers to a special researched briefing on a particular subject.

Stages of Financial Freedom®: A financial roadmap that depicts ideal and less than ideal financial trajectories through life. The image illustrates the foundation, early growth, growth, transition, security, and distribution stages of financial freedom. It also depicts what stagnation and depletion look like throughout life. Finally, it identifies the five distribution mode possibilities when you live (partially or fully) off of your financial resources (the maintenance, growth, or runaways growth distribution modes or the controlled depletion or uncontrolled depletion distribution modes). (See Mr. Janiczek's *Absolute Financial Freedom* book for a detailed explanation of each stage and path.)

Stakeholder Matrix: A TJI tool that facilitates great clarity regarding all those impacted and what they most care about, to help insure everyone wins.

Strategic Acceleration: The ability to expedite change and increase effectiveness more quickly, powered by clarity, engaged with focus, and converted into superior results via execution.

Strategic Acceleration **Studio:** Tony Jeary's private think tank, named after his best-selling book, *Strategic Acceleration*.

Strategic Altruism: Being intentional about helping others short- and long–term.

Strategic Goal-Setting: Being intentional about planning for what you want to achieve (have, share, experience, give, and become).

Strategic Health: Being intentional about your overall well being.

Strategic IQ: Intentional balance between your strategic and tactical activities.

Strategic Mindset: A well thought-out set of assumptions pertaining to thinking and beliefs, as well as balancing tactical and strategic efforts.

Strategic Parenting: Being intentional about raising exceptional, successful children.

Strategic Presence: Your Brand or reputation; how people perceive you personally. If you have a powerful brand (strategic presence), people are more likely to execute on your behalf. Be intentional and strategic about your brand/reputation or strategic presence.

Strategic Procrastination: A smart handle on both positive and negative procrastination, first introduced in Tony Jeary's best-selling book *Strategic Acceleration.*

Strategic Selling: Being intentional in the art of persuasion in order to get people to take action on your behalf.

Strategic Thinking: Another term for *Intentionally Strategic* (deliberate, planned, and intended use of overall thinking/planning).

Strength-Based Wealth Management® (SBWM): A comprehensive approach to building optimal levels of financial strength, agility, flexibility, and endurance to gain a powerful investment and financial advantage in the marketplace. The tenents of SBWM include actions to increase the Elastc Limit Wealth Threshold™ of your wealth (amount of stress your finances can withstand before becoming irrepairably damaged). (For more information, go to www.janiczek.com/sbwm.)

SWOT: An evaluation tool for the assessment of Strengths, Weaknesses, Opportunities, and Threats.

Targeted Polling: Calling on specific members of the audience and asking them to share their feedback, giving the presenter the ability to tailor the presentation to more successfully impact the audience; can be done before, during a break, or during an activity.

Trust Transference: The transfer of trust from one person's brand, reputation, and relationships to another.

Value Arsenal: A tool box of white papers, books, abstracts, and best practices of all kinds to help you be more valuable.

Values Clarification: An exercise that helps you define what matters the most to you.

Verbal Surveying: Asking questions of the audience during a presentation to obtain usable feedback and then adjusting accordingly (i.e., speeding up or slowing down for more or less detail).

Vision (Results) Boarding: A visual representation of goals and vision that motivates you to action.

Appendix A: Values

1. Accomplishments
2. Affection
3. Alignment
4. Altruism
5. Appearance
6. Appreciated
7. Attitude
8. Cleanliness
9. Congruence
10. Contentment
11. Cooperation
12. Creativity
13. Education
14. Effectiveness
15. Efficiency
16. Engagement
17. Fairness
18. Faith
19. Fame
20. Family
21. Financial Security
22. Freedom
23. Friendship
24. Fun
25. Generosity
26. Genuineness
27. Good Habits
28. Happiness
29. Harmony
30. Health
31. Honesty
32. Humility
33. Inner Peace
34. Inspiration
35. Intimacy
36. Joy
37. Knowledge
38. Lifelong Learning
39. Lifestyle
40. Loyalty
41. Loved
42. Motivation
43. Openness
44. Organization
45. Personal Brand
46. Personal Improvement
47. Personal Salvation
48. Philanthropy
49. Power
50. Productivity
51. Recognition
52. Relationships
53. Respect
54. Results
55. Routine
56. Romance
57. Security
58. See the World
59. Service
60. Significance
61. Simplicity
62. Solitude
63. Spiritual Maturity
64. Status
65. Thriving
66. Truth
67. Wealth
68. Wholeness
69. Winning
70. Wisdom

Appendix B:
35 Essential Strengths®

WEALTH OPTIMIZATION PLAN™ FOR HIGH NET WORTH INVESTORS

What does a plan to continually build and maintain an ultimate level of financial strength look like? What does an automated system and structure for analyzing, measuring and reporting strengths, weaknesses and vulnerabilities look like?

In this nine page folio, I provide an example of a Wealth Optimization Plan™ for high net worth investors. This plan includes the Five Guiding Principles™, 35 Essential Strengths® and an intuitive Wealth Optimization Dashboard™ designed to provide sophisticated and unsophisticated investors alike with a precise overview of their strengths, weaknesses and vulnerabilities. For information on a service that provides the system, structure, support and discipline needed to master this process across generations on an ongoing basis, see About Our Services section of this book or go to www.janiczek.com or call 303-721-7000.

FIVE GUIDING PRINCIPLES

1. Make your balance sheet, cash flow and portfolio your friend not your foe.

2. Compare your finances to standards of excellence and utilize them to direct you to making optimal enhancements.

3. Back-test and stress-test your plan under various scenarios to further reveal strengths, weaknesses, and possibilities.

4. Know what is pulling you forward, holding you back, and serving you best – essentials to having optimal energy, confidence, and focus supporting your plan.

5. Be specific and proactive by identifying and implementing the strategic actions that will result in the best permanent changes and advantages going forward.

THE FUNDAMENTALS (3 STRENGTHS)

Balance Sheet
- Having a strong balance sheet with all weaknesses or vulnerabilities eliminated or mitigated.

Cash Flow
- Living comfortably under your means with cushion, surplus, awareness, and control consistently serving you.

Portfolio
- Having a well allocated and performing investment portfolio generating current income and long term capital appreciation commensurate with your circumstances, objectives, risk temperament, and time horizon.

LIFESTYLE PROTECTION (9 STRENGTHS)

Liquidity
- Having an optimal level of liquid reserves—no less, no more.

Insurance
- Having an optimal level of insurance coverages—no less, no more.

Estate Plan
- Having proper estate-plan documents available at a moments notice to optimally serve you and your loved ones.

Semi-liquid
- Having an optimal level of unencumbered fixed income and equity securities.

Cash-Flow Resiliency

- Having relatively low levels of fixed expense obligations such that your outflow is easily sustainable, even in crisis conditions.

Portfolio Resiliency

- Having optimal portfolio risk/reward characteristics matched to your needs and circumstances and the prevailing investment climate.

Portfolio Accumulation

- Having accumulated an optimal level of semi-liquid and retirement portfolio assets in proportion to your standard of living and predictable passive-income sources.

Passive Income

- Having an ideal level of predictable passive-income sources in proportion to your standard of living.

Portfolio Distribution Rate

- Having a portfolio distribution rate that is sustainable even during extended bear markets.

ASSET OPTIMIZATION (4 STRENGTHS)

Portfolio

- Having an optimally structured and managed investment portfolio void of costly penalties, complexities, and inefficiencies.

Talent

- Putting your and others' endless energy, interest, and ability to work to optimally create wealth, multiply results, and better manage time.

Personal Property

- Having the optimal level of personal assets enhancing your lifestyle, yet void of harming your balance sheet or cash flow.

Non-Liquid Assets

- Having an optimal level of high-performing business and/or real-estate assets generating high levels of current income and long-term capital appreciation.

PORTFOLIO OPTIMIZATION (7 STRENGTHS)

Advisor

- Having a fiduciary, fee-only, full breadth lead advisor that provides the structure, system, support, and discipline necessary for long-term portfolio-management success.

Custodian

- Having investment accounts consolidated at a safe, efficient, unbiased, and robust custodian.

Efficiency

- Having optimal cost efficiency as an advantage in your portfolio management.

Diversification

- Having an optimal level of portfolio diversification—no less, no more.

Management

- Having an optimal level of value-added portfolio management, talent, and systems serving you.

Monitoring

- Having a consolidated monitoring system that provides you with performance, allocation, and tax clarity.

Customization

- Having your portfolio optimally customized to your needs and circumstances, on an ongoing basis.

ESTATE OPTIMIZATION (10 STRENGTHS)

Will/Trust

- Having well-prepared wills and trusts optimally customized to you, your current circumstances, and current laws.

Title
- Having optimal ownership and beneficiary elections that are co-ordinated with your overall estate plan.

Supplemental
- Supplementing your wills and trusts with other useful legal documents that serve you and your family in the event of disability, incapacitation, or death.

Protection
- Having optimal asset protection and family lifestyle protection commensurate with your risk and need profile.

Simple
- Having optimal, simple estate-planning techniques in place to minimize estate-taxation exposure to the fullest extent allowable by law.

Continuation
- Having an optimal continuation plan in place for your family and business(es).

Complex
- Further minimizing estate-taxation exposure to the fullest extent allowable by law by identifying, comparing, and implementing appropriate complex estate-planning techniques that build upon the success of simple techniques.

Family
- Assisting adult children and adult grandchildren in career development, personal development, and wealth mastery to the point of mitigating the risk of wealth depletion for generations.

Charity
- Enhancing your life and legacy and the lives of others with an optimal giving plan, structure, system, support, and discipline.

Blue Print
- Having a simple yet comprehensive document that provides you,

your spouse, and ultimately your legal representatives and loved ones with a complete schematic of your financial position, trusted advisor team, and estate plan.

BACK-TEST/STRESS-TEST (2 STRENGTHS)

Back-test

- Having back-tested your financial security to every forty-year period going back to 1900 with a 4 percent or less probability of depletion, even under worst 10 percent of conditions.

Stress-test

- Having stress-tested your financial security under challenging circumstances and still passing the above back-test.

WEALTH OPTIMIZATION DASHBOARD™ EXAMPLE

Following is an example of how this proprietary technology, exclusively available at Janiczek® Wealth Management, reports the results of an analysis of each client's finances in all thirty-five categories:

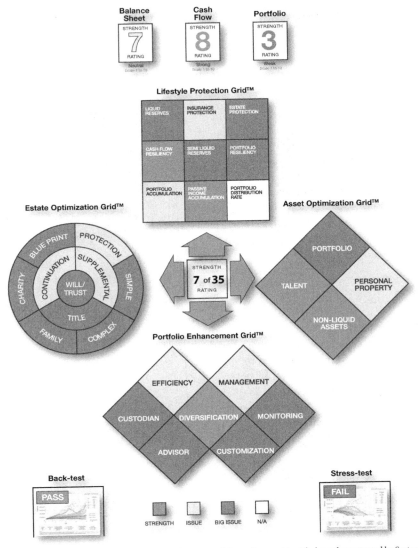

WEALTH OPTIMIZATION MAKEOVER

Here is a simulated example of what a Wealth Optimization Makeover might look like to a high net worth investor ($2-million to $20-million portfolio) or ultra-high net worth investor ($20-million+ portfolio). Notice how the 35 Essential Strengths™ turn from vulnerabilities and weaknesses to strengths in a relatively short period of time.

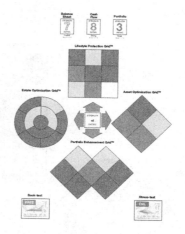

BEFORE

With less than one-third of the 35 Essential Strengths with a green (strength) rating, numerous issues (yellow) and big issues (red) are exposed, providing this investor with tremendous direction on eliminating vulnerabilities, weaknesses and complexities that have been holding them back.

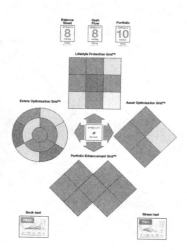

AFTER (6 months)

This investor took the analysis seriously and was highly motivated to bring their finances to a new level of optimization. They brought two-thirds of the categories into the green (strength) zone in just six months. This provided an even more focused plan of improvement for the year ahead.

AFTER (3 years)

This investor realized that mastering money is not as difficult as it seems when they have the right structure, systems, support, and discipline in place. Just three-years into the process they have 90% of the categories in green (strength) zone and are chipping away at the others. They know they are in a good place and know that they are Investing from a Position of Strength.

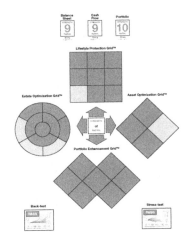

Appendix C:
Family Financial Manifesto

Here is a brief summary of what your Family Financial Manifesto can look like:

DOE FAMILY FINANCIAL MANIFESTO

(Date)

This Doe Family Financial Manifesto establishes specific standards of excellence we have thoughtfully considered and documented herein. It is to be utilized by us, our family, and our advisors in furthering our efforts to be exceptional stewards of wealth. Our hope is that these standards of excellence, written in the form of declarations, serves us and our family for generations.

1. We shall maintain a proper proportion of safety, market, and aspirational assets to match our lifestyle protection, wealth preservation, and long-term/ongoing wealth-creation goals and invest them under a prudent Evidence-Based Investing (EBI) approach.
    a. Our safety-assets proportion shall be adequately funded to insulate us from catastrophic risks, cash-flow crunches, and temporary waterfall-black-swan economic events.
    b. Our market-asset proportion shall be prudently funded and allocated to provide market returns (for a globally diversified equity/fixed income portfolio) and take advantage of documented premiums that reliable research indicates may be predictably gained over long periods of time.

       i. We shall maintain a strict rebalancing discipline, as follows (insert rebalance discipline you and your advisor mindfully select here).

       ii. We shall maintain a green "strength" rating on all seven Portfolio Enhancement Grid categories (see 35 Essential Strengths in the Appendix).

       iii. We shall maintain an "efficient" investment management standard (desired results with least effort) and avoid time-consuming, mind-consuming, and complex investment schemes.

       iv. In addition to traditional equity and fixed-income holdings, we shall allocate a modest amount of market assets for "satellite" investments like multi-family housing, commercial real estate, and/or other alternative asset classes that enhance market-asset performance and risk characteristics.

   c. We shall set aside a small proportion of assets for special non-liquid aspirational ventures that have a higher payoff possibility (can multiply the amount invested). The amount allocated here, if any, will be an amount that if totally lost or down for years, will not critically impact our financial security, lifestyle, and/or mindset. We will practice discipline or greatly limit or avoid this category altogether.

2. When it comes to investing we shall not:

   a. (List here things you want to avoid like "chasing hot money" or being lured or swayed away from your disciplines by fear, greed, noise, etc.). This list should take in account lessons learned from all past mistakes that you or others you know have made.

3. When it comes to working with advisors, we shall only work with a lead advisor who is: a) a fiduciary (legally has to do what is in our best interest); b) fee-only (no selling of products or making commissions whatsoever); c) full-breadth (Strength-Based Wealth Management [SBWM] and Evidence-Based Investing [EBI]) combined; d) full-disclosure (no undisclosed conflicts

of interest); and e) open-architecture (capable of utilizing best vehicles across full spectrum, not limited by brokerage or other conflicts or constraints).

4. We shall mindfully and carefully build and maintain an eight, nine, or ten green "strength rating" across the three "fundamentals" of our Wealth Optimization Plan (Balance Sheet, Cash Flow, and Portfolio). (See Appendix B.)

5. We shall consistently act to maintain nine out of nine Lifestyle Protection Grid categories as green "strength rating," swiftly identifying if/when we veer off track and course-correcting in a timely manner (inside one year).

6. Add more standards for wealth here that are related to being exceptional depletion-resistant stewards of wealth.

7. We shall diligently maintain a complete record of our finances on a highly secure online vault and maintain manually printed copies of important documents, our balance sheet, and our Life Team list in our physical vault.

8. Each Doe family member will be invited and encouraged to participate in the Complete Legacy Solution of our advisor; make progress mastering money; do the best with what they have, building rich, meaningful vocations and families; and avoid the pitfalls of arrogance, entitlement, over-spending means, under-developing/utilizing talent, and poor diligence.

9. The Doe family will generously give to charity under the following guidelines and standards:

    a. List you charitable giving goals and standards here.

This Doe Family Financial Manifesto is formerly adopted by John and Lisa Doe on _____ _____, 20_____.

Signed,

John Doe   Lisa Doe

Appendix D: Seven Rules for Developing New Habits

1. Focus on one new habit at a time. Choosing more than one new habit at a time defrays your focus, energy, and effort. Start by taking baby steps, one at a time. Then, as you see consistent progress and growing success, you'll develop confidence that you can achieve new habits in the face of adversity and chaos.

2. Break down a large complex habit into small sub-habits. As you master the smaller sub-components, the larger complex habit comes together. (Think about all the small habits you learned to help you master the automatic habit of driving a car successfully.)

3. Think of yourself as a pilot as you launch a new habit. During this burn-in period, you get results by muscling your way into them using considerable thought and effort. Like a pilot learning to fly, you turn on the full throttle to get airborne. You continue to exert tremendous energy to gain altitude, making it through turbulence and threats at lower altitudes. As you finally achieve the desired altitude and jet stream, you can turn down the throttle and achieve results with a fraction of the effort. You turn on the auto pilot (your programmed habit) and enjoy the rewards of the consistency it delivers.

4. Think forty days and forty months. Though some behavioral experts say it takes a minimum of twenty-one days of conscientious action to burn in a new habit, I believe the original burn-in period of a simple habit to be forty days, and for a complex/multiple habit to be forty months. Forty days takes you beyond a full month's cycle, and it's one-ninth of the year—plenty of time to make a habit

of whatever you want and test it beyond the initial novelty of the activity. Similarly, think of a complex habit made up of numerous sub-habits, such as financial mastery or healthy living. After forty months (a little over three years) of constant focus on building sub-habits, a high level of mastery is achievable for complex habits that would meaningfully change the course of your life.

5. To reinforce your effort, identify and build a team of mentors and peers to support you along the way. Going at a goal alone is the hard and lonely way; you need support and guidance to stay on course. Who do you know who has achieved success in the habit you are pursuing and would be a positive influence along your journey? What people can you read about who pursue excellence and will help you build your skills and confidence? What audios can you listen to that will reinforce your goals and habits?

6. Be a prime-time player. Make sure you devote quality prime time to master any new habit. That's when you have the energy, the concentration, the momentum, and the inertia to achieve great things—the time of day you are freshest and can focus on getting the result you want. If you give your prime time to everyone and everything else—and try to build a habit with the last ounce of energy you have at the end of the day—the odds stack up against you. Instead, wake up earlier and make sure you get your "habit" item into your day, first and foremost. You will be even more energized later in the day because of your success and confidence.

7. Eliminate, automate, delegate, and coordinate around your focus habits. When you focus on your habit, you will notice certain time-consuming activities you can eliminate or automate. For instance, if you're focusing on making a habit of saving, you can set up automatic savings out of your payroll check and into your 401(k) to free up time and achieve a habit. You can also use delegation effectively by building a value-added team around you, and you can coordinate your existing habits by attaching a new habit to one you already have.

By aligning your habits with your goals and values and following these steps to develop new habits that will change your life and your results, you will be able to pass along to your children a veritable wealth of practices that will take them a long way toward success.[9]

---

9 Joseph J. Janiczek, *Absolute Financial Freedom* (Denver: Prosperity Press, 2001), 118-127.

RESULTS FASTER!

The Results FASTER! digital course gives you access to the tools, skills, and techniques utilized by top companies, CEOs, and super achievers who embrace Tony Jeary's revolutionary "more results in less time" approach to goal achievement.

Following Tony's Results FASTER! success framework, you'll learn, develop, and implement actionable strategies guaranteed to keep the "results needle" in your life moving forward faster than you ever thought possible.

Join Tony for 7 weeks of video lessons as he takes you by the hand and guides you toward more of the ideas, people, and attitudes essential to your success. During your RESULTS FASTER journey, you'll develop a long-term *Results Blueprint* and measure your progress following Tony's Personalized Results Audit.

PRODUCT OVERVIEW

Develop an "Extraordinary Results" Mindset
- Build a solid foundation for immediate results in your personal and professional life.
- Attract more of the ideas, experiences, and people who matter into your life and career.
- Learn to positively impact others and lead them toward helping you realize success.
- Master results-oriented thinking and multiply your overall effectiveness.

Approach Your Goals with Clarity and Focus
- Create a clear vision for your future and discover all the steps you'll take to get there.
- Learn to focus your energy on the high-leverage activities that matter.
- Use "Force Multipliers" to put more time back into your day, even as you achieve more.
- Follow your personal Results FASTER! blueprint and consistently move forward.

Stop Waiting and Start Seeing Results
- Immediately turn your long-term dreams into achievable short-term goals.
- Astound others as you accomplish more with less by "creating time out of thin air."
- Realize what really matters to you and approach your goals with feel-good focus.
- Uncover the secret to long-term success and constant personal and professional achievement.

VISIT TONYJEARY.COM/RESULTSFASTERWEBINAR

Custom Corporate-wide Licenses Are Available.

SUCCESS
ACADEMY

RESPECTING TRUTH

Throughout history, humans have always indulged in certain irrationalities and held some fairly wrong-headed beliefs. But in his newest book, philosopher Lee McIntyre shows how we've now reached a watershed moment for ignorance in the modern era, due to the volume of misinformation, the speed with which it can be digitally disseminated, and the savvy exploitation of our cognitive weaknesses by those who wish to advance their ideological agendas. In *Respecting Truth: Willful Ignorance in the Internet Age*, McIntyre issues a call to fight back against this slide into the witless abyss. In the tradition of Galileo, the author champions the importance of using tested scientific methods for arriving at true beliefs, and shows how our future survival is dependent on a more widespread, reasonable world.

Lee McIntyre is a Research Fellow at the Center for Philosophy and History of Science at Boston University and author of *Dark Ages: The Case for a Science of Human Behavior* (2006). He is co-editor (with Alex Rosenberg) of the forthcoming *Routledge Companion to Philosophy of Social Science*. The author can be reached through his website at www.leemcintyrebooks.com.

Praise for this book:

"Lee McIntyre identifies the central problem of truth claims today—from global warming and GMOs to evolution and vaccinations—'willful ignorance.' *Respecting Truth* should be read by every member of Congress before voting on legislation, and they should do so based on the facts instead of party line. The problem is group think. The solution is having a 'designated skeptic'. I nominate Lee McIntyre."

Michael Shermer, *Skeptic Magazine, USA*

"This is a compellingly-written book that addresses a timely issue. It is well researched, tightly constructed, and insightful. It makes for an engaging, informative and eye-opening read. The prose is light and winning, and it provides an expertly-guided tour of an issue of profound importance to us all."

Andrew Norman, *Carnegie Mellon University, USA*

"McIntyre is very clear about the overall argumentative structure, and he provides excellent examples for each topic under discussion. Although the ideas being discussed are sometimes rather sophisticated, his exposition is very relaxed and casual."

Noretta Koertge, *Indiana University, USA*

RESPECTING TRUTH

Willful Ignorance in the Internet Age

Lee McIntyre

Routledge
Taylor & Francis Group

NEW YORK AND LONDON

First published 2015
by Routledge
711 Third Avenue, New York, NY 10017

and by Routledge
2 Park Square, Milton Park, Abingdon, Oxon OX14 4RN

Routledge is an imprint of the Taylor & Francis Group, an informa business

Library of Congress Cataloging in Publication Data
McIntyre, Lee C.
Respecting truth : Willful Ignorance in the Internet Age / Lee McIntyre.
pages cm
Includes bibliographical references and index.
1. Irrationalism (Philosophy) 2. Truthfulness and falsehood--Philosophy.
3. Self-deception--Philosophy. 4. Mass media--Objectivity. 5. Internet--
Psychological aspects. I. Title.
B824.2.M34 2015
153.4'301--dc23
2014044286

ISBN: 978-1-138-88880-7 (hbk)
ISBN: 978-1-138-88881-4 (pbk)
ISBN: 978-1-315-71316-8 (ebk)

Typeset in Bembo
by Taylor & Francis Books

Printed and bound in the United States of America by
Edwards Brothers Malloy on sustainably sourced paper

For Rich Adelstein
who taught me to stand up for what I thought was true,
even when he disagreed with me

In times of universal deceit, telling the truth will be a revolutionary act.

George Orwell

CONTENTS

PREFACE

In a previous book—*Dark Ages: The Case for a Science of Human Behavior* (MIT Press, 2006)—I wrote about how ideology was corrupting the standards for evidence-based belief in the social sciences. While the natural sciences seem firmly established as the arbiter of any serious dispute about how the natural world works, in the study of human behavior many feel it reasonable to substitute wishful thinking and intuition over empirical methods. If only the social sciences could be more like the natural sciences, I lamented, we would be in a better position to understand the true causes of some of the social problems that have continued to bedevil us over the centuries, and finally be in a position to address the source of so much human misery.

But by the time I looked up, the world had changed. Science itself was under attack, even in the study of the natural world, such that some political candidates, religious leaders, media commentators (and many others who should have known better) were now disputing not only specific scientific theories that did not match their ideological prejudices, but also questioning science itself as the basis for forming true beliefs about the world. Those who believed in reason, it seemed, were being dismissed as just another interest group and science as just another ideology.

How could this have happened?

True beliefs are adaptive, right? And science works. The methods of scientific reasoning have provided us with the bounty of modern human life that is too vast to enumerate; over the last thousand years science has lifted us out of the dark ages and brought us to a world in which most of our problems are caused not by ignorance of the natural world but by our stubborn inhumanity to one another. One would think that we would suffer, therefore, if we abandoned the most successful system that the human mind has ever invented for the discovery of truth, not only about the natural world but about ourselves as well.

Yet this is exactly where so much of today's public debate has landed us. Science (and the idea of using reason as the basis for human belief in general) is routinely questioned, resisted, denied, ridiculed, rejected, and outright disrespected at the hands of those who do not wish to believe the sometimes inconvenient conclusions that are forced on us by reason. Surely there is more to truth than that which can be determined by science. Yet today—when we have right-wing candidates for the Presidency of the United States who dismiss the scientific evidence for human-caused global warming as a "hoax" and many on the left who continue to believe that there is a medical conspiracy to deny the link between childhood vaccines and autism (even after that research has been debunked)—it is clear that the standards for human rationality are in trouble. For by making such blanket statements—with no credible evidence and no plausible theory about why the scientific community as a whole could get things so wrong—one understands that it is the soundness of science itself that is being questioned.

Of course, even though many may doubt particular scientific theories, they also understand at some level that we cannot do without science. They may question evolution or global warming when it suits their gut or their politics, but then without irony turn around and use Twitter or their iPhone to spread their medieval opinions. Captured by a benighted ideology, millions may wish to row away from science and reason when it is convenient, but they also want to keep the shoreline in sight.

How can we reach these people?

In this book I will argue that truth matters and that deep down most of us already know this. Of course, we may question inconclusive evidence and yearn for better theories, but that is allowable and even well-suited to science. Any reasonable standard of rationality should be able to handle such questioning, for criticism is at the very basis of rational belief formation. Instead, the biggest threat to truth in the twenty-first century, I maintain, is not skepticism or even outright rejection of specific scientific theories, but disrespect for the standards of truth that lie behind scientific reasoning in the first place. It is not crackpot theories that are doing us in, it is the growing prevalence of a dishonest attitude toward truth which says that one can embrace reason where it suits us and then reject it when the results do not match our preferred ideology.

Ignorance and falsehood are not the enemy. Instead we should be much more concerned about disrespect.

ACKNOWLEDGMENTS

It would be customary at this point for me to thank all those with whom I have ever discussed the ideas in this book. But I can't do that. The truth is that I have been thinking about the ideas in this book for virtually my entire working life, so that task would be impossible.

What I would like to do instead is single out a handful of people who have done the most to bring this particular book to fruition: my friend Jon Haber, who has read everything I've ever written and done me the honor of criticizing most of it; my teacher Rich Adelstein, whose influence on me has been so great that I dedicate the book to him; my friends and colleagues Dan Little, Mark Buchanan, Michael Martin, and Alex Rosenberg for at various times discussing with me the ideas contained here; and two anonymous referees for the publisher, who made such helpful comments on an earlier draft of this book.

The folks at Routledge have been a pleasure to work with and I would like to thank my editor Andy Beck in particular for his efforts on my behalf. Others who deserve thanks are Ruth Berry in production, Harriet Connor and Mike King in marketing, James Thomas—my copyeditor—who saved me from a number of mistakes and infelicities, and Laura Briskman for her all-around good cheer and hard work in seeing this project through.

I would also like to thank Alisa Bokulich, the Director of the Center for Philosophy and History of Science, for giving me such a wonderful home at Boston University; and my sister-in-law Pat Starr, who did not live to see the publication of this book, but took a special interest in helping me to see that my ideas could make a difference.

My daughter Louisa read every word of this book, then provided expert philosophical commentary that was uncolored by our relationship; I couldn't be more proud or more grateful. As I was writing this book, I often found myself thinking of my son James, knowing of his commitment to honest argument and making the world a better place. I hope I did you proud son. But, as always, my greatest thanks go to my wife Josephine, who has always believed in my work—and me—with an unshakable conviction that belies all obstacles and setbacks. They say that philosophers are professional skeptics, but there is one thing I've never doubted:

Doubt thou the stars are fire;
Doubt the sun doth move;
Doubt truth to be a liar;
But never doubt I love.

1

ATTITUDES TOWARD TRUTH

Willful Ignorance and the Last Glimpse of Shoreline

> All truth passes through three stages. First it is ridiculed. Second, it is violently opposed. Third it is accepted as being self-evident.
>
> Schopenhauer

The human relationship with truth is a complex one. On the one hand, most of us believe strongly in the concept of truth and may even grow upset when we feel that it is being withheld from us: when our government lies to us, when a doctor substitutes happy talk for a genuine diagnosis, when despite overwhelming evidence a child abuser pleads "not guilty" at trial. On the other hand, most of us can also be counted on to resist or even actively disbelieve in some truths that we just do not want to accept: that we cannot balance the federal budget unless we raise taxes *and* cut entitlement programs, that the mole on our back really is cancer, that even the most heinous criminals are entitled to a defense at trial. But what to say, then, about those cases in which—if we are rational beings—such dissonance should be resolved on the spot, *because we have the truth right in front of us* ... yet we resist it anyway? Why is there so much difficulty not only in *finding* the truth, but in *accepting* it once it has been discovered? It is the latter sort of problem that I will be concerned with in this book.

One might think that belief in truth—as opposed to its discovery—would be a fairly trivial matter. For despite our reluctance to hear unwanted truths, it seems plausible that the deep-seated countervailing human desire to *know* the truth would eventually result in acceptance, once things were demonstrated to us. But of course, with humans it is never quite so simple. As the history of science has shown us, the discovery of truth is hard, but the acceptance of truth can be even harder.[1]

But we have always known this. Even when science (and philosophy) were in their infancy, human nature was already going strong. In Plato's dialogue *Euthyphro*, we see the great Socrates admonish a callow young fellow for professing to know something that he is in no position to know: what is "righteousness"?[2] Throughout the dialogue, Socrates demonstrates again and again that Euthyphro has no idea what he is talking about, when he argues that it would be righteous for him to prosecute his own father for murder, given some pretty shoddy evidence and the fact that Euthyphro cannot even define the meaning of righteousness. One might think that Socrates is so adept at this kind of questioning and verbal humiliation—which is his standard method throughout the dialogues—because he himself knows the answers to the questions he is asking. But, when challenged in this way, Socrates always demurs and says that he himself has no wisdom, but is only a kind of "midwife" who can help others to seek it. Even though the goal of philosophy is to find the truth, Socrates customarily professes ignorance.

Why is this important? Here Plato is teaching a central lesson about the philosopher's search for knowledge that will have later ramifications not only for science but also for any subsequent quest for true belief. The real enemy of truth is not ignorance, doubt, or even disbelief. It is false knowledge. When we profess to know something *even in the face of absent or contradicting evidence*, that is when we stop looking for the truth. Which is more likely to stand in the way of truth, Socrates wonders, ignorance or the conviction that we do not need to learn anything new? It is the hubris of the latter point of view that is the real problem. If we are ignorant, perhaps we will be motivated to learn. If we are skeptical, we can continue to search for answers. If we disbelieve, maybe others can convince us. And perhaps even if we are honestly wrong, and put forward a proposition that is open to refutation, we may learn something when our earlier belief is overthrown. But when we are willfully ignorant—when we refuse to consider new data because nothing could convince us to abandon what we already believe—that is when truth is most in danger. When we choose to insulate ourselves from any new ideas or evidence *because we think that we already know what is true*, this is when we are most likely to believe a falsehood.

In the search for truth, it is not mere disbelief that explains why truth is so often disrespected. It is one's attitude.

The Problem of Willful Ignorance

Our problems with truth are many. Not only are we often ignorant of it, or careless in not bothering to use reliable methods to find it, but we also sometimes actively choose not to believe things even when we know full well that they are probably true or have within our reach easily available sources of information that would enable us to find out. In one of the 2008 Republican presidential primary debates, the candidates were asked to raise their hands if they did not believe in evolution; Senator Sam Brownback, Governor Mike Huckabee, and Representative

Tom Tancredo did so. In the 2012 political cycle, Sen. Rick Santorum, Rep. Ron Paul, and Gov. Rick Perry became fond of saying that global warming is a "hoax." When asked to clarify his views Perry said:

> I do believe that the issue of global warming has been politicized. I think there are a substantial number of scientists who have manipulated data so that they will have dollars rolling into their projects. I think we're seeing it almost weekly or even daily, scientists who are coming forward and questioning the original idea that man-made global warming is what is causing the climate to change.[3]

And while the eventual Republican nominee, Mitt Romney, had this to say in June 2011:

> I don't speak for the scientific community, of course. But I believe the world's getting warmer. I can't prove that, but I believe based on what I read that the world is getting warmer. And number two, I believe that humans contribute to that … so I think it's important for us to reduce our emissions of pollutants and greenhouse gases that may well be significant contributors to the climate change and the global warming that you're seeing.[4]

By August 2011, he appeared to have changed his position:

> My view is that we don't know what's causing climate change on this planet … and the idea of spending trillions and trillions of dollars to try to reduce CO_2 emissions is not the right course for us.[5]

That same month Jon Huntsman, the only Republican candidate who was willing to stand up for science, tweeted "I believe in evolution and trust scientists on global warming. Call me crazy." After polling in single digits for a few more months, Huntsman dropped out of the race in January 2012.

As if this sort of "head in the sand" approach to scientific evidence by our elected officials was not appalling enough, it is depressing to learn that the level of scientific illiteracy is perhaps even greater among the general public.

In a nationwide telephone survey conducted by the California Academy of Science in 2009, it was found that:

- 47 percent of American adults did not know how long it takes for the Earth to revolve around the Sun.
- 41 percent believed that the earliest humans lived on Earth at the same time as the dinosaurs.[6]

Add to this the equally depressing results of a 2007 Harris Poll which found that:

- 42 percent of American adults believe in ghosts.
- 32 percent believe in UFOs.
- 23 percent believe in witches.[7]

And, although it is true to say that Americans tend to be more skeptical of some basic scientific truths (like evolution) than residents of any other nation except Turkey,[8] the problem of willful ignorance is far from an American-only problem. In a 2008 British poll it was found that:

- 23 percent of Britons thought that Winston Churchill was a myth, while 58 percent believed that Sherlock Holmes was real.
- 47 percent thought that the twelfth-century English king Richard the Lionheart was a myth.[9]

But what makes us think that such incredible beliefs have anything to do with the problem of *willful* ignorance and are not just the result of plain old ignorance? Some of our fellow citizens and politicians, that is, could just be incredibly stupid when it comes to reasoning about scientific (and historical) matters. What is there beyond the falsehood of the views expressed above that leads us to believe that they not only contradict the truth, but show contempt for it?

Ignorance is the lack of true knowledge. Willful ignorance is something more. It is ignorance coupled with the decision to remain ignorant. In saying this, it is tempting to believe that if one is willfully ignorant then one must *know* that one is ignorant, thereby revealing a bit of savvy whereby, presumably, one knows that there is some truth out there that one wants to be insulated from. A good example of this might be our suspicion that a vast majority of the people who ran for the Republican presidential nomination in 2012 did not actually believe the nonsense that they spouted about global warming, but instead merely pretended to believe it, so that they would appeal to those voters who were actually ignorant.[10] But this is not willful ignorance; this is dishonesty. Instead, to be truly willfully ignorant, one could neither disbelieve in the truth (for, after all, one could simply think that one's mistaken beliefs were correct), nor affect the mere pretense of disbelieving (for that is to look at the truth with one eye and pretend not to see it). Willful ignorance is instead marked by the conviction to shut *both* eyes against any further investigation, because one is so firm in one's belief that any other sources of knowledge are not needed. Here one is not only ignorant but (like Euthyphro) prefers to remain so. One does not in any sense "know" the truth (even with one eye), even though one probably *does* suspect that there are further sources of contravening information out there. Yet these are rejected, because they might conflict with one's favored beliefs; if there are other sources of information, they must be ignored. This is why the false beliefs cited in the polling results show more than just ignorance. For when there are such easily available sources of accurate information out there, the only excuse for such stunning ignorance is *the desire to remain so*; one has actively chosen not to investigate. More than mere scientific illiteracy, this sort of obstinacy reflects contempt. But why would someone embrace such a hostile attitude toward the truth?

The answer to this question is complicated and will require the remainder of this book to address it fully. But already, we may settle the matter of whether willful ignorance is a reasonable approach to the problem of trying to form true beliefs, for most certainly it is not. To reject possibly refutatory sources of information—only because they might contradict one's beliefs—is wrong. Worse, it is irrational.[11] It is fundamental to scientific judgment that one could always be wrong. Because scientific judgment (and, one presumes, many other forms of rational judgment) are based on evidence, it is always theoretically possible that some further information will come along that will refute one's hypothesis. If one's beliefs are based on evidence in the first place, they should be open to revision or refutation based on further investigation. The problem with willful ignorance is not just that it will likely lead to false beliefs, but that it relies on a standard of reasoning that foregoes the possibility of correcting one's beliefs in the future. But we should not so easily give up on the search for truth. Instead, we should embrace the methods of critical reasoning that are used by science to make our beliefs better (and truer) over time. Even where we may not be able to find the truth, we can at least approach it.

To reject this method in favor of dogmatism is not just ignorant, nor even dishonest. It is instead to show contempt for the standards by which true beliefs are formed. Truth is not discovered by happenstance, nor merely by having the right theory. It is a result of openness to new data, whereby one is constantly correcting one's opinion over time, because this is a method that has proven itself in the past to lead to true beliefs. To shut oneself off from new sources of information is to be hostile to the truth. Even if one happened to be right about some matter of opinion (like the proverbial stopped clock that is right twice a day), one's opinions arguably still would not be "true" if they were arrived at by accident, rather than produced by a procedure that could be justified as reliable.

The problem with willful ignorance, therefore, is not mere ignorance of any particular facts about astronomy or biology, but rather a pervasive hostility to searching out reliable methods of gaining true beliefs, which demonstrates a lack of respect for the concept of truth in the first place. It reflects a willingness to cling to falsehood even when good sources of information are easily within our reach. Beyond being wrong, one's beliefs will likely end up being irrational. The problem with willful ignorance isn't mere ignorance of the truth; it is the "willfulness" that is troubling.

The Human Relationship to Truth

As we have seen, our relationship to truth is complicated. We can actively search for it, accept it when we see it, doubt it, reject it, disbelieve it, spin it, outright lie about it, keep it a secret, remain indifferent to it, choose to remain ignorant of it, or pretend that it isn't there. The interesting thing to note here is that whether or not we choose to inquire into the truth—or believe it when it is in front of us—our attitude toward truth can fall along either side of an axis marked by "respect" or "hostility" that has only an orthogonal relationship to the classic terms of "belief" and "disbelief."

Most people think of truth in terms of belief or disbelief, but this is far too simple. Even when we believe something that is true, we can misuse that knowledge in various ways, some of which are hostile to truth. Even true belief, that is, can be manipulated in a way that is not respectful. When we believe that something is true we can use that knowledge honestly, to correct our theories or even to change the world. But we can also use it dishonestly to deceive others, either by outright lying or simply misleading them, so that we may pursue some other attractive purpose. Alternatively, we can decide to suppress the truth, by keeping it a secret or pretending it isn't true. Even when we know the truth, we can fail to respect it.

Disbelief, too, can be complex. In some cases we may disbelieve something based on genuine, though perhaps faulty, judgments over whether it is true. That is fine and, even if we are wrong, this reveals a certain respect for the truth. But in other cases we may display a tendency to disbelieve something despite over-whelming positive evidence, such that it raises suspicions over our integrity.[12] In such cases, we may be in denial or find it attractive to equivocate or remain ignorant long past the point at which it would have been possible to ascertain enough evidence to settle the matter. (The example of the current "debate" over global warming here springs to mind.) In other cases, we may outright refuse to believe something that conflicts with beliefs that we find sacred. Such reactions, too, reveal a lack of respect for the truth.

So we see that, whether we believe in the truth or not, many of our reactions to truth can be hostile. If we believe something but use this knowledge to spin others, we are being hostile to the truth. If we reject the truth because we are afraid to engage in inquiry, we are similarly hostile. Indeed, anything short of the open and active pursuit of true beliefs, with the complete integrity of believing them if and only if we think that they are true, demonstrates some degree of hostility toward the truth.[13]

Of course, the majority of us fall short of this goal sometimes. Yet almost none of us dare express the sentiment that we do not care about the truth. Why is this? I think it is because deep down each of us probably does believe that truth matters, both that it exists and that the possession of it is valuable. Despite the fact that we sometimes treat it brutally, or only give it lip service, it is the rare individual who is prepared to embrace the idea that there is no importance in forming true beliefs. Although many treat it carelessly, few abandon the truth. Why? Because, as it turns out, the concept of truth is useful to the survival of our species and at some level most of us probably recognize that we could not have gotten to this point in our lives—or human civilization—without it.

As complicated as our brains may be in their patterns of denial and resistance, deception and rejection, the human brain is also possibly the single most carefully wired engine for detecting truth that has ever been seen in the history of the universe. And it is a good thing, for surely we would have perished long ago without it.

Notes

1 Giordano Bruno learned this when he was publicly burned in Florence in 1600 for his conviction that there were "other worlds," as did Galileo later when he was put under house arrest for his belief in the movement of the Earth.

2 The actual Greek word at issue in *Euthyphro* is "piety," which within this context may be loosely translated as "righteousness."

3 Jim O'Sullivan, "Perry tells N.H. audience he's a global-warming skeptic," *National Journal*, August 17, 2001, <www.nationaljournal.com/politics/perry-tells-n-h-audience-he-s-a-global-warming-skeptic-with-video-20110817>.

4 Louis Jacobson, "On Mitt Romney and whether humans are causing climate change," *Politifact.com*, May 15, 2012, <www.politifact.com/truth-o-meter/statements/2012/may/15/mitt-romney/mitt-romney-and-whether-humans-are-causing-climate/>.

5 Brad Johnson, "Romney flips to denial: 'We don't know what's causing climate change,'" *ThinkProgress* [blog], October 28, 2011, <http://thinkprogress.org/climate/2011/10/28/355736/romney-flips-to-denial-we-dont-know-whats-causing-climate-change/>.

6 "American adults flunk basic science," *Science Daily*, March 13, 2009, <www.sciencedaily.com/releases/2009/03/090312115133.htm>.

7 "Americans' belief in God, miracles and heaven declines," *Harris Interactive*, Harris Poll 97, December 16, 2013, <www.harrisinteractive.com/NewsRoom/HarrisPolls/tabid/447/ctl/ReadCustom%20Default/mid/1508/ArticleId/1353/Default.aspx>.

8 James Owen, "Evolution less accepted in U.S. than other Western countries, study finds," *National Geographic News*, August 10, 2006, <http://news.nationalgeographic.com/news/2006/08/060810-evolution.html>

9 "Nearly quarter of Brits think Churchill a myth: Poll," *ABC News* (Australia), February 3, 2008, <www.abc.net.au/news/2008-02-04/nearly-quarter-of-brits-think-churchill-a-myth-poll/1031856>.

10 Commentators sometimes called this "paying the crazy tax."

11 Of course, one may raise the objection here that I am using the standards of reason to critique non-reason, which begs the question. For a stirring discussion of the skeptical and reflexive problems that can arise in such a justification, see Michael Lynch's excellent book *In Praise of Reason* (Cambridge: MIT Press, 2012). My present goal, however, is not to provide a full-blown critical defense of reason, but rather to presume that even if philosophers have sometimes had a hard time providing a logical defense of it, in historical terms this debate was settled long ago. Science and reason have been at the foundation of Western culture since the Enlightenment. Yet *despite that*, some continue to doubt its results and question its methods, when it suits the purpose of their ideology. It is the latter issue that I am concerned with in this book and I refuse to allow those who reject the standard of rationality embraced by philosophy to somehow hide behind "skepticism" as convenient camouflage for their deeply anti-truth agenda.

12 Note that we are here talking about true statements, not false ones, so presumably there is some basis for believing them.

13 Truth is about more than the content of our beliefs, that is, but also about the attitude with which we approach the method by which true beliefs are formed.

2

THE VALUE OF TRUTH

Should My Genes Care Whether I Can Justify My Belief That a Tiger is Coming Toward Me?

Rather than love, than money, than fame, give me truth.

Henry David Thoreau

What use is the truth? Why should we value having true beliefs? Are true beliefs somehow adaptive or helpful to our species in its struggle for survival? And indeed, if this is so, wouldn't the tendency to look for and value true beliefs somehow be wired into our brains after all of these years of natural selection?

I believe that the answer to these last two questions is, for the most part, yes and that a compelling story can be told about human history that culminates in the development of the human brain's greatest truth-seeking invention: science. Science is the formal codification of the process of forming true beliefs about our world that has been selected for and wired into our brain over hundreds of thousands of years and has contributed to our survival and growth into the dominant species on this planet. Not coincidentally, I believe that science is also the best model of what it means to have a respectful attitude toward truth.

There are many misconceptions about how scientific beliefs are formed and of the standards by which scientific theories are evaluated. In the popular imagination, a scientist gathers evidence, tests a hypothesis, and then discovers "the truth." Any deviation from this fantasy, wherein one is forced to admit that a scientific theory is "not yet proven" or that "not all of the data are in yet," is sometimes taken by naive critics to show that a particular theory is "just a theory," which presumably has not yet gone through the rigorous assessment needed for scientists to show that it is actually "true." Such an ill-informed understanding of the process by which science actually works (or of what scientists mean when they use the word "theory" as opposed to "hypothesis") has probably led to many of the ignorant statements concerning the alleged lack of evidence for global warming or evolution that politicians love to bellow on the campaign trail.

But, to anyone who has bothered to study it, one understands that science is just not like this. It is not the *particular* theory of evolution or global warming that cannot be proven true but, if we get right down to it, actually *any* of the theories of science. But this is not because science is somehow a flawed process, which cannot lead us to better and truer theories. Instead it is just that science does not work like most people think it does. No scientific theory, no matter how well corroborated by the evidence, can ever be proven absolutely true. Not even gravity.

Although it is correct to say that science is "evidence based," it turns out that this is both a blessing and a curse ... the source of science's greatest strength and also its greatest perceived weakness. For being evidence-based means that no matter how well one's theory may fit with the current evidence, it is always possible that new evidence may come forward that will cause us to revise our current theories. *All* scientific belief, that is, is tentative and open ended. It is changeable and subject to revision because it is based on the possibility that we have not yet sampled all of the world that our theories are supposed to cover.

A scientific theory can no more be proven true than we can hope to make absolute pronouncements about the edge of the universe or what happens to us after death. We just have not been there yet. Part of this is due to the famous "problem of induction" that was put forward two centuries ago by David Hume, which shows that whenever we are generalizing based on a limited sample of data, our assertions must run the risk of being false. Only deductive statements—such as those in logic and mathematics—can be proven absolutely true, but this is because they are self-contained analytical systems whose truth is not based on correlation with the state of the world in the first place.[1]

Is this a weakness in science? Far from it. For in science we see that it is possible to contend with uncertainty in a positive way and learn to embrace the power of skepticism. Even if we are not prepared to believe that a theory is absolutely, provably true, it may remain worthy of our belief because it conforms with the best evidence that we are capable of gathering. This means, of course, that while science aims at truth, it can never technically speaking claim to have reached it. In science, truth is a guiding ideal, not a destination. But, outside logic and mathematics, what were we expecting? Like Socrates, we see that it is not doubt, disbelief, or even ignorance that stands in the way of using our inductive powers to learn more about the truths of nature; it is instead the refusal to consider new evidence because we are already sure that our theories are true in the first place. Yet how can we claim to discover truth about the world outside the examination of empirical evidence?

So we see that even if science cannot claim that every (or any) scientific belief is provably true, it nonetheless leads us *toward* truth and in doing so it is a model of respect for the formulation of true beliefs. Even when scientists refuse to believe something, they must do so in a respectful way, based on the principled desire to gain more evidence and do more testing. Indeed if they are not prepared to do this—as sometimes happens when scientists fabricate data or refuse to consider new evidence that confounds their favored hypotheses—it is not too strong to say that they have really given up on being scientists and have instead become ideologues, who contend that they somehow have special access to the truth outside hypothesis testing and corroboration by their colleagues. But, as Thomas Kuhn famously argued in his account of how earlier scientific beliefs are later overthrown by those who are willing to embrace new paradigms, there is a real danger in such cases that the "old guard" will get read out of the profession.[2] They become dinosaurs. And this, we may all agree, is not a good evolutionary move.

Evolutionary Psychology

The field of evolutionary psychology holds that we can understand human behavior only by attempting to explain it within the context in which the genes that govern human action were selected for by the environment. Why do men display so much sexual jealousy? Because those who were cavalier about their mate's extramarital friendships probably had their genes culled from the gene pool many generations ago. Why are parents so fond of their children, even to the point of sacrificing their own lives to save them? Because such devotion to one's offspring is an excellent way of getting one's genes into the third generation.

By the same token, we may conjecture that there is evolutionary value in seeking true beliefs. There must be. Otherwise we would have long ago seen less selective advantage for those who said "Yes, that really is a tiger! Run!" and more for those who said "I don't believe it. Let me take a closer look."[3] The ability to gather evidence from nature and formulate true beliefs on that basis is an evolutionary advantage that we see prized in humans and non-humans alike. Yes, that's a snake. No, don't eat that. What's that noise? These are the earliest rumblings of reasoning based on data from our environment that we inherited from our ancestors and so finely tuned into the majesty of science.

As Robert Park argues in his book *Superstition: Belief in the Age of Science*:

> Our ability to make sense of the world begins with the marvelous ability of the human brain to pick out patterns in the information collected by our senses. Recognizing familiar patterns in unfamiliar situations is the beginning of reasoning by analogy, and therefore of abstract thought. Our savage ancestors, living as hunter-gatherers in a Pleistocene wilderness, must have been very good at figuring out the behavior patterns of the animals they hunted as food, as well as those that hunted them for food. … Remarkably, it would turn out that the brain that was good at finding grubs and avoiding saber-toothed tigers could also recognize more abstract patterns in language and mathematics.[4]

Yet, given this, why do we so often refuse to believe something even in the face of evidence that it is true? If humans are wired up for pattern recognition, how did it happen that we have a conflicting tendency sometimes to resist or even to deny the truth? And if such a tendency exists, mustn't it also have been selected for by our environment? But what possible survival advantage might accrue from believing anything other than the truth? If truth-seeking is so valuable within the evolutionary context, then why do we have confirmation bias, cognitive dissonance, the gambler's fallacy, motivated reasoning, stereotype threat, and all of the other foibles of human reasoning that so vex social psychologists, unless those were *also* in some way valuable in the struggle for survival?[5] By the logic of evolutionary psychology, mustn't such truth-avoiding mechanisms *also* have a purpose? If not, why wouldn't evolution have culled them long ago?

Of course, there are some irrationalities that have clear survival value, like the placebo effect, where we find pain relief in a sugar pill merely because we *believe* that it is a powerful medicine. Perhaps there are evolutionary advantages to such mental structures—like pain minimization in the midst of a fight—that have helped us to survive. But wouldn't this mean that we should be prepared to defend *every* one of these mental "glitches" and show why each has specific survival value? Rather than discuss the problem of human irrationality as a whole, shouldn't we be prepared to show that every violation of logic must give its organism an evolutionary advantage? If so, it is hard to imagine the survival advantage of something like overconfidence bias (which is when we think we can do something that we probably can't), which has obvious evolutionary costs.[6]

Indeed, even in what might be thought of as an obvious case for the survival value of truth-avoiding mechanisms within the human brain, the purported benefits seem equivocal. In a study of adult survivors of childhood sexual abuse, researchers Melissa Himelein and JoAnn McElrath found that "well-adjusted" survivors tended to engage in four cognitive strategies: disclosing and discussing the abuse, minimization, positive reframing, and refusing to dwell on the experience.[7] Other research on victimized populations conducted by William Helmreich, who studied Holocaust survivors who had emigrated to the USA, found that many of them also employed mechanisms of psychological "distancing"—such as refusing to talk about their experiences or dwell on the past—that enabled them to cope surprisingly well with their trauma.[8] This sort of strategy—while not amounting to outright denial or resistance to the truth—did (according to Helmreich) enable these Holocaust survivors to do better than a control group of American-born Jews of the same age, as measured by low psychotherapy rate, more stable marriage, and low criminality. Robert Jay Lifton has identified such strategies to seal off part of one's emotions and memories as "psychic numbing," which Helmreich sees as a positive adaptation to trauma. Yet this is where the controversy arises, for one person's "tenacity" or "resilience" can be seen by another as symptoms of unresolved post-traumatic stress syndrome.[9]

Indeed, in other studies of Holocaust survivors, it was (perhaps unsurprisingly) found that most had deep psychological scars, which were sometimes passed on to a second generation.

What can we conclude from such cases? Are trauma victims who engage in truth-avoiding strategies such as "distancing" or "psychic numbing" respecting truth or not? Of course, even if they were not, one would be hard pressed to criticize them by insisting that everyone would be better off if he or she thought constantly about every painful truth. Sometimes the option to face truth is removed from consciousness, as seen in those cases where individuals experience personality splits, repressed memory, or other coping mechanisms wherein the psyche reacts to trauma by refusing to admit what is too painful to face. But what about the cases discussed above, where despite severe trauma the truth is *not* unavailable to consciousness, but it is nonetheless avoided, as victims choose to minimize the damage and get on with their lives? In such cases, perhaps the most important thing is whether the mechanism works. If it allows the victim to protect his or her psyche and move on to live as happily as possible, who are we to criticize? Survival value trumps epistemological consistency any day of the week. But isn't that the point? Why would *any* truth-avoiding psychological mechanisms be selected for? The point of evolution is to select what increases survival, and that is not necessarily in all cases the truth. Truth is sometimes—even often—valuable for survival. But where it is not, survival wins out. Is it possible then that the mind is wired primarily for survival, not truth?

Yet it is not so obvious that survival requires disrespecting truth. In cases of severe trauma, for instance, perhaps even truth-avoidance can be respectful of truth. The important thing to remember is that the survivors discussed by Himelein, McElrath, and Helmreich are not *denying* the truth or making up some falsehood in order to deceive others (or themselves), so much as they are making a conscious choice not to let it define the remainder of their existence. They are giving the truth its due and then moving on. One does not have to live with the truth every moment in order to respect it. There is nothing dishonest about choosing to focus on the future rather than the past. Indeed, we all do it every day of our lives.

A good example is the reality of death. Each adult probably remembers the exact moment in childhood when he or she figured out or was told the shocking truth that death is permanent and that it happens to everyone. Yet it cannot be correct to say that in order to respect this truth one must go through every waking moment of life with one's eventual death immediately present in consciousness. Of course, some do. (I had a distant relative who every night before going to bed put on the dress that she wanted to be buried in, thinking that she might be dead by morning. Of course, one night she was right.) But most of us happily choose, even in the face of our eventual annihilation, to live our lives. We adopt a dog. We eat an ice cream cone on a warm summer's day. We fall in love. Yes, we know that we will die someday, but this need not stop us from enjoying life. But isn't this precisely what the "successful" Holocaust survivors discussed by Helmreich were doing? They know first-hand not only that all of us will die, they have actually faced it. Yet they nonetheless want to live the rest of their lives. They don't want to let the worst thing that ever happened to them rob them of the pleasures that may come. They are not denying the truth, so much as refusing to let it define them. Thus they are both protecting themselves from the brutality of truth at the same time that they are respecting it, in an effort to live a life of hope and fulfillment.

Such an outlook might give us reason to appreciate the diversity of ways that it is possible to respect truth. But it still does not solve the problem of how it came to be that there exist so many *dishonest* ways of contending with the truth (denial, lying, covering it up) that are wired right in alongside the honest ones in the human brain.[10] There are so many of these, in fact, that it might make us question our original premise of whether truth has survival value, for if so then why haven't all of the fallacies and mistakes of human reasoning long since been eliminated by natural selection? But who ever said that the point of human reason was to discover truth?

Mercier and Sperber's Hypothesis

How can it be that truth-seeking and truth-avoidance both have potential evolutionary benefits that would explain their presence in the human psyche? One recent answer to this apparent conundrum has been provided by Hugo Mercier and Dan Sperber, who argue that the point of human reason is not and never has been to lead to truth, but is instead to win arguments.[11] If this hypothesis is correct, it would have the advantage of avoiding conflict between the simultaneous presence of truth-seeking and truth-avoiding mechanisms within the human psyche, by showing that the discovery of truth is not the point of human reason, but only a by-product. The point instead is to persuade others that we are correct (even if we are not). But what possible evolutionary advantage could this have for an individual?

The fundamental question that motivates Mercier and Sperber's analysis is this: if reasoning is supposed to lead to truth, and true beliefs have such great evolutionary value, then why do we reason so poorly? The fact that humans do reason poorly is beyond dispute. The psychological literature is replete with well-known examples of mistakes like "confirmation bias" (where we seek out information that confirms our preconceptions) and "hindsight bias" (where we rely on current knowledge to assume that something was predictable all along) and many others that go all the way back to Daniel Kahneman and Amos Tversky's groundbreaking work on human irrationality from the 1970s and 1980s.[12] Worse, many of these flaws seem to be an inalienable part of our cognitive make-up, such that even when we are informed that we are prone to these mistakes, we make them anyway. Why would this be? If true beliefs are the goal of reasoning then the presence of such glitches in the human mind would not make any sense in evolutionary context.

Hence Mercier and Sperber's thesis: reason is not intended to lead us to truth, but instead to win arguments. Now why would being a persuasive speaker be valuable within the evolutionary context? Here Mercier and Sperber tell a story about the importance of argumentation to the evolution of human communication. In a group setting, where people were not already inclined to trust the truth of what you said just because you said it, they would need some way of evaluating your claim. This is where arguments come in. Just to make an assertion does not rise to the level of overcoming the other person's "epistemic vigilance" over being deceived or manipulated. If you present the other person with the reasons for your belief, however, you have now given them the means to evaluate the truth of your claim and also, if you are right, presumably extend more trust to you in the future. Thus, according to Mercier and Sperber, the role of reason in allowing us to provide arguments for our beliefs facilitates both the quality and reliability of information that is shared in human communication.

According to Mercier and Sperber:

> [T]he emergence of reasoning is best understood within the framework of the evolution of human communication. Reasoning enables people to exchange arguments that, on the whole, make communication more reliable and hence more advantageous. The main function of reasoning, we claim, is *argumentative*.[13]

Later, they explicitly draw the connection to evolution.

> We view the evolution of reasoning as linked to that of human communication. Reasoning ... enables communication to produce arguments to convince addressees who would not accept what they say on trust; it enables addressees to evaluate the soundness of these arguments and to accept valuable information that they would be suspicious of otherwise. Thus, thanks to reasoning, human communication is made more reliable and more potent.[14]

Next, Mercier and Sperber proceed to outline a bold strategy. They say that if their hypothesis is correct, it should support several surprising *and falsifiable* predictions. Among these are that reasoning should produce its best results when used in argumentative contexts, most notably in group discussions, and do poorly outside these. They also predict that reasoning used to produce such arguments should exhibit a strong confirmation bias and be consistent with the "mistake" of motivated reasoning (which is when we allow our desires to influence our beliefs). Basically, Mercier and Sperber sum up their predictions with the claim that, if their hypothesis is correct, then "reasoning should do well what it evolved to do."[15]

The stakes of such a strategy are high. In addition to being a cognitive scientist, Sperber is a philosopher and therefore must know the great value that the famous philosopher of science Karl Popper put on judging the truth of one's hypothesis by whether it could survive attempts at refutation through falsifying one's predictions. Indeed, just in case we had any doubt about the stakes (or Mercier and Sperber's familiarity with Popper's work), they spell it out for us:

> It is ... crucial to show that [our hypothesis] entails falsifiable predictions. If the main function of reasoning is indeed argumentative, then it should exhibit as signature effects strengths and weaknesses related to the relative importance of this function compared to other potential functions of reasoning. This should be testable through experimental work done here and now. Our goal now is to spell out and explain what signature effects we predict to evaluate these predictions in light of the available evidence, and to see whether they help make better sense of a number of well-known puzzles in the psychology of reasoning and decision making. Should one fail, on the other hand, to find such signature of the hypothesized argumentative function of reasoning, and even more should one find that the main features of reasoning match some other function, then our hypothesis should be considered falsified.[16]

One must admire the courage of this strategy, especially in the face of the many criticisms (a plethora of which appear in the same issue of the journal as their original article) that the authors would anticipate.[17] But of course all that matters now is the quality of their arguments.

One of the most important results examined by Mercier and Sperber concerns the famous "Wason selection task," in which subjects were given four cards with the instruction that—although they could see only one side of the card—each had a number on one side and a letter on the other. The cards might read something like 4, E, 7, and K. The subjects were then given a rule such as this: "If there is a vowel on one side of the card, then there is an even number on the other" and asked to determine which (and only which) cards needed to be turned over in order to test the rule.

Subjects routinely found this test incredibly difficult. In the original Wason experiment and subsequent similar experiments, only around 10 percent of subjects got the right answer. The key, of course, is to realize that only the E and the 7 need to be turned over. The E obviously, because it might have an odd number on the other side, which would falsify the rule, but also the 7, for if there is a vowel on the other side of *that*, the rule is also falsified. Subjects tend to be flummoxed by the fact that the 4 does not need to be turned over. Those who have studied logic might understand that the 4 is irrelevant to the truth of the proposition; whether or not the other side has a vowel on it makes no difference, since the rule says only what must be the case *if* there is a vowel on one side of the card, not that an even number could not also be on the other side of a card that has a consonant. By the same token, K is irrelevant, because it is not a vowel and the rule says only what would follow if there is a vowel on one side of the card and nothing about what might follow if there is not.

The importance of this experiment for Mercier and Sperber's hypothesis is what comes next, when one asks subjects to solve the problem in groups. Here we find that 80 percent get the right answer. This is not, the authors tell us, merely due to everyone else in the group deferring to the "smartest person in the room." Indeed, this has been tested and it was found that even when none of the subjects in the room individually could solve the task, the group often could, resulting in what has been termed the "assembly bonus effect." What we see in this instance, Mercier and Sperber contend, is that only when the task is placed within an argumentative context (in a group discussion) do our better reasoning skills kick in. We test one another's hypotheses. We criticize one another's logic. We become persuaded by another person's reasoning. According to their thesis, this is precisely what one would expect, if reason had evolved primarily for the purpose of persuasion through argument. As individuals, we may feel little motivation to criticize our own arguments, even if they are wrong. In group settings, however, we have a much better chance of finding the truth. But this is not because someone in the back of the room has the answer. It is instead because our reasoning skills improve when they are placed within an argumentative setting.

One thing that happens in group settings is that our individual beliefs get challenged. And when that happens we routinely exhibit "confirmation bias." Mercier and Sperber tell us that "confirmation bias consists in the seeking or interpreting of evidence in ways that are partial to existing beliefs, expectations, or a hypothesis in hand."[18] In other words, once we have decided that something is true, we look primarily for evidence that confirms our existing belief, not evidence to disprove it. Although this is normally thought of as a "flaw" in human reasoning (according to some it is arguably why people think that they should turn over the card with the 4 in the Wason selection task), it is accepted by Mercier and Sperber as a predictable consequence of the production of arguments in group settings. We hate to be wrong, so naturally we are biased in favor of proving to others that our beliefs are true.

Although it would be better for the discovery of truth if we could mentally construct counterexamples and criticize our own hypotheses, this is just not something that we are motivated to do. Indeed, Mercier and Sperber claim that in cases of genuine confirmation bias, it is not that we *cannot* overcome this flaw, but that in most instances "an appropriate argumentative motivation is lacking."[19] Yet when we are working with a group in evaluating a hypothesis (as opposed to producing one), we perform much better at this task and confirmation bias is mitigated. Context is crucial. When we are alone, we just do not seem to be able to break our reasoning free from our motivation. When we face an audience, however, we are forced to be more rational. Mercier and Sperber observe that "when participants want to prove a conclusion wrong, they will find ways to falsify it."

A similar support for Mercier and Sperber's "argumentative theory" can be found in their discussion of the problem of "motivated reasoning." Here one is confronted with the fact that people routinely anticipate the defense of their beliefs. As such, they are motivated to find reasons that they are true, even if they originally embraced them for intuitive reasons. In anticipation of argument, we therefore have a tendency to look for reasons to justify the beliefs that we already hold.[20] Here Mercier and Sperber admit that the presence of this phenomenon can have "dire epistemic consequences" in our search for the truth, but once again they assert their claim that this is entirely consistent with the idea that reason evolved primarily as a tool of persuasion. Juries may jump to a conclusion. We may cling to fringe theories long after they are disproven. There may even be consequences for our moral attitudes, whereby we become more likely to "blame the victim" or find excuses for immoral behavior. This is all to be expected. As individuals—as we have seen throughout this argument—we are prone to horrible biases that interfere with our ability to find the truth. But as social animals—who expect that our beliefs on any number of topics will be challenged by other members of our group—this bias is exactly what one would expect. According to Mercier and Sperber, the role of reason is to facilitate our skills at argument, not to find the truth.

Near the end of their paper, Mercier and Sperber tell us that their hypothesis is in good shape because its predictions are "confirmed by existing evidence." They go on to equivocate, but only slightly:

> True, most of these predictions can be derived from other theories. We would argue, however, that the argumentative hypothesis provides a more principled explanation of the empirical evidence (in the case of the confirmation bias, for instance). In our discussion of motivated reasoning and of reason-based choice, not only did we converge in our prediction with existing theories, but we also extensively borrowed from them. Even in these cases, how-ever, we would argue that our approach has the distinctive advantage of providing clear answers to the why-questions: Why do humans have a confirmation bias? Why do they engage in motivated reasoning? Why do they base their decisions on the availability of justificatory reasons? More-over, the argumentative theory of reasoning offers a unique integrative perspective: It explains wide swaths of the psychological literature within a single overarching framework.[21]

Clearly, they believe that their hypothesis has done a good job of explaining why there are so many "flaws" in human reasoning. Their answer is that these sorts of flaws are not flaws at all, but just what one would expect if the role of reason were not to discover truth, but instead to facilitate argument.

It is now time to realize, however, that there is a lot that Mercier and Sperber have *not* done to advance their argument. For one thing, even if they are right in their overall claim (which I will challenge in the next section of this chapter), they must decide what to say about the specific evolutionary value of any "mistakes" in human reasoning. Similarly, they must find a better way to contend with how it came to be that reason does indeed *sometimes* lead to truth:

> ... individuals may develop some limited ability to distance themselves from their own opinion, to consider alternatives and thereby become more objective. Presumably this is what the 10% or so of people who pass the standard Wason selection task do. But this is an acquired skill and involves exercising some imperfect control over a natural disposition that sponta-neously pulls in a different direction. ... By anticipating objections, one may even be able to recognize flaws in one's own hypotheses and go on to revise them. We have suggested that this depends on a painstakingly acquired ability to exert some limited control over one's own biases. Even among scientists, this ability may be uncommon, but those who have it may have a great influence on the development of scientific ideas. It would be a mistake, however, to treat their highly visible, almost freakish, contributions as paradigmatic examples of human reasoning.[22]

To call accurate reasoners "freakish"—and assume despite their cogent perfor-mance that they must have cognitive biases anyway—is to draw a conclusion far beyond the data. Similarly, why assume without interviewing them that these skills were "painstakingly acquired" rather than natural, which would surely require an evolutionary explanation for why 10 percent of the human population apparently has this trait. Is truth an occasional by-product of human reason? Are mistakes in reasoning (which can lead to untruth) just irrelevant artifacts or are they somehow valuable in and of themselves? Isn't there a tension here between any alleged evolutionary advantages of mistakes in reasoning and the costs of foregoing truth?

Although they do not name them, there are several possible hypotheses that may provide an overall evolutionary framework to Mercier and Sperber's argument:

(1)   There is no adaptive value to mistakes in reasoning, but they are so unimportant that evolution hasn't bothered to cull them out; confirmation bias and motivated reasoning are the cognitive equivalent of vestigial organs.

(2)   There is no adaptive value to mistakes in reasoning in and of themselves, but they are linked to other traits that *do* have survival value.

(3)   Mistakes in reasoning are adaptive. They are selected for because they fulfill some evolutionary purpose that outweighs their costs to truth.

Mercier and Sperber say precious little that would allow one to discern an overall evolutionary strategy that would support their work, much less which of the three hypotheses conjectured above might motivate their views. But, since they explicitly frame their argumentative theory of reason within an evolutionary context, it seems fair to ask for more clarity from them and—in its absence—to use our own hypotheses above as a stalking horse to criticize their overall argument.

Criticisms of the Argumentative Theory of Reason

For the sake of completeness let's begin with the first hypothesis, so that we may immediately dismiss a misunderstanding that some may harbor about Mercier and Sperber's argument. If one hopes to put the argumentative theory of reason in evolutionary context—which Mercier and Sperber explicitly desire to do—it should be obvious that the "cognitive appendix" hypothesis makes no sense. If it were true that cognitive errors like confirmation bias and motivated reasoning had no cost in discovering the truth—or that belief in truth had no survival value whatsoever—then it might make sense to think that these sorts of mental mistakes could survive the culling process of evolution. But, given that at least *sometimes* it is valuable to believe in the truth (when the doctor tells you that you really must take your antibiotics on schedule; when your flight instructor tells you that you really don't have the skills to fly solo in current weather conditions), it stands to reason that any mental mistakes that undermined our survival *even to the slightest degree* would face relentless evolutionary pressure over the generations, such that these traits would be eliminated from the gene pool.

Evolutionary psychologists surely know that they cannot just wave their hands when a trait is difficult to explain. If the evolutionary hypothesis is strong enough to explain behavioral traits like altruism and homosexuality—which would seem to present a formidable prima facie case against evolutionary psychology—then surely one would expect them to be able to handle something like confirmation bias and motivated reasoning.[23] In short, if confirmation bias has survived in the human psyche all these years, it must have at least some survival value. It cannot be akin to some harmless, vestigial organ that evolution has not yet eliminated. Indeed, Mercier and Sperber themselves would seem disposed to recognize that even if such mental traits had costs at the individual level (i.e., for the discovery of truth) these must be balanced by advantages (i.e., in facilitating better communication and more reliable information sharing) at the group level.

This leads directly, however, to what may be thought of as a real problem with Mercier and Sperber's analysis, corresponding to the second hypothesis in our evolutionary framework, which says that even if there is no adaptive value to mistakes in reasoning in and of themselves, they may be linked to other traits that *do* increase survival value. Here one must ask a crucial question: survival value for whom? For the individual or for the group of which the individual is a member?

Are Mercier and Sperber claiming that mental mistakes like confirmation bias are (a) valuable to an individual (because it helps him to win arguments), (b) to the group that he is in (perhaps because it increases the fervor with which we defend our beliefs, which leads to spirited debate that helps to discover the truth), or (c) because even though it has no direct value whatsoever—to the individual or to the group—it has the collateral effect of facilitating communication *within* a group? Clearly (a) and (b) are linked with the third original hypothesis—that mistakes in reasoning are adaptive and are selected for because they fulfill some evolutionary purpose—which we have yet to consider. So for now, let's focus on (c), which seems part and parcel of hypothesis (2), which claims that even though there is no intrinsic benefit to mistakes like confirmation bias, they are linked to other traits that *do* increase survival value.

Again the crucial question: survival value for whom? It is a crucial flaw in Mercier and Sperber's analysis that, despite their desire to put their theory within an evolutionary context, they say far too little about the process of natural selection by which an individual who made reasoning mistakes like confirmation bias or motivated reasoning might benefit from such a trait. Even if the cultivation of argumentative skill led to group benefits (like better communication or group cohesion) in order for the traits to survive *in the individual* there would have to be some selective benefit for that individual as well.

Now perhaps Mercier and Sperber are making a sort of "group benefits" hypothesis, which is not unknown in the field of evolutionary psychology. As we just saw, this could not plausibly be a claim that a trait which benefitted one's group would be selected for unless it also benefitted the individual who held it, for without this it would be unclear by what mechanism such a trait would survive the process of natural selection. But perhaps a more sophisticated argument can be made here for how a trait that benefitted one's group could survive the evolutionary process. Indeed, one of the ways that theorists in evolutionary psychology have tried to explain traits like altruism and homosexuality is precisely through such a mechanism whereby, even if some traits did not directly benefit the individual who expressed them (presumably because altruism might get you killed and homosexuality is not a good way to pass along one's genes) these traits provided some sort of benefit to one's group (perhaps by raising an alarm call or providing redundant parenting within a society in which adult siblings were often killed). This might allow the trait to survive within the gene pool of others within the group, who presumably were somehow related to the individual whose life or genes were sacrificed. Here, of course, the level of selection is neither at the group nor the individual level, but at the genetic level, such that one might explain the survival of the "altruism gene" by suggesting that even if altruists are disproportionately killed, their genes enable the societies that contain such individuals to thrive, as compared to those that contain only narcissists. In short, groups containing altruists are more "fit" than those that do not. Even if the individual altruist may be killed, his genes will have a better chance of getting into the next generation if the members of his group (who presumably share some of his genes) survive.[24]

But if this is the sort of argument that Mercier and Sperber are making it is nowhere to be found in their essay. And if such a theory *were* to be advanced, it would be crucial to show that a group with better individual arguers was more fit than a group without them. But, unlike in the case of the altruist (either the alarm caller or the redundant parent), it is not clear that *any* direct benefit would accrue to someone other than the individual debater, *unless he happened to be arguing for something that was true.* Is there even a gene that controls for argumentative skill? And do those who argue well really take a greater risk of being culled from the gene pool (Socrates notwithstanding!), such that one would even need a "group benefits" hypothesis to explain how this gene would survive in one's relatives or progeny? Such an argument strains belief and would require careful articulation and defense, if that is even what Mercier and Sperber intend to hypothesize.

But there is another possibility, which is that the benefit of being a good arguer accrues just (or primarily) *to the individual himself.* Such a hypothesis seems much more in line with what Mercier and Sperber actually say in their paper, if only because they provide such an undernourished defense of the mechanism by which any group benefits like "social cohesion" or "enhanced communication" might drive the process of individual selection for argumentative traits. But if this is what they are saying, they must provide some explicit reason for thinking that *any* selective benefit accrues to an individual who argues well. As Andy Norman claims in his paper "Why We Reason: Intention-Alignment and the Genesis of Human Rationality,"

> [Mercier and Sperber's] hypothesis ... asks us to imagine that a reputation for argumentative prowess enhanced reproductive success. We understand that argumentative skill can bolster social standing in, for example, an academic setting. But it strains credulity to suppose that argumentative posturing carries significant reproductive rewards in a culture of Neolithic hunter-gatherers. ... A theory of reason's origins that rests on the supposition that, contrary to contemporary experience, Neolithic geeks got laid more frequently than their dialectically challenged contemporaries [is implausible].[25]

Perhaps Mercier and Sperber might make such an argument work—either to show that such an oratory advantage might confer direct reproductive benefits to the individual debater or, through inclusive fitness, to others who carried his genes, but so far they have not offered any such analysis.[26]

Where are we left, then, in analyzing Mercier and Sperber's theory? Next we must examine the third hypothesis in our evolutionary framework, which says that perhaps mistakes in reasoning *are* adaptive and are selected for because they fulfill some evolutionary purpose that outweighs their costs to finding truth. Recall here that such advantages might accrue either (a) to the individual or (b) to the group. But if that is the direction that this argument is going, it is important to remember that we must discuss not only the potential benefits of skillful persuasion, but also its costs. As Mercier and Sperber admit, there are distinct epistemic disadvantages to cognitive errors such as confirmation bias and motivated reasoning, if what we are trying to do is discover the truth. While it is true that these costs might be compensated for in group discussion, where others criticize our errors and we may all presumably enjoy the "assembly bonus effect," there are naturally some potential costs as well. And, for an evolutionary hypothesis to work, the benefits had better outweigh the costs.

In a critical piece that appeared as part of "Open Peer Commentary" in the same issue as Mercier and Sperber's original paper, Robert J. Sternberg published a brief note entitled "When Reasoning Is Persuasive but Wrong," in which he states that:

> Mercier and Sperber are correct that reasoning and argumentation are closely related. But they are wrong in arguing that this relationship is one of evolutionary adaptation. In fact, persuasive reasoning that is not veridical can be fatal to the individual and to the propagation of his or her genes, as well as to the human species as a whole.[27]

Focusing on the costs of overlooking truths that could pose a threat to our existence, Sternberg contends that individuals "who did not perceive things veridically would have been less able to reproduce than those arguers who did perceive things veridically. The brilliant reasoners who argued wrongly regarding threats had many more opportunities to perish before reproducing than those reasoners, persuasive or not, who saw threats as they were."[28] And, in fact, the same threat to survival may occur at the group level, where a persuasive charlatan may put the entire group at risk by convincing them that a wolf, for instance, is only a harmless animal or that cooling food has no effect on its preservation.

And in modern times, Sternberg argues, the stakes are even higher. If Mercier and Sperber are right that "the main function of reasoning is to produce arguments to convince others rather than to find the best decision" then "human survival is in serious jeopardy. [This use] of reasoning is not evolutionarily adaptive for survival in the long run."[29] Indeed, the stakes can be global:

> Consider global warming. Global warming threatens the existence of human and other life on the planet Earth, and yet deniers, including scientists, put the life of all human organisms on the planet—the replication of the species' genes and hence the survival of the species—at risk. Reasoning is being used in the service of argumentation, but not always for evolutionarily adaptive purposes, at least with respect to the genes of the individuals involved.[30]

One might here worry that Sternberg has confused "ought" with "is" and has put himself in the position of attacking Mercier and Sperber over how reason *should* be used, rather than their empirical claim that argumentation is the function for which reason actually evolved. This would not be the first time in history that our prehistoric traits—either physiological or behavioral—found themselves at odds with the selective pressures of a modern environment. Still, Sternberg has a good point, which is that it would not make evolutionary sense *even in the ancestral environment* for persuasive skill to be valued over truth.

Mercier and Sperber have likely overestimated the alleged evolutionary advantages of winning an argument *when one is not right*. Surely there is a potential cost to such error. Indeed, wouldn't the falsity of one's argument ultimately put selective pressure on the individual who made it and perhaps even on his group? Might the entire group get wiped out? If there were survivors, might they blame the person who made the false argument? How, one might wonder, can there be survival value to an argument that has no connection to truth?[31] Of course, perhaps it is not any *individual* argument that has to have a connection to truth, but merely the *propensity to argue*. Yet surely, over the long haul, an individual would be assessed on the quality of his arguments and what would this mean other than that his individual arguments more often than not corresponded to what was later found to be true?

Moreover, Mercier and Sperber overlook an obvious rejoinder to their theory of the argumentative theory of reason. For what could be more persuasive than the truth? If skill at argumentation tends to confer selective advantage, and belief in truth *also* tends to confer selective advantage, then why in the world would it *not* be the case that there would be some sort of evolutionary connection between reason and truth? Perhaps this is what the 10 percent of "freakish" individuals were about? Although evolution is a slow-moving process, it would be interesting to try to test whether *this* sort of adaptive trait conferred greater survival advantage and may be increasing over time.[32] Here one might be accused, I suppose, of making the perfect the enemy of the good. Surely it would be a selective advantage if humans could fly, but the fact that we cannot provides no good argument against evolution. Still, it seems curious that—as Mercier and Sperber admit—most classical theories tend to argue that reason is advantageous because it leads to truth, and *they* argue that reason is advantageous because it leads to better arguers, yet they downplay an evolutionary link (at least at the individual level) between skill at argumentation and the discovery of truth.

Of course, none of this suggests that the "classical" theory of reasoning is confirmed either. It has its own anomalies to explain, the most important of which is the question that motivated Mercier and Sperber in the first place: if reason is valuable because it helps us to discover truth (and true beliefs are valuable to us in our struggle for survival), then why are we so bad at reasoning? It is tempting here to quibble and make the claim that perhaps we are not so bad at individual reasoning as one might expect, especially if the alternative is to take the radical step of severing the tie between truth and reason. But of course there is always the claim that we could be better at it. Why *does* confirmation bias survive? Why *do* we engage in motivated reasoning? Yet evolution does not require perfection in order for a trait to be selected, only that it has survival value. And surely the ability to reason, despite problems such as confirmation bias and motivated reasoning, does confer *some* benefit. Or are we here again just making the perfect the enemy of the good, or perhaps merely telling another "just so" story?[33]

The best route may be to remember why we were initially attracted to Mercier and Sperber's hypothesis in the first place, which is that they could explain something that other theories could not. Even if Mercier and Sperber are wrong in their overall claim about the argumentative function of reason, one must still deal with their *results*. And we have not given them nearly enough credit thus far for one crucial finding: that humans are much better at using reason to find truth when we work in groups. But why would that be?

The Role of Groups in Scientific Reasoning

Mercier and Sperber hypothesize that the job of reason is more like a lawyer defending a case than an individual seeking truth. Even if they are wrong about this, however, perhaps they are right that even the most "truth-focused" individuals—such as scientists—can occasionally have selfish motives that get in the way. Even scientists, after all, want their own theories to be right. Some may even be in it primarily for the adulation. But here is the point. Science is a group process. It is not just about individual rationality or the attainment of individual rewards. Instead, scientific credibility (and rewards) comes about as a result of the judgment of others. Science is committed to the twin principles of peer review and the replication of experiments, both of which are ways for the scientific community to check the individualist/selfish motives that may have been wired into us by our evolutionary history. Is the scientist inherently more objective than his or her counterpart in the social sciences? Maybe, but it still helps to have someone looking over his or her shoulder.[34] This means that even if the individual scientist is not wired up exclusively to find truth, the *group* focus of science *is* well-suited to this goal.

Of course, there is still the possibility of mass delusion. Sometimes the entire scientific community can resist an idea that later turns out to be true (Wegener's theory of continental drift comes to mind). But in the long run, science as a whole is better equipped to make progress toward the truth than any individual seeker relying on his or her own reason. One would hope that individual scientists might eventually internalize and embrace the larger group values of science (and there is nothing like the fear of being shown to be a fool in front of your peers to encourage you to dampen any personal bias before it is made public), but it is still probably true that there is something to the "wisdom of crowds" effect in scientific reasoning. Yes, the entire group can make a mistake. But they also might catch our errors.[35]

Might one here borrow another page from evolutionary psychology and consider the concept of inclusive fitness as a potential explanation for the success of science?[36] Just as inclusive fitness sometimes trumps an individual organism's fitness in our gene's struggle for survival, maybe scientific rationality trumps individual rationality in the quest to find truth. The evolutionary advantage of forming true beliefs, that is, may be stronger for whole societies than it is for individuals. Does a society that produces science have a survival advantage over one that does not? And, through falsification, are individual scientific theories martyred for the progress of science?

It is fun to speculate about such hypotheses, but one needs to be careful that we do not here slide back into the swamp of the "group selection" hypothesis. Still it is intriguing to note that support for the "group benefits" (or "assembly bonus") hypothesis for the success of science comes directly from Mercier and Sperber's original paper. After presenting the bulk of evidence throughout their paper for the hypothesis that "people who have an opinion to defend don't really evaluate the arguments of their interlocutors in a search for genuine information but rather consider them from the start as counterarguments to be rebutted,"[37] near the end Mercier and Sperber draw the following conclusion: "in group reasoning experiments [however] where participants share an interest in discovering the right answer, it has been shown that *truth wins*."[38]

Can one imagine a better description of the scientific enterprise than this? Despite widespread flaws in individual reasoning and the probable harboring of petty agendas, in a group setting "truth wins!" Maybe Mercier and Sperber have made too little in their argument of the search for truth by individuals. And perhaps they have placed too much emphasis on the value of argumentative skill in the evolutionary context. But perhaps they are *right* about the importance of group dynamics in the search for truth. Even if they are wrong in their claim that individual reason does not primarily aim at truth, or is shaped by evolution for some other purpose, they may still be right that a group focus on reason explains a lot about the success of a truth-seeking process like science.

Near the end of their paper, Mercier and Sperber draw the conclusion neatly for science.

> The whole scientific enterprise has always been structured around groups, from the Lincean Academy down to the Large Hadron Collider. ... In group settings, reasoning biases can become a positive force and contribute to a kind of division of cognitive labor. ... By anticipating objections, one may even be able to recognize flaws in one's own hypotheses and go on to revise them. ... Even among scientists, this ability may be uncommon, but those who have it may have a great influence on the development of scientific ideas.[39]

We are social animals. It would make sense that even individual truth-seekers like the scientists of yore (Newton, Darwin, Einstein) would see themselves as working within a wider context where their ideas would be presented to and evaluated by a larger scientific community.

There is something enlightening about the idea of scientific fruit being borne from having a clash of ideas within a community. Right or wrong, isn't the scientific gadfly a spur to critical thinking? If so, this might offer at least some explanation for iconoclasm, if not the outright crackpot theories that may result from mental mistakes in our reasoning. If not for the contrarian who proposes a theory that seems crazy—yet may actually turn out to be true or at least be a spur to further hypotheses—would we not lose some of the clash of paradigms and fever to refute one another's theories that is the hallmark of science? Indeed, could such a beneficial effect perhaps explain the survival of individual mistakes in human reasoning through their beneficial effect on group processes?

If so, one would have to demonstrate that some sorts of "disrespecting" truth had positive effects on the search for truth itself, and I think we are still a long way from this. Yes, perhaps having people who deny global warming—damn the scientific consensus—may push the debate and convince scientists to work harder to prove that it is real, and thus have a timely effect on public policy and save the planet in the nick of time. Or perhaps not. When the habit of disrespecting truth becomes widespread it may lose its benefit as a spur to reason and may instead cost the rest of us our lives. That is the problem. Perhaps there is wisdom in crowds. But what happens when the balance tips and entire communities become so untethered from reality that they lose their way in the pursuit of truth?

Crowds, even of scientists, are nothing more than communities of individuals. And, as Mercier and Sperber admit, for good or for ill persuasive individuals can sometimes sway the thinking of entire groups. So *shouldn't* we care about the quirks and mistakes of individual reasoning, at least to the extent that these may interfere with the ability of scientists to do their jobs or inhibit the acceptance of scientific ideas once they are presented to a group? Even if truth is best discovered in groups, shouldn't we care about the mental mistakes that exist in individual rationality that may pose a threat to the discovery of truth at the group level?

Notes

1 Karl Popper famously tried to "resolve" the problem of induction and put science on firmer logical footing by offering his account of "falsification," whereby even though scientific theories can never be proven true, we may use evidence to show that some theories are definitely false. In this way, science may make progress toward true beliefs, even if they can never be "confirmed" by even the best scientific evidence, by jettisoning untrue theories.

2 Thomas Kuhn, *The Structure of Scientific Revolutions* (Chicago: University of Chicago Press, 1962).

3 Of course, one could argue that what is being selected for here is not the ability to discover truth, but perhaps an aversion to risk when something that is threatening *might* be true. Perhaps nature cares less whether we always get it right about whether there is or isn't a tiger in the jungle and more about whether—out of an abundance of

caution—our errors tend to be in the direction of thinking that there might be one, even when there isn't. See Michael Shermer, *The Believing Brain* (New York: Times Books, 2011), 60.

4 Robert Park, *Superstition: Belief in the Age of Science* (Princeton: Princeton University Press, 2008), 29.

5 Note that these are not trivial matters. While each of the aforementioned problems might individually be dismissed as a mere glitch in human reasoning, taken collectively we see that there are a plethora of such "foibles" in the way humans reason and that such tendencies are widespread within the human population. Given that these and other well-known human biases in reasoning (which will be discussed later in this chapter and in Chapter 3) act to steer us away from the truth, we may reasonably ask "why are they there?"

6 For a humorous and harrowing example of the potential cost of overconfidence bias see Robert Trivers's discussion of an incident from his own life when, in order to show off to his girlfriend, Trivers took the wheel from his nephew and almost drove the car off a cliff; *The Folly of Fools* (New York: Basic Books, 2011), 333–34.

7 Melissa Himelein and JoAnn McElrath, "Resilient Child Sexual Abuse Survivors: Cognitive Coping and Illusion," *Child Abuse and Neglect* 20, no. 8 (1996): 747–58.

8 William Helmreich, *Against All Odds: Holocaust Survivors and the Successful Lives They Made in America* (New York: Simon & Schuster, 1992).

9 Daniel Goldman, "Holocaust Survivors Had Skills to Prosper," *New York Times*, October 6, 1992.

10 I am not here saying that all truth-avoidance is dishonest. There are honest forms of truth-avoidance (like that practiced by the Holocaust survivors discussed by Helmreich, *Against All Odds*) and dishonest ones (which we will discuss in Chapter 3). So the point is not that we must seek truth every moment of our lives if we are going to respect it; it is that we should eschew those practices that disrespect truth.

11 Hugo Mercier and Dan Sperber, "Why Do Humans Reason? Arguments for an Argumentative Theory," *Behavioral and Brain Sciences* 34, no. 2 (2011): 57–111.

12 Daniel Kahneman and Amos Tversky, *Judgment under Uncertainty: Heuristics and Biases* (Cambridge: Cambridge University Press, 1982).

13 Mercier and Sperber, "Why Do Humans Reason?," 60.

14 Ibid., 72.

15 Ibid., 61.

16 Ibid., 60–61.

17 Of course, one might still quibble here over terminology. Strictly speaking, the effects that Mercier and Sperber (ibid.) "predict" are not predictions at all—because they were already well-known before they made their hypothesis—but instead are "retro-dictions," which, as Popper and others have pointed out, have much less confirmatory value. It is also curious to note that by using their "Popperian" strategy, Mercier and Sperber are engaging us in an *argument* that is intended to convince us that their theory is *true*, and they are using the tools of reason to do so, even while the content of their argument suggests that reason plays no role in leading us to truth!

18 Ibid., 63.

19 Ibid., 65.

20 There is a subtle difference, then, between confirmation bias and motivated reasoning, although they sometimes work together. With the former, we seek out reasons to think that we are right. With the latter, we allow our emotions to influence our interpretation of those reasons relentlessly in our favor.

21 Ibid., 72.

22 Ibid., 72 and 73.

23 For a discussion of the way that some evolutionary psychologists have tried to explain several traits like altruism and homosexuality—which seem at odds with the evolutionary

imperative of getting one's genes into the next generation—the classical source is E. O. Wilson's *On Human Nature* (Cambridge: Harvard University Press, 1978).

24 One should note, however, that there is furious debate within the field of evolutionary psychology over the mechanism by which something like this might take place. The original "group selection" hypothesis (which held that groups—rather than individuals or genes—were the unit of evolutionary selection) has been abandoned by most evolutionary psychologists in favor of the "inclusive fitness" hypothesis put forth by William Hamilton and developed by George Williams, which holds that one's genes can survive within a group that includes family members, even if the individual who carried the gene is sacrificed. Even here, however, there is debate over the exact mechanism at play, by which one's "altruistic" genes survive in one's family members.

25 Andrew Norman, "Why We Reason: Intention-Alignment and the Genesis of Human Rationality" (unpublished manuscript).

26 The reader may notice that for the last several pages I have been using only the male pronoun. In this I am following Mercier and Sperber's lead, for surely it is unclear from their analysis how the argumentative function of reason would at all increase the reproductive success of women! The image that they create of a silver-tongued charlatan, sitting around the fire telling half-truths in order to enhance his reproductive success just seems deeply sexist. They at least owe the reader an explanation for how such a non-truth-conveying rationale for reason could possibly enhance the evolutionary fitness of the other half of the population.

27 Robert J. Sternberg, "When Reasoning Is Persuasive but Wrong," *Behavioral and Brain Sciences* 34, no. 2 (2011): 88–89, at 88.

28 Ibid.

29 Ibid., 89.

30 Ibid., 88.

31 Consider, however, the following counterexample (which I owe to Andy Norman). What if you were able to persuade an entire tribe that the gods wanted you to have unfettered sexual access to all of the females in the group. Though false, this belief has obvious evolutionary advantage (at least for men).

32 But recall that Mercier and Sperber appear to dismiss this line of investigation by arguing *without evidence* that such abilities are "acquired" rather than innate, and so presumably would have no role in evolutionary explanation ("Why Do Humans Reason?," 72–73).

33 Although truth-seeking is, no doubt, favored by evolution, it is not exclusively favored. From an evolutionary perspective, survival is more important than truth. Perhaps this is why we have some built-in cognitive biases; where there is risk in believing something that is true, perhaps survival wins out. Must something like confirmation bias then have survival value independent of its link to truth? This claim will be explored in Chapter 3. In the meantime, it is important to note that even if truth-seeking were not a hard-wired raceway in the human brain, we nonetheless may still have a *choice* about whether to seek truth.

34 In his fascinating book *The Folly of Fools*, Robert Trivers argues that replication of experiments in science helps to guard against *self*-deception as well (p. 305).

35 In *The Folly of Fools*, Trivers offers support for this hypothesis when he tells us that "in interactions with group members, self-deception is inhibited by two forces. Partial overlap in self-interest gives greater weight to others' opinions, and within-group feedback provides a partial corrective to personal self-deception" (p. 252).

36 Recall here that inclusive fitness is the idea that one may increase the prospects for the survival of one's genes through one's group, even if the individual perishes.

37 Mercier and Sperber, "Why Do Humans Reason?," 72.

38 Ibid., 72 (emphasis in original).

39 Ibid., 72–73.

3

THE ROOTS OF HUMAN IRRATIONALITY

Behavioral Economics, Self-Deception, and Lawn Chair Larry

> The first principle is that you must not fool yourself—and you are the easiest person to fool.
>
> Richard Feynman

Is it possible to disrespect truth unintentionally? For the last thirty years or so, the fields of behavioral economics and social psychology have detailed the ways in which human beings make a series of obvious and predictable mistakes in the way that we reason. In topics ranging from why we are so prone to procrastinate in saving for retirement to why we sometimes have such a hard time choosing among a large display of items in a grocery store, our brains just seem inclined to fool us in the way that we reason about the world. But so what? Isn't all of this unconscious? Even if we have a tendency to make such mistakes, how can it be contemptuous of truth if we do not even know that we are doing it?

Until recently, this question might have seemed enough to close the matter. But recent work at the intersection of behavioral economics and neuroscience has suggested that a good deal of human irrationality may be wired into our brains. Although it may be unconscious, it is also perfectly predictable (to those who know what they are looking for) and so possibly within our ability to understand and control for these kinds of errors. Our failure to do so, therefore, suggests a certain hostility toward choosing a path that has better prospects for leading to truth.

Behavioral Economics

There are a plethora of mistakes in human reasoning that can stand in the way of the discovery of truth. Some of these are quite small (such as the human tendency to estimate when faced with more than seven objects), but some are large and can result in major errors that have tragic costs both for the individual and for society. On August 22, 2005, at the height of the Iraq War and a growing national debate over why we were there, President George W. Bush gave a speech in which he made reference to the 1,864 American deaths in Iraq and said "Each of these men and women left grieving families and loved ones back home. ... We owe them something. We will finish the task that they gave their lives for."[1] With no credible link between Saddam Hussein and Al Qaeda, and no WMDs found in Iraq, apparently the best way to honor the dead was to keep fighting in their name, which resulted in an additional 2,624 deaths before the end of that conflict, making this one of the most disastrous examples of the "sunk cost fallacy" in recent history.

It is important here to differentiate between ignorance and irrationality. The sort of problems that are identified by behavioral economics are not just instances where we don't know some crucial piece of information which, if we did, everything would be all right. Neither is this field an examination into the personality type of those who are extremely stubborn, incurious, or incapable of learning from new information. It is instead an analysis of a set of structural problems in the human mind that are shared by all of us, which affect how we process and use information to make sense of the world. Just as there are well-known *perceptual* illusions, that flummox the brain into thinking that some equal lines are not the same length, that identical shapes are not the same size, or that grey dots hover and disappear at the intersections of a black and white grid, we are now faced with the idea that there can be *cognitive* illusions as well, where the brain makes predictable mistakes in reasoning and leads us to conclusions that are unsupported by the evidence. Although there are of course individual differences, as there are for most psychological phenomena, experiments have found that these sorts of irrationalities can be found in most people. They seem wired in: a part of what it means to be human.

The discovery of these "errors" in human cognition began in the field of psychology, which is where behavioral economics got its start. Under the old "neoclassical" model of economics, theorists felt forced to make a number of simplifying assumptions (such as perfect information and perfect rationality) in order to make the mathematical model of "rational economic man"—who maximized utility in all situations—work out to produce reasonable answers to questions about prices and the efficiency of markets. It was an open secret that people did not actually reason in the way that this economic model mandated. But just as physics had occasionally used simplifying assumptions about "frictionless" systems or the reduction of gravitational pull to an infinitely small point, neo-classical economists felt that their assumptions were warranted in order to facilitate the scientific status of their work.

Then the lid came off. Based on the work of Daniel Kahneman and Amos Tversky, culminating in their classic paper "Prospect Theory: An Analysis of

Decision under Risk,"[2] economists began to feel growing pressure to account for a body of experimental work which showed that humans make a series of predictable mistakes in the way that we reason. In the quest to produce a science of human behavior, the carefully controlled studies of Kahneman and Tversky, and others (fêted in their 1982 collection *Judgment under Uncertainty: Heuristics and Biases*), began to look like the gold standard for how one should *actually* conduct an empirical study of human action. Even more revealing, many of Kahneman and Tversky's results directly undermined the simplifying assumptions that had been used in neoclassical economics.

A few examples will suffice.

One of the most important early findings of Kahneman and Tversky was that when we reason we tend to use "heuristic" short cuts, rather than engage in exhaustive rational analysis. Some of these heuristics, however, can lead to outright errors. One of the most blatant is the "anchoring" heuristic, whereby we become unduly influenced by the first piece of information that we learn—for example a price—which then becomes an "anchor" for our subsequent decision. A good example here might be buying a new car. The salesman knows better than to ask "what do you think this car is worth?" If asked such a question, we might suggest a figure that was far too low, which would then serve as the base for our negotiations. Instead, the salesman is trained to show us the "manufacturer's suggested retail price." This is customarily highly inflated (both over what we may feel is fair value for the car and also what anyone but a fool would pay for it), but once we have heard the anchor, that then becomes the starting point for our negotiations. Indeed, it has been shown experimentally that we are much more likely to pay a higher price for an item when we are primed with a higher figure, *even if that prime has nothing whatsoever to do with the value of the item.* In a fascinating experiment, Daniel Ariely has shown that when experimental subjects were asked to record the last two digits of their social security numbers, and then bid on an item, those with higher social security digits bid more than those with lower digits.[3]

In other work, Kahneman and Tversky introduce the "representativeness" heuristic, which can lead to erroneous judgment by tempting us to disregard the base rate probability of something occurring and instead be unduly swayed by whether a factor *sounds* influential. In one example Kahneman and Tversky consider whether a man who is "meek, quiet, and introspective" is more likely to be a farmer or a librarian. Subjects overwhelmingly said that the man was more likely to be a librarian even though (at that time) there were twenty times more male farmers in the USA than male librarians. In an even more controversial example (that is not tied to subjects' perhaps spotty knowledge of the base rates for given professions), Kahneman and Tversky showed that the representativeness bias was powerful enough even to overcome logic. Consider the following description:

> Linda is thirty-one years old, single, outspoken, and very bright. She
> majored in philosophy. As a student, she was deeply concerned with

issues of discrimination and social justice, and also participated in antinuclear demonstrations.

The subjects were then asked to judge which alternative was more probable:

Linda is a bank teller
Linda is a bank teller and a feminist.

The fact that 85 to 90 percent of undergraduates at several major universities chose the second option reveals the devious power of the representativeness bias.[4]

Perhaps the most powerful demonstration of heuristic bias, however, came from Kahneman and Tversky's later work on "loss aversion" coupled with "framing bias." Here experimental subjects were faced with the following scenarios:

Problem 1:

Imagine that the US is preparing for the outbreak of an unusual Asian disease, which is expected to kill 600 people. Two alternative programs to combat the disease have been proposed. Assume that the exact scientific estimates of the consequences of the programs are as follows:

If Program A is adopted, 200 people will be saved.
If Program B is adopted, there is a one-third probability that 600 people will be saved and a two-thirds probability that no people will be saved.
Which of the two programs would you favor?

In this problem, framed as one in which lives could be saved, 72 percent of subjects were risk averse and chose Program A, with only 28 percent opting for Program B. Now consider an alternative:

Problem 2:

If Program C is adopted, 400 people will die.
If Program D is adopted, there is a one-third probability that nobody will die and a two-thirds probability that 600 people will die.

Here, with the problem framed as one in which some people may die, only 22 percent of subjects chose Program C, with 78 percent choosing Program D. The problem, of course, is that Programs A and C are mathematically identical to one another, as are Programs B and D.[5]

Our deep-seated propensity for loss aversion is here beautifully illustrated by the irrational rejection of an identical scenario, merely because it is framed differently. Indeed, some have suggested that this illustrates the cognitive problem behind the sunk cost fallacy, which so famously tempted President George W. Bush in his 2005 speech.

Kahneman and Tversky's work thus opened a pandora's box of irrationalities in human judgment, which other researchers in a wide range of fields have now explored, with seminal consequences for psychology, economics, sociology, philosophy, and a range of other subjects. In Chapter 2, we saw how Mercier and Sperber attempted to account for the problems of motivated reasoning and confirmation bias. But there are literally hundreds of other biases that have now been discovered, the cumulative effect of which may make us wonder that human beings can make any rational decisions at all![6]

Outside psychology, the greatest influence of this work by far has been in the field of behavioral economics, where the discovery of such biases directly undermined the standard economic model's assumption of rationality. Behavioral economics got its start when Richard Thaler, who was then a young economist at Cornell, contrived to spend the 1977–78 academic year at Stanford, so that he could meet and talk with Kahneman and Tversky, who were visiting fellows at the nearby Center for Advanced Studies in the Behavioral Sciences.[7] The three of them met regularly over that year, sharing ideas across psychology and economics. Then, in 1980, Thaler published a paper entitled "Toward a Positive Theory of Consumer Choice," which Kahneman has called "the founding text in behavioral economics."

Since then, the field has exploded, with behavioral economists teaching at Harvard, MIT, Berkeley, Stanford, Chicago, Princeton, and elsewhere, studying everything from how to get people to use less electricity, drive less in the city, sign up to be organ donors, and save more for retirement. Successful applications based on some of this work have even found their way into public policy. Indeed, in 2009 the Obama administration hired Cass Sunstein (Thaler's co-author of the highly influential 2008 book *Nudge,* which President Obama had read) to head the Office of Information and Regulatory Affairs. The influence of behavioral economics began immediately, with the April 2009 payroll tax cut meant to stimulate the economy, where Obama decided against sending one-time rebate checks (which research had shown people were more likely to save than to spend), instead opting for decreased paycheck withholding.[8] In his 2010 budget, Obama again relied upon behavioral economics, when he sought a mandate for the Department of the Treasury and the Internal Revenue Service to provide preapproved language for employers so that they could more easily set up automatic enrollment for their employees in 401(k) plans, to encourage more people to sign up for them. (However, this initiative—and budget—did not pass Congress.)

This prescriptive use of behavioral economics to enable gently paternalistic social planners at all levels of government to "nudge" their citizens in the direction of making better choices is classic for the discipline, and can be seen most clearly in two of the most interesting and highly influential research programs in the field: Sheena Iyengar's work on the "paradox of choice" and Richard Thaler's work to increase retirement savings called "Save More Tomorrow."

Believe it or not, the classic work on choice involved choosing jam. In 1999, Sheena Iyengar and Mark Lepper published a study in which they sought to test how even a simple decision might be effected by our number of choices. The experiment took place in a grocery store that was set up with a booth where shoppers were offered the chance to taste different kinds of jam. In the initial display there were twenty-four choices of jam. In the experimental condition this was decreased to six options. The displays were rotated every few hours (to ensure that virtually no shoppers remained from one experimental condition to the next) and other scientific controls were also instituted. Iyengar and Lepper then measured how many jams people chose to taste from each display and gave everyone who stopped at the booth a coded coupon, so that the researchers would be able to measure their later purchasing behavior.

And what they found was nothing short of amazing. Even though the more extensive array of jams attracted slightly more initial interest from shoppers, their subsequent purchasing behavior was radically diminished. In each display, about an equal number of people tasted the same number of jams. But when the researchers later measured the results they found that those shoppers who had visited the booth with twenty-four choices used their coupons only 3 percent of the time, whereas those who had visited the booth with six jam choices used their coupons 30 percent of the time.

In their analysis of these results, Iyengar and Lepper speculated that the complexity of the first task must have overwhelmed the shoppers. They couldn't be sure that they had chosen the best jam, so many chose not to buy any at all. But in the second condition they were thought to be better able to handle the choice. As it turned out, more choices were not necessarily better. Although few would probably have articulated it this way, people seemed to want *fewer* choices. Indeed, when the task was set up this way, consumers actually bought more jam.[9]

Now the interesting thing about this work is that it has such wide application to non-condiment social topics. One perennial social problem is why people save so little in their 401(k) retirement plans—in some cases even foregoing employer matching funds, leaving money on the table. This may sound like a trivial social problem when compared to the yawning ones of war, terrorism, budget deficits, and entitlement reform, but the human misery of not saving enough for retirement should not be underestimated. With the current push for privatization of retirement plans, lots of corporations have stopped offering defined benefit pensions to their employees, preferring instead to make defined contributions and then let their employees manage their investment options—and take all of the risk—themselves.

The dilemma is a familiar one. On the first day of a new job we are likely faced with a stack of papers to get back to Human Resources by the end of the week. One of them inevitably involves choosing whether to participate in the employer's 401(k) plan and, if so, at what percentage reduction to our salary and among what investment options. As we look over the forms, the choices are formidable. Is 5 percent enough to withhold? Is 10 percent? How much will I need to retire? And how can I possibly choose between the fifty or so investment options? Will the more conservative ones allow me to save enough? But if I choose a riskier one, what is the likelihood that I might lose my money? Is it any wonder that a significant number of us elect to put the decision off until later (which effectively means choosing not to enroll)?

In the application of her "jam" work to saving for retirement Iyengar collaborated with two new colleagues in order to investigate just this problem.[10] Just as with the jam studies, the underlying problem was due not to some deep-seated irrationality or mistake in reasoning, but the simple human tendency to put off a decision where one might make a mistake, especially when we feel overwhelmed by too many choices. And, once again, the results were stunning. Iyengar and her colleagues found that for every increase of ten investment options, the participation rate fell by 1.5 to 2 percentage points. But the solution turned out to be easy. As with the jam, people apparently wanted fewer choices.

Here the story continues with the work of Richard Thaler in his Save More Tomorrow program, which directly addresses the problem of how to get more people to enroll—and choose better options—for their retirement plans. The first decision, of course, is whether to participate in an employer's 401(k) plan at all. Here Thaler recommends the ultimate reduction in choice: automatic enrollment. The idea here is not to force someone to enroll in a retirement plan against his or her will, just to change the default option so that if someone procrastinates and does not turn in the paperwork, they automatically become part of the company's plan. The choice that they face, therefore, is not whether to join the plan, but whether to opt out. By changing the default, Thaler found that the participation rate shot up by more than 30 percentage points.[11] The employees still had a choice, but it was a radically restricted one, and they ended up being much better off for it.

The next choice involves how much to save for one's retirement plan, and here the benefits of the Save More Tomorrow plan really kick in. It turns out that even when employees chose to participate, they were inevitably put off by the idea that they would have to reduce their salary to do so. Consequently, many chose a salary reduction that was far too low. To address this Thaler came up with the idea that although one could choose to participate now, the effect of that choice would be more palatable if it kicked in only later, especially when coupled with a raise. Given that the average raise is 3 percent, Thaler's program offered participants the option of committing themselves to increase their contribution level by 3 percentage points every time they got a pay raise; thus they would not see the effect of this decision as a reduction on their paycheck. For those employers who instituted this program, contribution levels quadrupled.[12]

The final decision is how to invest one's money, especially when faced with an overwhelming array of possible investment options. Recall from Iyengar's work that our ability to choose the "best" option in such a case often shuts down. And if the default option is to put all of our money into the most conservative investment option—usually a money market fund—there is an excellent chance that unless we later modify this we will not reach our retirement goal.

Thaler's solution again relies on the simple idea of changing the default option. Once federal law was changed in 2006 (so that employers were no longer legally responsible for investment losses under automatic enrollment), the prospect of simplifying investment choice opened up. With this came the introduction of "target date" investment funds, in which the employee had only to choose the year in which he or she would likely retire. These plans had the advantage not only of diversifying one's initial investment allocation into a basket of stocks, bonds, and cash options (based on age), but also gradually changed this allocation over time, to become more conservative as one's retirement date grew nearer. By making these sorts of funds the default option (again, allowing employees to opt out of them), Thaler discovered a plan that allowed employees to make investment decisions that were more in line with historical trends that have provided reliable growth for retirement savings (such as diversifying and putting more of one's investment into equities and eschewing overinvestment in one's company stock). By focusing on psychological research into the human tendency for procrastination, loss aversion, inertia, and dislike of too many options, behavioral economics has thus discovered not only some of the irrationalities behind human behavior, but how to change the "choice architecture" so that we will be able to live better despite our irrationalities.

What does all of this have to do with respecting truth? For one thing it is important to note that behavioral economics is based on the idea that there *is* a truth about human behavior and that it can be discovered only when we admit that this is an apt subject for scientific investigation. As such, we need to learn to put our intuitions and assumptions about human behavior on hold, in order to learn from experimental evidence what actually motivates us and shapes our decisions. As we've seen, once these truths are discovered they can help us to implement a more effective public policy, as enlightened social planners learn how to "nudge" us in the right direction.[13] One needs to know the truth before one can use it.

But it is also important to recognize that this sort of knowledge can be misused as well. If we are unaware of the unconscious forces that influence human behavior, then we cede knowledge—and control—to those who do understand them. As such, the irrationalities behind human action provide a means for us to be manipulated by those who seek to exploit our cognitive foibles in order to get us to do what is in *their* interests, rather than our own. If the behavioral economists are right that there is a set of predictably irrational forces that influence human action, isn't it best for us to know about them? Part of respecting truth means acknowledging that we don't know everything and understanding that this is unlikely to change unless we gain enough knowledge to put ourselves in the driver's seat.

Manipulating Belief

Does anyone seriously doubt that there are forces out there who are seeking to get us to believe what they want us to? Political campaigns, advertisers, industry, partisan think tanks, and some of the media have clear vested interests not just in shaping our actions, but in getting us to believe that certain things are true (even when they are not). Some of the most striking demonstrations have come from psychological studies of political belief.

In one study, Brendan Nyhan and Jason Reifler exposed political partisans to mock newspaper stories, which included claims that were provably false.[14] For conservatives, they provided false stories about how there were WMDs in Iraq and how the Bush tax cuts increased government revenue. For liberals, the stories claimed that the Bush administration had imposed a *total* ban on stem cell research. Next they exposed the subjects to direct contradictory evidence, such as a speech from Bush in which he admitted that there were no WMDs in Iraq. And the results were shocking. The researchers found not only that exposure to contrary facts did not necessarily convince subjects to change their false beliefs, but that in some cases they produced a "backfire effect" *in which the erroneous views became more hardened once subjects were exposed to contrary truthful evidence.* Worse, this effect *increased* with one's level of education. Is it any wonder that in the 2012 presidential campaign, *Time* magazine published an October 15, 2012, cover story called "The Fact Wars" in which they decried that neither political campaign seemed to be paying a price for false or misleading claims in their political advertisements? As one Romney advisor put it: "we're not going to let our campaign be dictated by fact checkers."

Perhaps the reason is that both campaigns were familiar with other research which has found that repeated exposure to the same message makes us more likely to believe it, *even when the message is untrue.*[15] Of course, knowledge of this phenomenon is not new, as evidenced by the infamous quotation from Hitler's propaganda minister Joseph Goebbels who said, "A lie repeated often enough becomes the truth." When coupled with the phenomenon of "source amnesia" (where we tend to remember only the content of a message and forget where we heard it—or whether the source was reliable), one is confronted with a formidable set of barriers to having truthful beliefs, *even when one is willing to gather evidence.*[16]

As with the results from behavioral economics, it is easy to imagine how these cognitive foibles might be dangerous in the wrong hands. In political campaigns, where they may be trying to get us to forget the all-important context of an opponent's inflammatory statement—or in an advertisement where we are hammered again and again with the name of a product—or in partisan news media where we are told that the "fact checkers" are biased—we see the effect of these phenomena. Yet part of respecting truth means being aware of our cognitive weaknesses and understanding how our mind works. Unless we are prepared to accept that we are prone to such biases and admit that we do not automatically understand everything about ourselves just because we are human, we will constantly be fooled and exploited by those who have mastered these effects. Human intuition can take us only so far. Free will, if we have it, is useless unless we understand the way that the human brain reacts to choice. As we've seen, not all of our mistakes are due to ignorance; some are due to our unconscious irrationalities. But what to do, then, when confronted with these irrationalities? Should we remain ignorant or pretend that they do not apply to us?

This is one reason why I have argued in favor of a science of human behavior.[17] Once we have a better understanding of the causal influences behind human action, we will be in a better position to improve social ills and live a more enlightened existence. Once we have studied our behavior scientifically, we will be in the driver's seat for social change, rather than allowing ourselves to be pushed around by seemingly random social forces that no one understands or exploited by those who understand them all too well. Whether we think that we should be in charge of our own destiny—or put our faith in a paternalist government whom we hope has our best interests at heart—what seems clear is that knowledge of human irrationality is out there, waiting for us to discover it. We can either resist such knowledge or embrace it, but the only way to keep from being manipulated is to admit our ignorance and learn the truth about ourselves. Respecting truth counsels the latter path.

The Problem of Self-Deception

One lingering problem is self-deception. Sometimes we are fooled not just by others, but by ourselves. Just because there is a truth about our behavior doesn't mean that we are prepared to admit it (or recognize it). When someone lies to us, it makes us angry and we want to expose them. As it turns out, there are good behavioral techniques—such as reading facial microexpressions—that can help us to detect when someone is lying.[18] These are now used by the TSA (Transportation Security Administration) in the prevention of terrorism or the detection of smuggling. But what happens when the person who is trying to fool us is ourselves?

In his book *The Folly of Fools: The Logic of Deceit and Self-Deception in Human Life*, Robert Trivers explores the fascinating problem of self-deception.[19] According to Trivers, there is a solid evolutionary argument for why self-deception should never occur, for there is likely to be a heavy tax on survival when we are alienated from reality. If we are prone to believe things that are untrue, how would we survive the negative consequences of this tendency and pass our disposition for delusion down through our genes to future generations? And yet we deceive ourselves every day. Why? The answer is that there must be a corresponding benefit to self-deception, which outweighs its evolutionary cost. In his book, Trivers develops a compelling evolutionary argument for the benefits of self-deception and the likelihood that such unconscious biases guide a good deal of human behavior. The short answer (though I heartily recommend reading

Trivers's entire book) is that sometimes the best way to fool others is first to fool ourselves.

One example—which works as well for animal behavior as for our own—may serve to illustrate the argument. Consider the problem of overconfidence:

> [T]wo animals square off in a physical conflict. Each is assessing its opponent's self-confidence along with its own—variables expected to predict the outcome some of the time. Biased information flow within the individual can facilitate false self-confidence. Those who believe their self-enhancement are probably more likely to get their opponent to back down than those who know they are only posing. Thus, nonverbal self-deception can be selected in aggressive and competitive situations, the better to fool antagonists.[20]

Even though this example is drawn from non-verbal, animal behavior in a physical encounter, it is easy to imagine how its applications could be extended. Two prisoners in the recreation yard fighting over turf? Two university professors in a public spat over who is the more eminent figure in his field? The analogies are endless.

Of course it cannot be a comfortable thing to realize that one is being deceived, even by oneself, despite seemingly good evolutionary reasons behind the deception.[21] Consider the case of "implicit racial bias." Most people are routinely shocked and embarrassed to discover the depth of their prejudices. Some of the most popular and well-known work on this topic has been done by Mahzarin Banaji, a social psychologist at Harvard, who (along with Brian Nosek and Anthony Greenwald) has invented the Implicit Association Test (IAT) by which we may allegedly measure our biases on a host of subjects. In the most controversial test, Banaji purports to be able to measure whether someone is a racist.[22] The key point here is *not* that subjects are reluctant to admit *to others* that they have racial biases. Banaji argues that many people do not even know that they have such biases until they take her test, because biases are unconscious.

In a typical test, subjects were presented with a series of words such as "glorious," "failure," "wonderful," and "hurt," and were then asked to sort them according to whether they were "good" or "bad" words by pressing the "e" key on the computer with one's left hand for one categorization and the "i" key with the right hand for the other.[23] Although it is possible to make a sorting mistake (and the computer will catch you if you do) what is actually being measured is not one's accuracy in categorizing "wonderful" as a "good" word or "hurt" as a "bad" one, but rather *how long it takes to get the right answer*. The test then moves on to a series of "European" and "African American" faces, where the left and right sorting continues. Next, the categories are paired, such that "European" faces and the "good" words are on one side, with "African American" faces and the "bad" words on the other.[24] Then the moment of truth arrives; the pairing is reversed. Now the European faces must be paired with the bad words and the African American faces must be paired with the good ones.

Again, the crucial measurement here is the time that it takes to do an accurate sorting, on the theory that—if one is an implicit racist—it will allegedly take more time to pair the good words with the African American faces than it will the converse. And this is precisely what Banaji and her colleagues have found. As Banaji is fond of saying, the measurement at hand is not subtle: "a sundial will do." Most subjects—including over half of African American ones—show an implicit bias for European faces on this test.

What does this show?[25] Is this a new result in line with behavioral economics, where we have used scientific procedures to discover an unconscious truth about ourselves? Banaji appears to think so, and has agreed to testify as an expert witness in at least one case where there were allegations of race bias on a jury.[26] And her results have been used by others for everything from corporate training to diversity education in university orientations. But one should pause here for a moment and consider a problem. Aside from the moral question of whether one should be considered guilty of "thought crime" merely for a result on a test, one wonders whether the results of this test have been shown to be valid, by correlating with "racist" behaviors by those who do poorly on them.[27] To her credit, some of Banaji's recent work has investigated these issues, though the results remain equivocal.[28]

But there is a larger issue here of methodology. Although it is rarely a welcome conclusion that one is a racist, many in the media and in the academy have rushed to embrace Banaji's results, without questioning whether there are scientific flaws in her work. One potential flaw, involving the order of presentation of the pairings, seems potentially significant. If one first learns from the test that European faces are to be associated with good words (so press the "e" key) and that African American faces are to be associated with bad words (so press the "i" key), *and then these are reversed*, there is naturally going to be a prior association at work, not necessarily based on one's cultural or implicit associations, but from the first half of the test itself. In the FAQ section of her website Banaji calls this the "order effect" but it is more well known in the psychological literature as "perceptual set" and can be experienced by anyone who has learned to do something one way and is then forced to do it another. Someone who has learned to type on a QWERTY keyboard (as nearly everyone does), for example, will find it almost impossible to make the transition to a Dvorak keyboard, even though it is superior in both speed and accuracy for those who start with it. Indeed, it is harder to learn to type on a Dvorak keyboard for someone who has already learned QWERTY than it is for someone who has never learned to type at all.

Banaji admits on her website that the order of presentation on the IAT *does* make a difference in some tests, but she goes on to explain that "the difference is small and recent changes to the test have sharply reduced the influence of order." She goes on to explain that the test has now been changed so that the order of presentation is *random*, and that "with the revised task design, the order has only a minimal influence on task performance."[29] Curiously, she then states that one may check whether order had any effect on one's own test by taking it again and that if there is a different result, the true answer probably lies halfway between them. This is a ridiculous statement, however, in light of the previous discussion of the order effect, for the order in which one takes the *tests* (and not just the order of the tasks *within* a test) may also suffer from the same problem of the "order effect." Of course, this is a straightforward matter to discover, for one could just compare the implicit bias results for a large number of subjects, each of whom is taking the test for the first time, half of whom were shown the associations in one order and half in the other, to see whether the effect is diminished or might even disappear altogether. The FAQ discussion of this problem on the IAT website lists a paper by Nosek, Greenwald, and Banaji as "in press," so one cannot see the data nor learn if these findings can be replicated by other researchers.[30] Critics of this work, I am sure, will welcome the chance to do so.

But there is another potential methodological flaw with the IAT which, to my knowledge, has never been tested. In October, 2003, I was in the audience when Prof. Banaji gave her implicit race bias test to a ballroom of people at a conference at Harvard. The results were predictable. Afterward, during the Q&A session, I asked whether the effect might be due to the well-known psychological phenomenon of "inhibition," whereby our performance is degraded when we are under stress. In a public demonstration on such a "hot" topic as race bias, surely the task of correctly categorizing words with faces is complicated by the fact that one is attending to one's performance at the same time that one is performing the task. If one does not want to be thought of as a racist, this feedback loop might well interfere with the result, creating a self-fulfilling prophecy. In short, nobody wants to be thought a racist, so if you're sitting there timing yourself, your ears get hot and your face turns red and it takes longer for you to perform the task because you are inhibited by how your answers look to others (or to yourself).

Prof. Banaji's response was instructive: "Racists' ears don't get hot." But of course this is a logical error. I did not say that if one is a racist then one is not inhibited; I said that if one is not a racist (or didn't want to be thought to be one) then one *would* be inhibited. Note that this effect could be experienced even if one were taking the Implicit Association Test in private. Surely, if we do not want to be a racist, it is our own opinion of ourselves that we fear as much as the opinion of others. When the task on the computer begins, and we must now pair African American faces with good words, we all know what the "right" answer is supposed to be. And our ears *do* get hot. We say "uh oh, I hope this test doesn't show that I have racial bias; I'd better be careful," which of course increases our "cognitive load" and has the potential to interfere with our performance. At various times during the task, if one takes too long on any given pairing, one cannot help but think of the negative effect that it will have on one's own overall assessment, which of course only makes the problem worse and lengthens our time to get the "right" answer.[31]

Another possible criticism along these lines is the (perhaps ironically named) phenomenon of "stereotype threat," whereby one's expectations regarding one's performance can affect it. In a groundbreaking study, Kelly Danaher and Christian Crandall found a difference in girls' performance on the AP Calculus AB exam based on the seemingly trivial matter of whether they were asked to fill in the demographic bubbles (including one about gender) *before* they took the test or afterwards. By priming thoughts of their gender before the test, perhaps triggering the gender stereotype that "girls aren't as good at math as boys," Danaher and Crandall hypothesized that this might negatively affect performance, which it did.[32] Thirty-three percent of girls scored worse on the test when demographic information was requested before the test began, rather than after.

Analogously, one wonders whether knowing that the IAT is a test of implicit racial attitudes *before the test* might trigger negative thoughts of "oh no, I hope it doesn't show that I'm a racist," which could affect performance.[33] Where is the "null hypothesis" in testing implicit racism? Although racial bias may be unconscious, our knowledge of what is being tested surely is not. Don't we need some way to test subjects without their knowledge of what is being tested, so that we could neutralize any effects of inhibition and stereotype threat?

After the ballroom demonstration, I suggested to Prof. Banaji that she consider a test where the associations might seem dissonant, but the valence was not so "hot." This might eliminate the problem of being embarrassed, either in front of others or to oneself at getting the "wrong" answer. Perhaps one might have word pairs like "loving" and "affectionate" juxtaposed with dog breeds like "pit bull" and "golden retriever." Unless one were worried about being judged a "doggy racist" I think that the results of this test might be very instructive in sorting out the issue of inhibition.[34] Better, one might consider a "null hypothesis" test, where one performed the IAT with a series of zero-valence shapes like rectangles and triangles, to see if there was any effect (and, if so, whether there was an order effect as well). Or, if one prefers to stick with "hot" topics, perhaps the subjects' autonomic responses might be measured for an increase in respiration or blood measure, to see whether they were stressed when faced with the "racist" task. These days, one could even hook them up to an fMRI and measure blood flow to different parts of their brain, to see how "hot" they actually were. To my knowledge, such tests have never been performed.

Finally, let us return to the question of what is actually being measured by the IAT in the first place. Suppose that any given test *does* show that certain pairings take longer than others. Is this necessarily reflective of bias? Why not suppose that there is a mere cultural association that we have internalized after long exposure, even though we may disagree with it? Consider, for example, an IAT that juxtaposed the word "stove" with the word "snow." Both are fairly neutral words and have a host of mildly good and bad associations. But I would bet that it is more difficult to pair "stove" with "good" words on the IAT than with the bad ones. Why? Because of the cultural association we all learned at an early age from our parents between stoves and fire, which is dangerous. But does this mean that we are biased against stoves? Does it even mean that we prefer snow to stoves? Thus even if there is a learned cultural association between African American faces and "bad" things, does this mean that the person who learned it is biased? If so, what are we to say about the more than 50 percent of African Americans who show implicit bias against their own race?

We face a sometimes slippery slope when dealing with the scientific study of irrationalities that involve self-deception. When we have an unconscious bias and *we are not aware* that we are being judged for our "poor" performance—such as when we are choosing a jar of jam or we are procrastinating in signing up for a retirement plan—our mental awareness does not alter our behavior or get in the way of its measurement. When we are being deceived by *others* (e.g., the researchers who are secretly looking to see whether we are buying any jam), our behavior is unaffected. But when the situation changes to one of *self*-deception and *self*-awareness (when we understand that our behavior is being measured—by others or by ourselves—in comparison with some normative standard) our behavior may be altered. The problem of self-deception, like any of the rest we have considered from behavioral economics or evolutionary psychology, is a scientific issue and I do not mean to suggest that the answer to these questions is unavailable to further scientific inquiry. I do, however, offer the warning that just because a result is measurable, and produced by "social scientists," does not mean that the finding is methodologically sound nor the result valid. As Matisse once said, "exactitude is not truth." Like natural scientists, social scientists must have enough respect for truth to criticize their own hypotheses.

For every social scientific breakthrough about procrastination or the irrationalities of choice, there is another layer to the onion of self-deception. It is important to keep peeling these away until we discover which findings are genuine and which are not … which truths we may be resisting and which ones we are prepared to accept. The discovery of truth is not automatic, even if we are using science. As Trivers has shown, human survival depends on a melange of competing interests and the discovery of truth is only one of them. As such, it is not surprising that our brains are not wired exclusively for the discovery of truth. But this does not mean that we cannot *choose* truth. Despite our irrationalities and mental foibles, it has been demonstrated throughout human history that we are capable of inventing institutions—like science—that allow us to sort through the prejudices, wishful thinking, and mistakes that may clutter individual thinking. And this seems as true of our investigations into ourselves as it does the patterns of nature. Of course, we are right to be skeptical of the idea that every alleged scientific breakthrough reveals a truth. As in natural science, we must be on guard against mistakes. But, where the work is good and it has been adequately conducted, there is no reason to continue down the path of resistance and denial.

Self-deception may be an inherent part of human bias—and thus perhaps itself a suitable topic for behavioral economics—but this does not mean that we are stuck with it when deciding what to believe. As with other irrationalities, once we become aware of our cognitive limitations, we should try to overcome them in the pursuit of truth.

Conspiracies, Rumors, and Other Barriers to Truth

There is one more category of irrationality that we should now consider: the crackpots. Although they tend not to be studied very much by behavioral economists or social psychologists—because their beliefs are so widely skewed from the norms of human society—they deserve to be considered here, if only because a surprising (and growing) number of our fellow citizens seem to buy into such beliefs every day.[35]

First, there are the "true believers," who desperately cling to a set of beliefs or doctrine that is completely at odds with reality, not to mention any rational standards for the revision of one's beliefs in the face of contrary evidence. There are literally hundreds of examples of this phenomenon throughout human history, but one of the most recent and bizarre was the 2011 "doomsday prophecy" of Harold Camping, an evangelical minister and host of the Family Radio Worldwide network. Based on his study of Christian scripture, Reverend Camping predicted that the world would end on May 21, 2011. His followers were exhorted to spend their life savings on billboards to announce the coming Judgment Day and drive around the country to spread his message, which many did. It is estimated that more than $100 million was spent on such efforts.

As it turns out, this was not the first time that Camping had predicted the apocalypse; decades earlier he had predicted the end of the world on September 6, 1994. When that didn't happen, he claimed that he had made a mathematical error. But this time, he assured his followers, he knew that May 21, 2011, would be the day. When the day came with no apocalypse, Camping's followers were puzzled. Some said that perhaps the calculations were merely wrong again. Others said that their faith had delayed things, so that more souls could be saved. But the idea that captured Camping himself was that he had been correct and that Judgment Day *had* actually happened, but that it had been a "spiritual judgment day" with no destruction of the Earth. That was still coming, he warned, and would occur on October 21st, 2011. But, since no more salvation was possible, there was no point in continuing to tell anyone, so his radio station stopped its warnings and simply began to play Christian music until the rapture that would arrive on October 21st. Over the summer, Camping had a stroke and dropped out of sight while his following dwindled. After October 21st passed without incident, he apologized for his error and said that his Christian critics had been right all along to quote the words of Matthew 24:36: "of that day and hour knoweth no man." The end of the world was still coming, he believed (along with millions of Christians worldwide), but it had been arrogant of him to try to predict the date.

If this were an isolated incident, perhaps we could let it pass. But it is intriguing to note that the scenario just described is almost identical to one that occurred in the 1950s when a group called "The Seekers" sold all of their possessions and waited on a mountain top for a space ship to rescue them. Their leader, Dorothy Martin, had allegedly transcribed an interstellar message through automatic writing that the world would end on December 21, 1954. When that didn't happen, Martin greeted her devotees with a new message: that their little group had believed so hard and spread so much light to the world that God had decided to save the planet! They were overjoyed.[36]

The latter incident was studied in its own day by the eminent social psychologist Leon Festinger, who marked it as one of the classic examples of "cognitive dissonance." Cognitive dissonance occurs when we have two or more beliefs that conflict with one another, which threatens our ego. This makes us stressed. We strive to reduce this stress by changing one of our beliefs to achieve harmony again, normally in a way that denies that there was ever any dissonance. So is this sort of "true belief" abnormal or not? Is it deviant? According to social psychologists we all experience the phenomenon of cognitive dissonance. Although it is easy to laugh at such extreme examples as the doomsday prophets, it is probably wise for us to be on the lookout for times in our own lives when we also engage in more subtle forms of disrespecting truth.

Consider, for example, conspiracy theories. Surely there are too many of these to mention. The US government is responsible for (or at least knew about) 9/11. Barack Obama was not born in the United States. The Bureau of Labor Statistics faked the unemployment rate drop from 8.1 to 7.8 in the month before the 2012 Presidential election. What do all of these beliefs share? The idea that there are brilliantly competent but evil forces at work, who are colluding to keep us from knowing the truth. In fact, these forces are so good at their jobs that they have managed to suppress most of the evidence and keep their co-conspirators quiet. The fact that there is so little evidence for these beliefs, therefore, is testimony to the genius of those who are covering them up. Nonetheless, if one is paying attention, any member of the public can easily "connect the dots" and see that there *must* be a conspiracy at work.

That there are believers of such nonsense strains credulity. Yet it is curious, for our purposes, to note that these folks at least *want* to know the truth! But do they respect it? Hardly. Respecting truth means having at least some faith in the laws of probability. Coincidences do happen. In fact, they are predictable. Which is more likely: that the unemployment rate actually dropped from 8.1 to 7.8 in October 2012, or that a government agency which employs thousands of people—both Democrats and Republicans—managed not only to manipulate economic data, but keep it a secret?

Customarily, such ideas are understood to be the province of cranks and spread no more harm than infecting the minds of those who are addicted to late-night talk radio. But occasionally there is genuine harm that results. All that is necessary for such deviant beliefs to become virulent is for one person in a position of power to believe them. Take, for example, those who deny that HIV causes AIDS. Although this belief has roots in America, it has had its deadliest effect in South Africa, which has the world's largest population of those who are infected with HIV. During the period from 2000 to 2005, South Africa's president Thabo Mbeki denied that HIV caused AIDS. He argued that antiretroviral drugs were part of a "Western plot" by pharmaceutical companies and Western governments to poison the people of Africa. Instead, he recommended treatment with garlic, herbs, and lemons rather than AZT. The Harvard School of Public Health estimates that 365,000 people died as a result.[37]

Unfortunately, we have now begun to experience the negative consequences of such deviant beliefs about medicine—though thankfully on a much smaller scale—in America as well. The idea that childhood vaccines cause autism may at some point have been a credible scientific hypothesis. Although the mechanism was unclear, a 1998 study by Dr. Andrew Wakefield was published in the respected British medical journal *Lancet*, in which he proposed that there was a linkage between the MMR vaccine and autism. The resulting outcry—driven by concerned parents, some of whom were Hollywood celebrities—was enormous. Vaccination rates began to drop in some communities to levels where experts worried about "herd immunity." If only one child is unvaccinated, the concern may be slight. But if multiple families stopped vaccinating their children, could the recurrence of childhood diseases be far behind?[38] This is exactly what occurred in Ashland, Oregon, where exemption rates for childhood vaccinations reached as high as 30 percent, and in Marin County, California, where 7 percent of children showed up to kindergarten without state-mandated vaccinations. Consequently, whooping cough, measles, and mumps are making a comeback after virtually disappearing in the United States.[39]

Meanwhile, scientists began a desperate search for any linkage between vaccines and autism. As a precautionary measure, many pharmaceutical companies stopped using thimerosal in MMR vaccines, due to concerns about mercury. When it was later found that Wakefield's work was flawed, the shift from public health to conspiracy theory began. That Wakefield's hypothesis has now been scientifically discredited is beyond dispute. Although it is scientifically impossible to "prove a negative" (that vaccines do *not* cause autism, that garlic does *not* prevent AIDS), the question becomes how to assess the probabilities, based on the evidence. First came the suspicious circumstances. Wakefield's research was based on interviews with just twelve families, which seemed too few to support such a sweeping hypothesis. Then it was learned that Wakefield had a serious undisclosed conflict of interest due to his patent application for a measles vaccine that would have competed with the classic MMR shot. Ten of the thirteen authors of the original paper retracted their contributions. Next came the substantive challenges.

> Epidemiologists in Finland pored over the medical records of more than two million children … finding no evidence that the [MMR] vaccine caused autism. In addition, several countries removed thimerosal from vaccines before the United States. Studies in virtually all of them—Denmark, Canada, Sweden, and the United Kingdom—found that the number of children diagnosed with autism continued to rise throughout the 1990s, after thimerosal had been removed. All told, ten separate studies failed to find a link between MMR and autism; six other groups failed to find a link between thimerosal and autism.[40]

Ultimately, the *Lancet* retracted the paper and the British medical association revoked Wakefield's medical license. Still the drumbeat of conspiracy continued. If thimerosal did not cause autism, why was it removed? What were they hiding?

A 2004 report from the Centers for Disease Control, which discredited any link between autism and thimerosal, became a flashpoint for controversy, raising suspicions of a governmental cover up. US Representative Dan Burton, R-Indiana, held emotionally charged hearings.[41] Robert F. Kennedy Jr. said that the report proved that "the CDC paid the Institute of Medicine to conduct a new study to whitewash the risks over thimerosal." When confronted with the CDC report, actress Jenny McCarthy said, " … we vaccinated our babies and something happened. … My science is named Evan and he's at home."[42]

At what point does "skepticism" become crackpot? How long before the preference for anecdotal over scientific evidence tips the balance toward a conspiracy theory that ranks with AIDS deniers and those who believe that NASA faked the Moon landing? Conspiracy theories are one of the most insidious forms of disrespecting truth for, even while they profess to be guided by the fervent desire to *discover* a truth that someone else is hiding, they simultaneously undermine the process by which most truths are discovered. Conspiracy theorists are customarily proud to profess the highest standards of skepticism, even while expressing a naive credulity that the most unlikely correlations are true. This is disrespect, if not outright contempt, for the truth.

Finally, we turn to the problem of rumor. After the foregoing account, it may seem that belief in rumors has nothing much in common with the set of irrational beliefs that we have dismissed so far as "crackpot." Yet rumors too can be dangerous and far-fetched. In the absence of reliable sources of information, rumors can tempt us to believe things that in less exigent circumstances we would be highly likely to dismiss.

The best example in recent years is the list of atrocities that allegedly occurred in New Orleans just after Hurricane Katrina. Armed gangs were beating and raping tourists in the street. Snipers were shooting at rescue workers. Inside the

Superdome—which was home to some 25,000 refugees—muzzle flashes were said to portend mass killings with bodies piling up in the basement. Children's throats were slit. Women were being dragged away from their families and raped. A seven-year-old girl was raped and murdered. Two babies had their throats slit.

The consequences of these reports were dire. When Governor Kathleen Blanco sent the National Guard in to restore order, she did so with a stark message to the perpetrators: "I have one message for these hoodlums: these troops know how to shoot and kill, and they are more than willing to do so if necessary, and I expect they will." She and Mayor Ray Nagin called off rescue efforts to focus on protecting private property. Helicopters were grounded. The sheriff of one suburb that had a bridge to New Orleans turned back stranded tourists and locals, firing bullets over their heads. New Orleans had become a prison city. A team of paramedics was barred from entering the suburb of Slidell for nearly ten hours based on a state trooper's report that a mob of armed, marauding men had commandeered boats. An ambulance company was locked down after word came that a firehouse in Covington had been looted by armed robbers.[43] New Orleans police shot and killed several lawbreakers as they attempted to flee across the Danziger Bridge.

The problem is that none of the reported atrocities just described actually occurred. None. Three weeks after the storm, police superintendent Edwin P. Compass III, who had initially provided some of the most graphic reports of violence, said "we have no official reports to document any murder. Not one official report of rape or sexual assault." During the alleged six-day siege inside the Superdome, Lt. David Benelli (head of the New Orleans Police Department's sex crimes unit) *lived with his officers inside the dome* and ran down every rumor of rape or atrocity. At the final count, they had made two arrests, both for attempted sexual assault, and concluded that the other rumored attacks had not happened.[44]

The snipers who were shooting at rescue workers turned out to be a relief valve on a gas tank that popped open every few minutes. The men commandeering boats turned out to be two refugees trying to escape their flooded street. The report of the robbery at the firehouse was simply false. When the giant refrigerated trucks backed up to the Superdome to haul out the bodies, there were only six: four had died of natural causes and one from suicide, with only one dying of gunshot wounds.[45] The child who was raped—and indeed each of the rapes in the Superdome—turned out to be untrue. So did the story of the murdered babies. Despite police commitment to investigate, no witnesses, survivors, or survivors' relatives ever came forward.[46]

What was very real, however, was the aftermath of the city's stalled rescue efforts and the crackdown on all those alleged lawbreakers. The people who were shot by police on the Danziger Bridge turned out to include a middle-aged African American mother who had her forearm blown off. The other was a mentally disabled forty-year-old man on his way to his brother's dental office, who was shot five times and killed. A teenager was also killed.[47] And thousands of people suffered with little food, water, or medical attention for days inside the Superdome. Yes, there were confirmed reports of widespread looting after the storm, mostly for food, water, and other necessities. And there was some violence. But how did such small incidents get so wildly exaggerated? How did we all become so easily seduced into believing the worst about the refugees in New Orleans?

In a city that was two-thirds African American before Katrina hit, and substantially less diverse in the population of refugees who could afford to put thirty gallons of gas in their SUVS and flee the approaching storm, one doesn't need to take an IAT to understand that racial bias may have had something to do with it. Indeed, many experts now feel that the power of rumor to feed into pre-existing racial stereotypes likely led to one of the most tragic instances of "confirmation bias" ever to play out on the world stage. And the tragedy is that the effect of this bias was borne by the refugees themselves, who had done nothing wrong and were begging for help. They were stranded not merely due to poor federal disaster planning and lack of supplies, but also by the palpable hesitancy of public officials to expose rescue workers to the kind of "animals" who would commit such atrocities.

What to say about those of us who were nowhere near New Orleans? Are we off the hook? Yet how many of us *even to this day* knew that the reports of violence in New Orleans were untrue? Although the press bears some responsibility for not reporting the retractions with as much vigor as the alleged atrocities, the corrected stories were out there. Yet how many of us read them? How many of us were sufficiently skeptical of such incredible claims even to look? Will Rogers famously quipped that "a lie gets halfway around the world before the truth can get its pants on." Yet if we respect truth, isn't it important to engage our critical faculties and search out better information?

Rumor has the power to keep us from looking for the truth only if we are willing to suspend our critical faculties. In a life-threatening situation, it is probably understandable to take rumors seriously. If we do not know what is going on and we are scared, we may feel that we cannot afford the risk to be gullible. Survival comes first. But when the danger has passed, or we are far removed from it, don't we have an obligation to try to replace rumor with fact?

Truth may be the first casualty of war, but *respect* for truth must survive the conflict. We may not like to think of ourselves among the "Seekers," "Birthers," "Truthers," or other conspiracy theorists, but the fact is that we are all probably capable of believing in crackpot theories if the circumstances are right. We demonstrate respect for truth when we are willing to resist such pressure.

Conclusion

As we have seen in this chapter, there are a lot of mistakes in individual human reasoning. And we now face an extremely important but rarely asked question that has hung over this entire chapter: why are there *any* irrationalities behind human action? What possible survival value could there be for the type of cognitive biases that we have here investigated, such that evolution would not already have weeded them out? Here it is important to remember the crucial insight offered by Robert Trivers. It is not that there are no *costs* to human irrationality. It is just that there must also be *benefits* that outweigh them.

Clearly, some people do pay the price for their stupidity. Since 1993, there has been a dubious annual honor called "The Darwin Awards," which is bestowed on someone who has done something so spectacularly idiotic that it resulted in his or her death. The Darwin Awards are "named in honor of Charles Darwin, the father of evolution, [to] commemorate those who improve the gene pool by removing themselves from it."[48] The website includes such famous stories as "Angry Wheelchair Man," "Chainsaw Insurance," and "Dynamite Rancher." The most famous, however, was bestowed on a man who was only worthy of an honorable mention category called "at-risk survivor," because he lived. In 1982, Larry Walters (dubbed "Lawn Chair Larry") fulfilled his boyhood dream of flight by attaching 45 helium-filled weather balloons to his lawn chair. Armed with sandwiches, beer, and a pellet gun, Larry cut the anchor, thinking that he would merely hover a few feet off the ground and enjoy the flight. Instead, he rocketed into the stratosphere above Los Angeles, eventually reaching a height of 16,000 feet, where he remained for fourteen hours. Eventually, when he crossed the glide path of several jets, Larry finally worked up the nerve to shoot a few of his balloons. When he came back to Earth he was fined by the FAA and said, "A man can't just sit around." Could there be a more compelling example of overconfidence bias than this?

Yet clearly most people (even Larry) do not die of their stupidity. More important, even if some do die, the potential survival value of our irrational biases must be powerful enough that they normally get passed down to our descendants. But why? What possible survival value could there be for a cognitive "mistake"? Here one is reminded of an earlier hypothesis: that the brain is wired for survival, not truth.[49] Although true beliefs have obvious potential survival value to an organism, this is not always the case. Indeed when there is a conflict between survival and truth (say when one is judging whether there is a tiger in the bushes or not) it is safer to go with the low-risk strategy, even if it subverts the truth. It is just not worth the risk to be right in one's judgment when the evolutionary price of a mistake may be death. Thus it would not be surprising if our brains allowed us to overlook some truths. In some situations truth may be a luxury that we cannot afford. Over the centuries, our brains therefore would have evolved in response to all of these selective pressures, until today, when we have a skill set that values truth, but also includes a vast array of (presumably useful) cognitive biases as well.

But how to explain the evolutionary benefits of cognitive irrationalities? Recall here the hypothesis from Chapter 2 made by Mercier and Sperber, who felt that they could explain the cognitive biases of confirmation bias and motivated reasoning by pointing out the potential evolutionary advantages for persuasive speaking. If persuasive speaking were an important skill in the struggle for survival—as they argue—this would be one such example. Given that I pointed out some problems with their argument, however, it seems only fair that I now attempt to provide an alternative hypothesis.

Consider here Andy Norman's example of a Neolithic hunter-gatherer named Glog, who found it difficult to improve his reproductive success solely through persuasive speaking.[50] Suppose that the material fortunes of Glog's entire society have now improved to the point where they live in an agricultural community that has just discovered corn. One day Glog sees a snake with three bands of color (red, yellow, and black) go into the cornfield where his friend is picking corn. He hears his friend yell "snake" and his friend later dies. Glog wisely decides not to go back into the cornfield. Some of the other villagers, however, ultimately decide that they are hungry enough to take the risk. Glog watches them go into the cornfield, where some of them are bitten by snakes and die. Glog grows thin. One day he hears a rumor that not all of the snakes in the cornfield are poisonous. Some people have gone in and come out safely. Why is that? Because they were lucky or because not all of the snakes are poisonous? Over time, Glog watches the snakes who go into the cornfield and he notices that they come in two patterns: (1) red, yellow, black, yellow, red, (2) red, black, yellow, black, red. He forms an idea that maybe one snake pattern is poisonous and one is not. Should he test his theory personally? That is too risky. If he's wrong, the price might be death. So he continues to watch the snakes and some brave villagers who go into the field every day. One day he notices that someone goes into the cornfield just after one of the red, black, yellow, black, red snakes and the person lives. Glog forms a rule in his head "red touch yellow, kill a fellow; red touch black, venom lack." He watches more and more people go into the cornfield and he confirms the rule. When people go in with the red-touching-yellow snakes they sometimes die. But when they go in with the red-touching-black snakes they never do. Now he can safely go back into the cornfield.

Clearly there is survival value to Glog's confirmation bias. Once he had his theory, Glog looked for examples to prove that he was correct, before he was confident enough to go back into the cornfield himself. Of course, he still hasn't completely tested his theory. What about the people who went in with the red-touching-yellow snakes who lived? Maybe only *some* of those snakes are poisonous. But what does he care? The safer path is only to enter the cornfield with the "red-touching-black" snakes. That part of his theory has been well-confirmed by positive instances and so far there have been no negative ones. Survival comes first. Perhaps in the long run it may matter to him to learn the truth about the snakes for, if he did, he could sometimes have the whole cornfield to himself. But for now, at least he can eat again.[51]

This is only one (and perhaps not even a very compelling) example of a possible evolutionary advantage for a single cognitive bias. Surely further work is needed at the intersection of behavioral economics and evolutionary psychology to investigate the possible survival advantages of many others: motivated reasoning, procrastination, the anchoring heuristic, loss aversion, belief in conspiracy theories, belief in rumors, etc. Even if Mercier and Sperber are wrong (and I am too) about our specific hypotheses of potential survival advantages for particular cognitive biases, couldn't there be better ones? Indeed, shouldn't there be *some* answers to these sorts of questions before any evolutionary hypothesis about the brain and the value of its irrationalities would make sense? I believe so, and hope that there will someday be more work on this compelling question.

In the meantime, on the supposition that better answers might someday be had, what would this mean for respecting truth? Should we be mere slaves to evolution? No. Truth is a choice. Even if we are not wired to get the correct answer every time, this does not mean that we cannot pursue a path that might lead to better answers than those that are supplied automatically by the "fast" part of our brain, which is prone to make reasoning errors. Truth may not be automatic, but it is still an option. We are no more a slave to evolution in reasoning than we are in morality. Few would argue that we are genetically programmed to be moral. We may have all sorts of wired-in responses to do things that might increase the survival value of our genes (like rape), but we do not do them, because they are immoral. We can make a rational choice. And if we can exercise our will and our reason over what evolution has given us in the domain of morality, why not in other areas?

This is what makes us human. We have the power to decide for ourselves how we will live our lives. What makes us human (fortunately) is not our perfect brains, but instead the ability to choose how we are going to live despite the fact that our reasoning is imperfect. We can choose to behave morally or not. Likewise, we can choose whether to respect truth or not. Even in light of the irrationalities of the human brain, it is still open to us to choose a path that leads to respecting truth.

Notes

1 Elisabeth Bumiller, "Citing sacrifice, president vows to keep up fight," *New York Times*, August 23, 2005.
2 Daniel Kahneman and Amos Tversky, "Prospect Theory: An Analysis of Decision under Risk," *Econometrica* 47, no. 2 (1979): 263–292.
3 Ariely is quick to point out that this does not mean that we are doomed to pay more if we have higher social security digits: we must be primed with them—or indeed with anything—for the effect to occur. A full description of the experiment can be found in *Predictably Irrational: The Hidden Forces That Shape Our Decisions* (New York: HarperCollins, 2008), 23–34.
4 Daniel Kahneman, *Thinking Fast and Slow* (New York: Farrar, Straus and Giroux, 2011), 156–58.
5 Ibid., 436–37.
6 "Cognitive Bias," *Wikipedia*, <http://en.wikipedia.org/wiki/Cognitive_biases>.

7 Alix Spiegel, "Using Psychology to Save You from Yourself," *NPR*, June 8, 2009, <www.npr.org/templates/story/story.php?storyId=104803094>.

8 Michael Grunwald, "How Obama is using the science of change," *Time*, April 2, 2009.

9 Sheena Iyengar and Mark Lepper, "Rethinking the Value of Choice: A Cultural Perspective on Intrinsic Motivation," *Journal of Personality and Social Psychology* 76, no. 3 (1999): 349–66.

10 S. Iyengar, G. Huberman, and W. Jiang, "How Much Choice Is Too Much? Contributions to 401(k) Retirement Plans," in *Pension Design and Structure: Lessons from Behavioral Economics*, ed. O. Mitchell and S. Utkus, 83–95 (Oxford: Oxford University Press, 2004).

11 Richard Thaler and Cass Sunstein, *Nudge: Improving Decisions about Health, Wealth, and Happiness* (New Haven: Yale University Press, 2008), 109.

12 Ibid., 114.

13 Thaler and Sunstein (*Nudge*) call this "libertarian paternalism," because it implies a sort of benign guidance, while respecting our freedom to opt out.

14 Brendan Nyhan and Jason Reifler, "When Corrections Fail: The Persistence of Political Misperceptions," *Political Behavior* 32 (2010): 303–30.

15 R. Hertwig, G. Gigerenzer, and U. Hoffrage, "The Reiteration Effect in Hindsight Bias," *Psychological Review* 104, no. 1 (1997): 194–202.

16 Sam Wang and Sandra Aamodt, "Your brain lies to you," *New York Times*, June 27, 2008.

17 Lee McIntyre, *Dark Ages: The Case for a Science of Human Behavior* (Cambridge: MIT Press, 2006).

18 Sheena Iyengar, *The Art of Choosing* (New York: Twelve, 2010), 126–28.

19 Robert Trivers, *The Folly of Fools: The Logic of Deceit and Self-Deception in Human Life* (New York: Basic Books, 2011).

20 Trivers, *Folly of Fools*, 13.

21 It is also demonstrated, in Trivers's work (*Folly of Fools*), that overconfidence bias can have its evolutionary costs as well—such as when JFK Jr. felt that he could fly a plane in dangerous weather after only minimal training. Trivers does not deny this, but argues that the cost of such disasters is on the whole outweighed by its advantages, which is why the tendency is passed down in our genes.

22 Although Banaji is careful with the word "racist," instead preferring to discuss one's "implicit racial bias," this has seemed to many (especially in the media) to be a distinction without a difference. On the question of whether biased attitudes are correlated with biased behavior see M. R. Banaji, B. A. Nosek, and A. G. Greenwald, "No Place for Nostalgia in Science: A Response to Arkes & Tetlock," *Psychological Inquiry* 15, no. 4 (2004): 279–89. For a more recent statement, which draws an explicit link between the IAT and discriminatory behavior, see Mahzarin Banaji and Anthony Greenwald, *Blindspot: The Hidden Biases of Good People* (New York: Delacorte Press, 2013), 47–52.

23 A version of the test is available online at Project Implicit, <https://implicit.harvard.edu/implicit/>.

24 Although the words in any particular test are sorted left and right, the FAQ section of the website explains that this is random, in order to eliminate right-handed bias.

25 Even if the tests are reliable, there is controversy over what they measure. Do they measure implicit bias in one's own racial attitudes or merely implicit associations that one has internalized from one's culture?

26 Jonathan Saltzman, "Jury in Cape murder ordered back to court," *Boston Globe*, November 30, 2007.

27 Harvey Silverglate, "Thought reform in disguise," *Boston Globe*, May 29, 2005.

28 One barrier here has been Banaji's past reluctance to seek such correlations, for fear that they might result in the IAT being misused as a proxy to measure racist behavior. See Shankar Vedantam, "See no bias," *Washington Post*, January 23, 2005. In more

recent work, however, Banaji appears to have no such qualms in drawing a correlation between findings of implicit racial bias on the IAT and racism, claiming that the IAT can predict discriminatory behavior. See Banaji and Greenwald, *Blindspot*, 47. This finding is disputed, however, by H. Blanton, J. Jaccard, J. Klick, B. Mellers, G. Mitchell, and P. E. Tetlock, "Strong Claims and Weak Evidence: Reassessing the Predictive Validity of the IAT," *Journal of Applied Psychology* 94, no. 3 (2009): 567–82.

29 See "FAQs," *Project Implicit*, <https://implicit.harvard.edu/implicit/demo/background/faqs.html>.

30 In her book with Greenwald, Banaji does reverse the order of the IAT tasks, but these are mere demonstrations for the reader. What one desires is more empirical research that measures this effect in a controlled setting. On p. 220 of *Blindspot*, Banaji and Greenwald admit that order can have "a small effect," but claim that fifteen years of research show that it could not account for the entire result.

31 See here Daniel Kahneman's recent discussion in *Thinking Fast and Slow* about the "automatic" brain versus the "rational" brain, where too much attention even to a well-learned task—such as swinging a golf club—can be inhibited by too much thought about our performance. Indeed, Banaji unwittingly demonstrates the possibility of this effect *when she reports on her own experience the first time she took the IAT*: " ... when I took the test ... it was stunning for me to discover that my hands were literally frozen when I had to associate black with good. It's like I couldn't find the key on the keyboard, and doing the other version, the white-good, black-bad version was trivial. So the first thought I had was: 'Something's wrong with this test.' Three seconds later, it sunk in that this test was telling me something so important that it would require a re-evaluation of my mind, not the test" (Carolyn Y. Johnson, "Everyone is biased: Harvard professor's work reveals we barely know our own minds," *Boston Globe*, 2 May 2013, <www.boston.com/news/science/blogs/science-in-mind/2013/02/05/everyone-biased-harvard-professor-work-reveals-barely-know-our-own-minds/7x5K4gvrvaT5d3vpDaXC1K/blog.html>). Surely this type of self-reflection and angst *during the test* represents a significant cognitive load that might affect performance.

32 K. Danaher and C. Crandall, "Stereotype Threat in Applied Settings Re-examined," *Journal of Applied Social Psychology* 38, no. 6 (2008): 1639–55.

33 Precisely this effect was found by Cynthia Frantz, Amy Cuddy, *et al.*, "A Threat in the Computer: The Race Implicit Association Test as a Stereotype Threat Experience," *Personality and Social Psychology Bulletin* 30, no. 12, (2004): 1611–24.

34 On the IAT website, Banaji does have a test of attitude toward flowers versus insects, but is this perhaps merely a measure of preference rather than bias? A better test might be to measure a "hot" question of bias, where subjects are simply unembarrassed by their prejudice. One way might be to test reciprocal attitudes of warring factions, where the culture is similar and bias is genuine, but inhibition is presumably muted. Are Tsutsis biased against Hutus just as Hutus are biased against Tsutsis? Studies of reciprocal bias might go a long way toward diminishing the effect of inhibition (because not everyone agrees that a particular bias is wrong) and it might tease out the effect of mere cultural association as well.

35 Note that I am not here discussing people who are mentally ill, which is the province of abnormal psychology. Instead I am considering the weird, deviant, and false set of beliefs that are shared by those whom we would still consider sane.

36 Chris Mooney, "The science of why we don't believe in science," *Mother Jones*, May/June 2011, <www.motherjones.com/print/106166>.

37 Michael Specter, *Denialism: How Irrational Thinking Hinders Scientific Progress, Harms the Planet, and Threatens Our Lives* (New York: Penguin, 2009), 184.

38 Specter, *Denialism*, 57–101.

39 Jennifer Steinhauer, "Rising public health risk seen as more parents reject vaccines," *New York Times*, March 21, 2008. In early 2015, there was a measles outbreak with

over 100 confirmed cases across 14 states in the USA, which followed a resurgence of 644 cases in 2014. See Mark Berman, "More than 100 confirmed cases of measles in the U.S., CDC says," *Washington Post*, February 2, 2015.

40 Specter, *Denialism*, 71.

41 Despite earlier speculation in "The Science of Why We Don't Believe in Science," that the vaccine-autism hypothesis provided evidence that there might be such a thing as a *left-wing* conspiracy theory, in his later book *The Republican Brain: The Science of Why They Deny Science—and Reality* (New York: John Wiley, 2012), Chris Mooney admits that polling data do not support this claim and that belief in the link between vaccines and autism is bipartisan, 232–34.

42 Specter, *Denialism*, 73–79. Although such stories are heartbreaking, they hardly rule out the possibility of naive correlation, given that childhood vaccines tend to be given at about the age when autism is diagnosed. But this does not mean that vaccines cause autism any more than that colonoscopies cause Alzheimer's. Also, note that even if there *were* a linkage between vaccines and autism, the question of whether to stop immunizing one's child might remain open, for there is still the issue of which is the greater risk: childhood disease or autism.

43 Jim Dwyer, "Fear exceeded crime's reality in New Orleans," *New York Times*, September 29, 2005.

44 Ibid., 2.

45 Rebecca Solnit, "Four years on, Katrina remains cursed by rumour, cliche, lies and racism," *Guardian* (London), August 26, 2009.

46 Gary Younge, "Murder and rape—fact or fiction?" *Guardian* (London), September 6, 2005.

47 Solnit, "Four years on," 2.

48 *Darwin Awards: In Search of Smart*, <www.darwinawards.com>.

49 Michael Shermer, *The Believing Brain* (New York: Times Books, 2011), 59–62.

50 Andy Norman, "Why We Reason: Intention-Alignment and the Genesis of Human Rationality," (unpublished manuscript).

51 Of course, one might argue that Glog has already taken the first step toward being a scientist by looking for counterexamples at all. If even one person had died after going into the cornfield with a "red-touching-black" snake, he likely would have abandoned his hypothesis. Although this is a step in the right direction, it is still not enough to overcome his confirmation bias toward the "red-touching-yellow" snakes, so he falls short of truth.

4

THE ASSAULT ON TRUTH AND THE TRIUMPH OF IDEOLOGY

The Flying Spaghetti Monster, Climate Change, and the "Myth" of Race

> The problem with ideology is that it gives you the answer before you look at the evidence.
>
> Bill Clinton

In the last chapter we saw that many of the problems we have with truth are a predictable result of built-in biases that we inherited from an ancestral brain that was wired for survival rather than the exclusive search for truth. Does this mean that truth is not useful in our struggle for survival? Certainly not. It's just that when there is a conflict between survival and truth, survival wins. Thus it is sometimes the case that we "disrespect" truth without even knowing that we are doing it, as a result of the unconscious biases and reasoning mistakes that have been handed down to us through the process of evolution.

But this does not mean that we cannot overcome these biases and learn to reason better than we do. Just because we are not naturally built to reason flaw-lessly does not mean that we cannot learn to develop better reasoning skills any more than the fact that our bodies are naturally fairly slow and inflexible means that we cannot learn to do gymnastics. But first we had better try to get a handle on some of the *conscious* assaults on reason that many of us suffer from as well. If we expect to overcome the sort of unconscious biases that we examined in Chapter 3, the first order of business should be to understand and eliminate those conscious biases that can harden into ideologies if we are not careful to recognize their threat to truth.

But of course the problem here is that many people do not *want* to overcome these biases. For whatever reason, some are so committed to a favored worldview that they do not even question it and may in fact be prepared to lie, deny, mislead, or spin away any contradicting information in order to protect their beliefs. Such unreasoned commitment to one's prejudices may be defined as "ideology," which is the unquestioned acceptance of a system of belief—even when it may be contradicted by relevant evidence—because it pleases us to think that it is true. The attraction here is that ideology appeals to our emotions and makes us feel that we are reasoning even when we are not; it tells us what to think, without bothering us with the hard work of actually reasoning, so that we can feel justified in believing what we want to and rejecting what we don't. As such, ideology erects a significant barrier to the formation of true beliefs.

Some of the best examples of ideology come from religion and politics, where we find biases on both the right and the left. As we saw in the 2012 American presidential election, many on the right do not believe in the truth of evolution by natural selection or in human-caused global warming. On the left, there is widespread acceptance of the idea that race is a biological myth. That there is evidence against each of these beliefs does not, for many people, enter into the equation. They refuse to believe what they find intellectually repugnant. And that, perhaps, is the surest indication that one is dealing with unreasoned opinion. When one finds oneself saying "I just don't believe it!" even in the face of contradicting scientific evidence, there is a good chance that one has entered the realm of ideology.

Presumably, many such convictions are made with a degree of foreknowledge by their proponents, who should know or at least suspect that there is relevant information that they are ignoring. Still, there is a problem here, and it is a familiar one from the last chapter: self-deception. What is conscious and what is not? When is the line crossed between lying to oneself and lying to others? As we learned from Robert Trivers, there may be a fine line between these and it may not always be obvious when we are engaging in self-deception. In those cases where we are genuinely in denial and cannot admit the truth to ourselves, this probably falls into the category of irrationality that we considered in the last chapter. But this still leaves plenty of room for those who know full well what they are doing, yet cynically spin and distort the data in order to protect their favored beliefs. A good deal of disrespect for truth surely falls into the latter category, where we make assertions which we know we cannot defend, yet we make them anyway. In such cases of conscious acceptance of dubious empirical beliefs, where we either know or *should know* that we are cutting corners in our reasoning, let us call this ideology. By contrast, when we succumb to a mental mistake that is outside our conscious awareness (which, if we knew about it, we would probably want to correct), let us call these irrationalities. The difference between ideology and irrationality, then, lies in the potential effect that conscious awareness might have on their influence over our behavior. With irrationalities—once we discover that we are making a mistake—we would probably want to change our beliefs. With ideology, we probably would not care.[1]

Religious Ideology

The number of Americans who are willing to say that they are atheists has shown a marked increase in recent years (from 1 percent in 2005 to 5 percent in 2012), but the USA is still a majority-religious country.[2] Still, it is remarkable that public opinion—or perhaps just the level of comfort with coming out of the closet as an atheist—has changed so much in less than a decade. Perhaps some of this has to do with a tide of "new atheist" books that appeared from 2004 to 2007. Sam Harris, *The End of Faith: Religion, Terror and the Future of Reason* (Norton, 2004), Daniel Dennett, *Breaking the Spell: Religion as a Natural Phenomenon* (Viking, 2006), Richard Dawkins, *The God Delusion* (Houghton Mifflin, 2006), and Christopher Hitchens, *god is not Great: How Religion Poisons Everything* (Twelve, 2007), each in his own way added one more brick to the pile in arguing that belief in God is not only irrational but can even be dangerous.

It is important to make clear, however, that *none* of these authors takes himself to be arguing that God does not exist. That is an empirical claim that could scarcely be proven, short of providing extraordinary evidence, any more than those who argue in favor of God's existence could hope to defend their claims based on anything more than faith. Instead, each of these authors is basing his argument on the fundamental irrationality of believing in something for which there *is* no evidence, especially if one is hoping to make an empirical claim that passes muster with scientists.

Although none of these authors draws the analogy directly, it seems to me that the best way of understanding faith-based claims about the existence of God is to draw a parallel to the sort of conspiracy theories that we dismissed as irrational in the last chapter. Anyone who claims the existence of an omnibenevolent, all-powerful, all-knowing deity, who could very well reveal his existence but chooses instead to cloak it behind a series of obscure clues that can only be decoded by the faithful, has made an assertion so incredible that we should not waste much time trying to refute it. It is just another conspiracy theory. We do not need to prove that it is wrong in order to justify ignoring it. As Christopher Hitchens so aptly put it, "what can be asserted without evidence can also be dismissed without evidence."[3] This argument is consonant with the idea that much of religion seems like made-up stories, drawn from the infancy of human thought, engineered precisely to address the sort of fears that multiplied in our ignorance of what caused natural disasters, disease, famine, eclipses, and death.[4] But we have outgrown that now. When we have better sources of information on those subjects, so the argument goes, there is no need for faith-based superstitions about empirical matters. We can gather evidence and use our brains instead. We need no longer believe in fairy tales, nor engage in disputes with other religions over whose imaginary friend is superior.

Let me concede that there are surely some truths that cannot be fathomed by science, because there just isn't any evidence. This is not to say that there could not *be* any evidence or that the evidence could only be understood by believers. It is to assert that in some cases we merely find ourselves in a position where the relevant evidence is not available. Such an example, I maintain, is found in the question of life after death. Every one of us will die, but we have absolutely no idea, outside of what happens to our bodies, what that means. Does this mean that we are free to form beliefs about this topic based solely on faith or speculation? I don't think so. There is an answer to what happens to us after we die. We just don't know it yet. But the problem is that there seems to be no way, short of dying, of finding out. Here I maintain that the best path is one of true agnosticism, where we suspend judgment.

In his book *The God Delusion,* Dawkins has some quite harsh things to say about agnosticism, as compared to atheism, when it comes to the question of the existence of God. Roughly, he argues that agnosticism is only warranted in those cases where the outcome seems equiprobable and—in the lack of evidence—God's existence certainly does not fit this bill. It is intriguing that Dawkins defends, however, the idea that we *should* be agnostic about the possibility of extraterrestrial life, based on the inaccessibility of the evidence. But is this really 50 percent likely? How can one tell? Better, I think, is to take the distinction between agnosticism and atheism to be one between instances where belief is withheld because the evidence is unavailable versus when disbelief is warranted because the evidence is either inade-quate or held to be irrelevant. Belief in God, I think, is thus an entirely different matter from belief in the possibility of extraterrestrial life or the possibility of an afterlife. If the faithful take themselves to offer any sort of evidence (including their own private experiences) for God's existence, then we are free to evaluate that evidence and reject it if we find it lacking. Alternatively, if they claim that evidence is irrelevant in this case—that faith is enough—then disbelief seems warranted. One cannot support an empirical claim based on faith. Atheism seems an appropriate response to such irrationality. But with claims where it is admitted that evidence *would be relevant but there just is no evidence*—as in the case of extraterrestrial life or the possibility of an afterlife—I believe that agnosticism is the appropriate path. There may be a truth out there, but science just is not able to reach it.

Some skeptics would scoff at this, and insist that disbelief is more warranted than agnosticism in a case like this, because the possibility of an afterlife is so unlikely. But unlikely compared to what? Our existence in the first place is pretty incredible. Is it really so unimaginable that we might also exist outside the material sphere? Can we really assign a percentage to this kind of thing? Just as believers are wrong to say that they have warrant to believe in an afterlife (based on their faith or personal experience), I think that skeptics would be wise here to embrace a true agnosticism, where we admit that there is a right answer to this question, but that it is unavailable to science, because the evidence cannot exist during our lifetime.[5]

What to say, then, about the legions who believe that the phenomena of near-death experiences (traveling toward a bright light, hovering over one's own body, seeing dead relatives, feeling the presence of a welcoming spirit) provide evidence for the existence of an afterlife? Of course these experiences are subjective and the evidence they provide—like faith—is unshareable. And every one of them may have a material explanation. Hypoxia? Ketamine? There are many current proposals that purport to give a scientific account of such phenomenal experience.[6] But, it should be remembered that, even if they cannot, there is a difference between near-death and actual death, and the mental leap from an experience that one has when one is nearly dead to what must exist on the other side of death is a large one.[7]

But even if one is clinically dead and comes back to life, it is still possible that any remembered phenomenal experiences might have occurred during the periods before actual death or immediately following resuscitation. Nonetheless, whether a patient is dead or near-dead, the issue is whether such experience would indicate anything about an afterlife. As such, one might expect these experiences to include information that was unobtainable unless one had experienced disembodied existence. Are there any documented cases of patients who were dead or near-dead and came back to report information that would not have been available to the living? Actually there is one case.

In an example that has been touted as the "best case" for corroborated veridical near-death experience, we learn of a patient named "Maria" who had a cardiac arrest at a Seattle hospital in 1977 and later reported an out-of-body experience in which she viewed a tennis shoe with a worn toe and its lace stuck under it, on a ledge outside the hospital, that was allegedly unobservable from her floor. A few days later, she confided in her social worker, Kimberly Clark, about what she had experienced, and begged her to go look for the shoe as confirmation of her claim.[8] When Clark found it, in just the condition and position where Maria had reported it, this was hailed as evidence of the truth of her near-death experience claim.

Balderdash. Coincidence. Mere anecdotal evidence provided by one person who may have been motivated to lie about it. Where is the science? As it turns out, this claim was investigated by a team of psychologists from Simon Fraser University, who interviewed Clark and visited the hospital where the incident took place, and found that the shoe would have easily been visible to many people both inside and outside the building. If Maria were bed-bound, could she have actually seen it? Maybe not, but she easily could have overheard other hospital workers talking about it and later unwittingly incorporated it into her near-death experience, in much the same way as we commonly take experiences from our day and incorporate them into our dreams. The researchers noted, too, that Clark had not reported this incident until seven years after it had happened and had misremembered some of the details about the location of the windows in the building and other physical details of the scene. In the intervening years Clark had, moreover, become a minor celebrity and published a book about this, making it much more likely that even if she were not lying about the incident, she was subject to motivated reasoning.[9]

Have the researchers then "debunked" near-death experiences, such that we should *disbelieve* in an afterlife? Not at all. First, note that the connection between near-death experiences and the existence of an afterlife was tenuous to begin with. Even if near-death experiences are veridical *and have no immediate naturalistic explanation*, one might doubt whether they increase the probability that there is life after death. And, if they are absent, does this decrease its possibility, any more than the refutation of ubiquitous and dubious claims about "seeing little green men" decreases the possibility that there is extraterrestrial life? Second, even if the "Maria" case has now been debunked, it opens a fascinating door on the possibility of obtaining empirical evidence for claims of out-of-body perception, whether they are linked to the possibility of an afterlife or not.

One ongoing study along these lines has been conducted since 2008 by Dr. Sam Parnia, a specialist in resuscitation medicine, who has pursued the question of whether it is possible to gather scientific evidence of near-death claims.[10] Zeroing in on the "out-of-body" experience (since this is one of the few objectively measurable pieces of data) for near-death experiences, Parnia has designed an experiment involving twenty-five hospitals and thousands of patients, where his team installed small shelves containing pictures very high over patients' beds, which would only be observable if they were hovering near the ceiling. No longer do we have to rely on anecdotal reports of patients who see a bright light and are carried off to perform a life review with dead relatives. If they can see the picture, perhaps we should take seriously their claim that their spirit left their body. If not, then perhaps such negative evidence might push us from agnosticism to disbelief.

In *Erasing Death*, Parnia reports that due to the small number of cardiac arrests that lead to near-death experiences—let alone the fewer reports of out-of-body experiences that accompany near-death experiences—there have so far not been any such events in rooms that have been equipped with picture shelves.[11] He reassures the reader that the study is ongoing and that when they have actual data from the rooms with the shelves, he will report the results in a peer-reviewed journal. Until then, one can only anticipate the results and look forward to the day when other researchers might try to reproduce any results.

This is welcome respite from the customary, stale back-and-forth between believers and skeptics in the absence of testable evidence. For some truths, there may be no evidence. But perhaps, after all, the question of near-death or out-of-body experiences is not one of them. Respecting truth counsels a default position of agnosticism until the evidence is in, and skepticism if it proves unconvincing. But it should be remembered that respecting truth also counsels the wisdom of an attitude that inclines toward the investigation of even extraordinary claims, where testable evidence is obtainable.

To some, this may sound dangerously close to making accommodation for spirituality. But I fail to see how those who have faith in the existence of God have a monopoly on insight into what happens to us after death (or, if an afterlife were discovered, how it would automatically support the existence of God; if one does not feel that *this* life needs the existence of a deity to explain it, why would our existence on another plane need one either?). There is a relevant distinction to be made here between beliefs based on faith and those based on evidence. When we are talking about empirical matters, I would argue that there is no room at all for faith; when we have evidence, or even when there exists the theoretical possibility that there *could* be some evidence, it seems unreasonable to base our beliefs on what we hope to be true rather than on data. And, when we are talking about non-empirical matters, I would argue that the appropriate response is to use reason where we can and remain agnostic where we cannot; faith still has a questionable role in determining truth. In either case, we should not succumb to ideology, which tempts us to slide over into letting our beliefs be dictated by what we *want* to believe rather than what we have reason to believe.

Indeed this, to me, seems the real danger of religious ideology. It is not that faith cannot be personally meaningful or a guide to one's inner life (or even occasionally support a lucky guess about some empirical matter). On the question of personal values or the choices that one makes about how to dress or what to eat, there seems little danger to religious beliefs, even if they are strange, because there is no scientific question of how to determine the "right" beliefs on these matters in the first place.[12] But when it comes to making claims about matters that are capable of being proven right or wrong based on tests or experiments—when we are trying to say something about what is true in the world—I think there is no room for religious ideology. In saying this, I do not mean to argue that people should not take their personal experiences of enlightenment seriously. If they have faith, I suppose that is a kind of evidence and they would be foolish to ignore it (even if, just as with our sensory evidence, we ought to regard it critically lest it lead us astray). But what I do not agree with is the idea of using someone else's personal faith as a kind of trump card for what the rest of humanity should believe about the world. If one has faith, surely it should be recognized that this is a personal matter and will not be convincing to those who do not share it. Instead, we should look for better and more reliable ways to test an empirical claim—in science or otherwise—than to rely on someone's private conviction.

The implications here for belief in God seem obvious. If theists care to make an assertion about the actual metaphysical existence of God, they have two choices. Either they can claim that belief in God is purely a matter of faith—in which case we can safely dismiss their desire to make a scientific claim—or they can claim that there is actual evidence for God's existence—in which case they need to share it with us, while recognizing that their personal faith is not evidence for anyone but them.[13]

Here is where religion gets into a turf battle with science. If we are going to make the clash between religion and science one about evidence for what is true about the world, it is likely to be a blow out. Is evolution by natural selection true? There is a profound consensus in the scientific community that it is, and one's ideology really does not matter. Is global warming real? Ditto. Galileo long ago warned the church that it should avoid these sorts of head-to-head confrontations with science, because religion would lose. "The Bible tells us how to go to heaven, not how the heavens go," said the deeply religious Galileo. Unfortunately, the Catholic Church did not take Galileo's advice and instead imprisoned him, then spent the next three centuries fighting what Freud called a "series of pitiful, rearguard actions" in the shadow of the success of science. As many religious and non-religious thinkers alike have realized, there is no room for faith in science. When we are talking about truths that can be settled by consulting the facts, the faithful have no business offering their opinions on matters of objective empirical examination.

Why not? *Because even if religion takes itself to have discovered the truth, it is not scientific truth unless it is open for public inspection.* Scientific evidence must be capable of being tested by others who may not share one's beliefs or opinions. This is how science makes progress. Religious ideology is based on faith. It is based on our personal convictions about what we hope to be true. But science is not ideological. It is based on the idea that our beliefs about the empirical world should depend on what we have evidence to believe, based on testing our hypotheses against the sensory evidence that can be gleaned from observation or experiment, subject to correction by those who may disagree with us. And that method has worked. Whereas religious ideology has been forced to defend a dwindling piece of real estate over the last three centuries, science has flourished.

What to say about those areas in between science and religion, where we do not have empirical evidence? Here we must use reason. We should try to settle the matter by argument, based on logic, and not by the strength of one's personal convictions. (Where this fails, we should probably embrace a true agnosticism, where we agree to withhold belief because the truth cannot be discovered). For science and reason to be convincing, they must appeal to shared norms covering how one goes about verifying the truth of one's beliefs. We start with a shared set of assumptions about what counts as evidence and how we will verify the other side's claims. There is no room for appeal to unreproducible or private experiments in science, just as there is no defense for using non-standard chains of logical deduction in philosophy. This is how one respects truth, by showing respect for the *method* by which true beliefs are formed. Those who disagree with our theory must be able to look at the evidence and examine our reasoning. And we must offer the other side a chance to prove us wrong. Faith may comfort us in our hopes and prejudices—and it may even occasionally stumble upon some truth—but *as a method of discovering empirical truth*, it is so unreliable that religious ideology must be dismissed as having no relevance in learning the truth about the material world.

Unfortunately, adherents of religious ideology have sometimes misunderstood this basic point about the public nature of scientific evidence and have tried to ram their "truths" down everyone else's throat, even to the point of claiming that certain faith-based beliefs are scientifically respectable (or that science is just another ideology). This has culminated in recent years in the attempt to get ID (intelligent design) theory (the latest incarnation of creationism) taught in the public school *science* curriculum. But this is a travesty that represents the highest level of disrespect—indeed outright contempt—for truth. For whatever ID theory is, it is not science.

Creationism in a Cheap Tuxedo

Say what you will about the intellectual dishonesty of the intelligent design movement, their strategy is shrewd. They understand that they cannot just appeal to their faith in the creation story in the Bible and expect this to make it into the science classroom. They know this because earlier attempts to do precisely this were met with outright defeat when the question was litigated in court. In an earlier book *Dark Ages: The Case for a Science of Human Behavior* (MIT Press, 2006), I told the story of this battle, leaving off with the then-current state of play in 2005, when creationism had rearmed as ID theory and found itself back in court. But a lot has happened since then and in order to understand it one must know the history. Here I will briefly recount that, then bring the story up to date.

In 1981 the state of Arkansas passed Act 590, which required "balanced treatment" for "creation science" and "evolution science" in public school science classrooms. It is clear from the act that—in order to avoid entanglements with federal law—religious instruction was not to be offered outright, but only the "scientific evidence" for creationism. Indeed, the act went so far as to argue that the extant model of teaching only "evolution science" in Arkansas classrooms *itself* violated the separation of church and state, in that it would provide an environment hostile to "Theistic religions" and would give preference to "Theological Liberalism, Humanism, Nontheistic religions, and Atheism in that those religious faiths generally include religious belief in evolution."[14] The strategy here is clear. If one could make the theory of evolution by natural selection itself look like religious ideology, then there would be no argument against considering the "scientific evidence" offered by alternative religious ideologies, such as Christianity.

The hubris of such an argument was savaged in court by a panel of legal, scientific, and philosophical experts—and ultimately by Judge William Overton himself—who ruled in *McLean v. Arkansas* that creationism "is simply not science" and that "the Act was passed with the specific purpose ... of advancing religion." Relying heavily on the testimony of Michael Ruse, a prominent philosopher of biology, Judge Overton spent an important part of his decision outlining what he took to be the essential characteristics of science, stating that "a scientific theory must be tentative and always subject to revision or abandonment in light of facts that are inconsistent with, or falsify, the theory. A theory that is by its own terms dogmatic, absolutist and never subject to revision is not a scientific theory."[15] Thus was the attempt to offer "creation science" as a contender to evolution in the science classroom exposed as a masquerade. Later, when Louisiana passed a similar law in 1987, the Supreme Court ruled in *Edwards v. Aguillard* that teaching "creation science" was unconstitutional, thus closing the door on this intellectual fraud.

Or did it? Over the next few years the creationist movement regrouped. In *Edwards,* the Supreme Court ruled against the Louisiana law that had mandated teaching creationism alongside evolution, but left the door open for teaching alternative theories by stating "we do not imply that a legislature could never require that scientific critiques of prevailing scientific theories be taught. ... Teaching a variety of scientific theories about the origins of humankind to schoolchildren might be validly done with the clear secular intent of enhancing the effectiveness of science instruction."[16] Coincidentally, at exactly this time, the draft of a creationist textbook (tentatively titled *Biology and Origins*) was being shopped around for a publisher. As a direct result of the *Edwards* decision, approximately 150 individual changes were made to the draft of this book, whereby the word "creation" and "creationist" were changed to "intelligent design" and "design proponent," which the book's author, Charles Thaxton, had overheard being used by a NASA engineer. In one of the most telling details of how superficial these changes had been, it was later discovered that, save for these word substitutions, the subsequently published book *Of Pandas and People* was a nearly word for word copy of the original manuscript, except for one mistake in which the word "creationists" had been accidentally replaced with "cdesign proponentsists."

This charade was not enough, apparently, to dissuade the creationist movement from embracing this book as the centerpiece of its new strategy, which was to get the newly minted "intelligent design theory" into the nation's science classrooms as quickly as possible. And with the founding of the Discovery Institute in Seattle in 1990, the intelligent design movement now had an intellectual home. With generous financial backing from conservative Christian groups, the Discovery Institute offered fellowships and grants for those scholars who were interested in doing academic work that would either attack evolution or advance intelligent design. If evolutionary biology had panels of scientific experts, the Discovery Institute would have its own. If pro-evolution scientists could write books and publish papers, they could too. This was all part of the new "wedge strategy" (revealed through a leaked memo in 1999) which aimed to show that evolution was a "theory in crisis" and that there were holes in it large enough to justify teaching an alternative theory alongside it in science classrooms, just as the *Edwards* decision had allowed. No longer satisfied with the old creationist strategy of showing that evolution was religion, the new goal was to show that evolution was bad science and that intelligent design was a suitable alternative. Hoping to raise enough doubts about evolution by suggesting that it was "just a theory," that it had gaps, and that some scientists had rejected it, the intelligent design mantra became one to "teach the controversy," in the name of educational freedom and scientific openness.

This, of course, was a sham and was understood to be so by virtually every learned commentator who was not already beholden to creationist ideology. For one thing, to say that evolution is "just a theory" is to misunderstand the basis of scientific reasoning. Everything in science is "just a theory." The theory of gravity is "just a theory." The idea that the Earth is round instead of flat is "just a theory" as well. In science, we can never completely dispel uncertainty. No matter how good our evidence—even if it is overwhelming—there is always the possibility that our theory can be proven wrong. This means that no scientific theory, no matter how wonderfully it fits with the data, can ever be accepted as "proven to be true."[17] Just ask Isaac Newton.

Science progresses by new theories coming along and explaining anomalies in the old ones, which sometimes results in a revolution in our understanding of the universe. That is just the way of scientific reasoning. It is empirical, not deductive. Could this happen too with evolution? Yes, of course it is possible. Yet it is also extremely unlikely. But the standard of considering and teaching alternative scientific theories has to be based on something more than grasping at straws of uncertainty in current theory or the conspiracy theorist's lament that their own theory "could be true." Indeed it might be, but evidence is required. Einstein did not overthrow Newton merely by pointing out that Newtonian mechanics could not explain the perihelion advance of Mercury; he offered an alternative explanation that was borne out by prediction and fit with the data. Has intelligent design done that? Has it said even one word to raise our confidence that even if there were "holes" in evolutionary theory, they have a better scientific way to explain them?

And what of these "holes" in the first place? It is important to understand that the alleged holes in evolutionary theory are not holes at all, but well-known research problems that were well on their way to being addressed even in Darwin's time. The argument that the eye was too complex to have been the product of gradual evolution was not only mentioned by Darwin, but the problem that it allegedly creates for evolutionary theory has since been resolved by Richard Dawkins. In his book *Climbing Mount Improbable*, Dawkins provides an explanation of how the flatworm eye (which can detect light but no image) would have been useful even if it were not as complex as the human eye, undercutting the idea that the eye would only be adaptive once it was fully formed. Dawkins devotes an entire chapter to showing how it would be easy for something as complex as the eye to evolve gradually. In another chapter, he does the same thing for a bird's wing.[18] So much for creationist arguments concerning "organs of extreme perfection."

What about the "missing link" or the problem of gaps in the fossil record? As Dawkins observes, "creationists adore 'gaps' in the fossil record, just as they adore gaps generally," thinking that if such gaps exist, the only suitable explanation is divine intervention.[19] But, as Dawkins points out, it is ridiculous to demand fossils at every stage of evolutionary transition, given that only a small fraction of animals fossilize in the first place and that, even if we had no fossils, there is still evidence for evolution from other sources, such as molecular genetics.[20] It should go without saying that it is naive to suggest God's existence as a better explanation of any gaps.

It is even more compelling to note that whereas the absence of any specific fossil does not discredit evolution, the presence of even *one* fossil in the wrong geological stratum would blow the theory out of the water.[21] To those who sometimes grumble that evolution does not itself fulfill the lofty scientific standard of falsifiability that Judge Overton borrowed from the philosophers, it is crucial to note that evolution by natural selection *does* make risky predictions. "Fossil rabbits in the Precambrian," J. B. S. Haldane famously responded—when asked whether there was any possible evidence that, if found, could falsify the theory of evolution. Despite creationist fairy tales of human footprints in the same stratum as dinosaurs, no such fossils have ever been found.[22] What *has* been found in recent years, however, is a serious candidate for one of the "missing links" between fish and humans. In 2004, a team led by Neil Shubin discovered the fossilized remains of a 375-million-year-old "fishapod" named the Tiktaalik, which had shoulders, elbows, legs, a neck, and a wrist.[23] The alleged "holes" in evolutionary theory seem to be filling in fast.

On the other side of the ledger, it is important to realize that there is not and never has been any credible scientific evidence in favor of intelligent design. As creationist theory dressed up in scientific clothes, ID theory relies heavily on the idea that design is the only conceivable alternative to "random chance" as an explanation of biological complexity. As such, it just might qualify as one of those "scientific critiques" that the Supreme Court had allowed under *Edwards*. But, once again, Dawkins shows that natural selection—which is *not* a random process—is a better explanation than either design or chance, in that it reveals how complexity might result from the cumulative building of incremental advantage in successive forms over a long period of time.[24] Intelligent design, as it turns out, offers a vastly inferior (indeed substantively empty) *scientific* explanation for complexity.

All of this came to a head in 2004, when the Dover (Pennsylvania) Area School District voted to mandate the teaching of "intelligent design" as part of its science curriculum, with the textbook *Of Pandas and People* as a reference. Eleven parents sued the school district and the case *Kitzmiller v. Dover Area School District* was tried in federal court before Judge John E. Jones, a conservative Republican who had been appointed by President George W. Bush. In an opinion remarkably similar to Judge Overton's ruling in *McLean v. Arkansas*, Judge Jones ruled for the plaintiffs, concluding that intelligent design was "not science" and that its attacks on evolution had been successfully refuted by the scientific community, while intelligent design had itself failed to generate any peer-reviewed publications or scientific tests of its own substantive claims. ID theory, in short, was revealed to be nothing more than the "progeny of creationism," serving as a pretext to teach religion in the public schools. Judge Jones went on to cite the "breathtaking inanity" and "striking ignorance" of the Dover school board's actions, reprimanding them for wasting the taxpayers' time and money. As a result, the Dover Area School

District was ordered to pay over $1 million to the plaintiffs, despite the fact that all of the school board members who had voted for the original mandate were turned out of office at the next election.

Now it must be over, right?

Suffice it to say that such a verdict (and payment of damages) probably made any future state school board pause before they voted to mandate the teaching of intelligent design in their science classrooms. And indeed that seems to be just what happened when in 2007 the Kansas School Board voted to amend its earlier 2005 decision (which was made just before the *Kitzmiller* verdict came out in December 2005), which had mandated the teaching of ID theory alongside evolution in Kansas public schools.

But maybe there was another factor at work as well.

In January 2005, a twenty-four-year-old physics student from Oregon State University named Bobby Henderson sent an open letter to the Kansas School Board in which he demanded equal time for his own self-created religion of "Pastafarianism" (based on the gospel of the "Flying Spaghetti Monster") who had created the universe and, he said, presumably also the laws of evolution. Framing his theory as consistent with the doctrine of intelligent design, Henderson argued that like ID theory, his theory was not based on faith, but scientific evidence. After a lengthy description of how the Flying Spaghetti Monster is capable of changing any carbon dating or other scientific measurements by touching them with "His Noodly Appendage," Henderson goes on to explain that the scientific aspects of his theory should be taught alongside evolution and ID theory in the science classroom, but that it is disrespectful to teach this material without wearing His chosen outfit: full pirate regalia. Henderson closes the letter by providing a graph showing that his theory can explain global warming and other natural disasters as a function of the decline in piracy since the 1800s.[25] Based on this "scientific evidence," Henderson ends with a plea that if the Kansas School Board is going to mandate teaching ID theory alongside evolution, they really must include Pastafarianism as well. It would be unfair if they didn't. Henderson suggests one-third time for each. "Teach the controversy."

A more brilliant satire of the intellectual bankruptcy of ID theory is hard to imagine. Unfortunately (before the *Kitzmiller* ruling), this was not enough immediately to convince the Kansas School Board, who voted in November 2005 to mandate teaching ID theory in science classrooms in Kansas, in order to increase "balance." After this, Henderson put his Flying Spaghetti Monster letter online, where it became an Internet phenomenon that later turned into a book: *The Gospel of the Flying Spaghetti Monster* (Villard Trade Books, 2006). In the book Henderson claims 10 million adherents to his new religion and includes glowing testimonials from numerous renowned scientists who provide comical "proofs" of his claims for Pastafarianism. To say that Henderson's theory has now surpassed ID theory in its popularity is perhaps not an exaggeration; on the website one can buy car magnets and mugs with photos of the Flying Spaghetti Monster and His Noodly Appendage.

The fallout from such a clever and strategic skewering of the scientific status of ID theory eventually made an impact on the debate when some of Henderson's fans—dressed in full pirate regalia—gave public testimony at a Polk County (Florida) School Board meeting in 2007 and convinced them not to include ID theory in their science classes. One board member complained that the intervention had made a "mockery" of her school board (which was probably the point), but she eventually capitulated and dropped the intelligent design mandate in the glare of negative public opinion. Eventually, as noted, the Kansas School Board came around too when the new board members voted in 2007 to amend the earlier 2005 mandate. One does not know, of course, whether this had more to do with Pastafarianism than it did with the *Kitzmiller* decision, but the trend line was now clear. ID theory had become a laughing stock.

Incredibly, this is not the end of the story.

The creationist/intelligent design strategy has shifted once again and now focuses on protecting the academic freedom of public school teachers who wish to "teach the controversy" on evolution and a handful of other "controversial" scientific subjects. In 2008, a bill entitled the "Louisiana Academic Freedom Act" was filed with the Louisiana Senate. It states that "the teaching of some scientific subjects such as biological evolution, the chemical origins of life, global warming, and human cloning can cause controversy [and] some teachers may be unsure of the expectations concerning how they should present information on such subjects." The bill goes on to argue that Louisiana's teachers should be free to help students to "understand, analyze, critique, and review in an objective manner the scientific strengths and scientific weaknesses of existing scientific theories pertinent to the course being taught."[26] After a complex set of parliamentary procedures, all references to evolution and other specific scientific subjects were removed from the bill and it was renamed the "Louisiana Science Education Act" and passed with overwhelming support and signed into law by former Rhodes Scholar and Republican Governor Bobby Jindal in 2008. Despite cosmetic changes to avoid the appearance of promoting creationism/ID theory, the intent of the law was clear. It was intended to provide legal cover for teachers who wished to mislead their students about the alleged "controversy" surrounding scientific issues that were well settled, but still politically radioactive.

Although a similar bill had already gone down to defeat in Florida in early 2008 (once state Democrats seized on the academic freedom tactic to insist that any such bill should also protect teachers who wished to teach birth control, abortion, and sex education) the precedent set in Louisiana could now be followed by other states. Even though similar bills have died in the legislature in Missouri, South Carolina, and Iowa, it is my duty to report that in April 2012, a bill that protects "teachers who explore the 'scientific strengths and scientific weaknesses' of evolution and climate change" was signed into law in the state of Tennessee.[27] By January 2013, four other states had attempted to follow suit, with "academic freedom" bills pending in the legislatures in Colorado, Missouri, Montana, and Oklahoma.[28]

The inclusion of climate change in the Tennessee law is of course troubling, as the intelligent design lobby seeks support for its religious ideology among those conservatives whose political ideology commits them to a similarly empty critique of any science that they do not like. Yet one also sees hope in the strategy used in Florida, where the Pandora's box of academic freedom brought with it a host of "controversial" topics about reproductive freedom that Republican legislators just could not stomach. One wonders whether someday a clever teacher might choose to test the limits of one of these bills by teaching Pastafarianism!

Yet this clearly isn't funny. How can one profess to care about academic freedom when one has so little respect for the truth? It is of course depressing to note the ridiculous amount of time, money, and effort that has gone into proving that faith is not science and that religious (and now perhaps political) ideology has no business in the science classroom. And that battle is not nearly over yet. After so many defeats, how can religious ideologues still not understand that creationism/ ID theory isn't science? Of course, they probably *do* understand that very well. They would just rather posture that they are protecting science rather than eroding it, so that they can promote their religious ideology. But in doing so they reject what every thinking person must know: that we cannot teach every crackpot theory in the science classroom, because that would be misleading and contemptuous of the methods of scientific discovery. For a theory to be taught in science class it has to have at least some evidence in its favor to *earn* its place at the table, and ID theory (like Pastafarianism) has none. Academic freedom does not and should not protect dishonest attempts to shoehorn ideology into the classroom. Nor should it protect outright lying by those who seek to manufacture a scientific controversy where there is none.

The idea that we need to "teach the controversy" on scientifically bankrupt theories is blatantly exposed by the Flying Spaghetti Monster parody. As Dawkins argues, we might as well teach flat-Earth theory.[29] There just *is* no scientific controversy over the truth of evolution by natural selection. The eminent biologist Theodosius Dobzhansky was taken by many to speak for the profession when he said, "Nothing in biology makes sense except in light of evolution."[30] And obviously there is no scientific controversy over ID theory, for it *has* no scientific evidence to be considered. Given that, the repeated attempt to put creationism into the nation's classrooms must be seen for what it is: a blatant fraud perpetrated by those who wish to smuggle religious ideology into the schools by any means possible. This is not science. This is not respecting truth. Indeed, this is *contempt* for truth of the highest order.

At this point it would be easy to declare victory and stop fighting. As Thomas Henry Huxley once said, "life is too short to occupy oneself with the slaying of the slain more than once." If we have not yet convinced religious ideologues that faith is not science, we never will. Worse, they probably already know it, but cynically prefer to push ahead anyway, in service to their ideological agenda. So should we quit and just laugh at them? That would be a mistake. Although ridicule is a powerful weapon, we cannot grow complacent. If we don't fight ignorance and unreason it will fester and begin to erode the standards for truth. Where falsehood goes unchecked it may metastasize. The battle for truth, science, and reason is eternal. And if it will never be over then we should never stop fighting.

The latest skirmish over intelligent design also must be put in historical perspective. Although it may seem incredible to us, this is actually par for the course in the history of science. Religious ideology is just displaying its old tactic of making a conscious attempt to undermine scientific belief. Remember that they burned Giordano Bruno and imprisoned Galileo; suddenly, trying to shoehorn creationism into the nation's science classrooms doesn't seem so threatening. Yet, once again, religion has chosen the wrong foe. As we saw, Galileo warned long ago that, for its own protection, religion should not trespass on the turf of science. And as the religious debate now morphs into a political one, it will be necessary for those who respect truth to remain committed to fighting this hydra wherever it pops up. Just as the creationists and global warming deniers are not respecting truth when they subvert the process by which true beliefs are formed, those who wish to support science and reason must not themselves disrespect truth by failing to fight for it. Even if the creation story from the Bible were true, it is clearly not science, not only because there is no evidence in its favor but because faith has no role in settling empirical matters. If one wishes to believe things about the world based on faith that is one's business. But the long battle against religious ideology that has been fought all the way from Galileo to the Flying Spaghetti Monster has provided mountains of evidence that this is *not* a reliable route to the discovery of empirical truth, and it is therefore disrespectful to truth to leave it unchallenged. One cannot create one's own reality just by desiring it. Though, in recent years, some have certainly tried.

Political Ideology

Unfortunately, religious ideology is not the only "faith-based" school of thought that has intruded itself into factual debates in recent years. Over the last few decades, the growth of political ideology has presented itself as an alternative system of belief to facts and evidence on a range of subjects.

The guilt for this exists on both the right and the left. But let's not pretend in any way that the blame is equal. One failure of the media in recent years is that when they seek to criticize one side in a partisan debate (for instance Romney's claim that Obama went on an "apology tour" just after he was elected President in 2008) they seem obsessed with trying to balance it with some overstatement or distortion on the other side (for instance Obama's claim that if Romney were elected we would have had an "outsourcing pioneer" in the White House).[31] But this is just misleading. Although it is regrettable that one can point to *any* lies told by either campaign, this does not mean that on every "partisan" issue—especially those that concern science—there are two equal sides, both of which have a reasonable claim to truth.[32]

The majority of bias against science and reason in recent years has been overwhelmingly Republican. For the definitive study on this point, one may read Chris Mooney's devastating account in *The Republican War on Science* (Basic Books, 2005). This is not, of course, to say that there has been no bias on scientific topics that has come from the left and it is intellectually instructive to identify these. Later in this chapter I will consider one such case of left-wing bias. For now, however, we should start where the majority of ideological bias against science can be found and that is with the conservatives. There are literally dozens of examples to choose from: stem cell research, food contamination, birth control, environmental protection, oil drilling, etc. But I will choose the most egregious example in recent years: the denial of evidence for global warming.

Climate Change

The "debate" about global warming, it should be made clear from the outset, is not a scientific debate but a political one. Ever since the Intergovernmental Panel on Climate Change (IPCC) released their 1995 report, which suggested that "the balance of evidence suggests that there is a discernable human influence on global climate," the evidence has only grown stronger. In 2004, Naomi Oreskes published a literature review in the prestigious journal *Science*, which found that between 1993 and 2003 there were 928 peer-reviewed scientific papers on the general topic of "global climate change" and that exactly *zero* of them disagreed with the idea that human-caused global warming was occurring.[33]

This did not mean, of course, that there was no debate—even furious debate—that had already started in the halls of government and in the media over whether global warming was real. In a 2003 Gallup Poll, 33 percent of the American public said they believed that the seriousness of global warming had been exaggerated.[34] In 2003, US Senator James Inhofe (R-Oklahoma), the new chair of the Senate Environment and Public Works Committee, took to the floor of the US Senate to give a speech aimed at blocking a bipartisan bill that "would have created the first caps on greenhouse gases emissions ever agreed to by the U.S. Government."[35] After stacking a Senate panel with climate change skeptics, Inhofe made his own speech, which included the statement that global warming was "the greatest hoax ever perpetrated on the American people." The bill was defeated.

In years since, global warming has grown to be a deeply partisan issue. A 2012 Pew Research Center poll showed that only 48 percent of Republicans think there is "solid evidence" that the Earth is warming (compared to 85 percent of Democrats), and that while 63 percent of Obama supporters think that this warming is caused mostly by human activity, only 18 percent of Romney supporters agreed with that statement. On the question of whether they thought that *scientists* were divided over these same issues, 70 percent of Republicans said that they were, while 42 percent of Democrats agreed with them.[36]

Scientists actually betray no such diversity of opinion. The IPCC, the National Academy of Sciences, the American Meteorological Society, and the American Geophysical Union all agree that human activity is causing global climate change.[37] The most recent comprehensive poll of Earth scientists found that 90 percent answered "yes" to the question of whether mean global temperatures had risen over the last 200 years and 82 percent said "yes" to the question of whether human activity was a significant contributing factor to this.[38] When the results were further analyzed into categories of those who specialized in climate science and had published more than 50 percent of their recent peer-reviewed publications in this area, they rose to 96.2 percent who agreed that global warming was real and 97.4 percent who thought this was caused by human activity.

What might a political ideologue do to fight such widespread scientific consensus? Challenge the science! Now it is important to note here that the only reasonable challenge to a scientist's views about empirical matters is to challenge them scientifically, with more and better science, published in peer-reviewed scientific journals. This, however, was not the tack taken by partisan conservatives who wished to dispute the facts about global warming. Instead, through the subtle use of corporate money, ideological "think tanks," lobbyists, op-eds, partisan media, and friends in high places, the "skeptics" about global warming have managed in the last decade to create the impression *through public relations* that there is a scientific controversy where none actually exists. As with the "debate" over evolution, the controversy over global warming has taken on a partisan edge and focused on raising spurious doubts, so that the mainstream media will be forced at every turn to pronounce the issue "controversial" when it reports on the subject. Sadly, this strategy has largely worked.[39]

This strategy, of course, is not new. We saw it in the intelligent design advocates' efforts to change the curriculum in the public schools and we have also seen it used over the last few decades on "debates" over whether tobacco causes cancer, whether there is acid rain, the feasibility of President Reagan's "Star Wars" missile defense system, what to do about the hole in the ozone layer, and whether physical and mental harm results from abortion or the Plan B pill. Any one of these topics would make a good case study of the role that political ideology has in disrespecting truth. And they have.[40]

On the topic of global warming, one should realize that such political push-back against unwelcome scientific conclusions is just the latest iteration of a well-worn conservative strategy to challenge and obfuscate facts that one does not like. The specific story on this with respect to global warming (and other topics) has been well told not only by Chris Mooney and Naomi Oreskes, but also by James Hansen in *Storms of My Grandchildren* and by James Hoggan in *Climate Cover-Up*.[41] The story of how ExxonMobil and other corporations funneled money to conservative "think tanks," who then hired their own "experts" to challenge scientists in the popular press, is a shocking story of manipulation and dishonesty that must be read to be believed. Below, I will tell just a bit of this story, but since my job in this book is to defend the general idea of respecting truth, it is important to note two obvious facts: (1) such ideological manipulation of the scientific process does *not* respect truth and (2) there is no widespread dissent in the scientific community over the truth of anthropogenic global warming. Indeed, since the real measure of scientific dissent is to be found not in public opinion polls, political speeches, or newspaper articles, *but only in peer-reviewed scientific papers*, one notes that the most recent literature review—which sought to update Oreskes's 2005 finding—found that of 13,950 peer-reviewed articles on climate change from 1991 to 2012, only 24 of them (0.17 percent) rejected global warming.[42] This while 43 percent of the American public continues to believe that scientists disagree on this subject.[43]

Such blatant disrespect for the methods of science reveals a deep hostility to the concept of truth and a willingness to put political ideology (and profits) before facts.[44] To say that global warming is "just a theory," or to say that we cannot move forward with any policy proposals until the science is "certain," is to misconstrue a fundamental truth about science. As we saw in the challenge that intelligent design put up against the theory of evolution by natural selection, *everything* in science is just a theory; *nothing* in science can ever be completely certain. The method of science just does not allow for absolute verification, no matter how good the evidence. But this does not mean that there is any real doubt about the truth of global warming. Scientists are always criticizing one another's theories. When done in a spirit of openness and honesty, this facilitates the search for truth. When done for ideological purposes, however, this open and critical aspect of science can be exploited by those who wish to fan the flames of uncertainty in service of a private agenda.

Now to put it this way may be slightly unfair to the handful of climate change skeptics who are respected scientists. It is true that there is not yet as much consensus on the topic of global warming as there is on evolution. Perhaps the most famous skeptic on the topic of global warming is MIT Professor of Atmospheric Sciences and member of the National Academy of Sciences, Richard Lindzen. Although Lindzen believes that global temperatures are rising and that they are a result of human activity, he is still taken by many as a skeptic in this debate, because he believes that we need not worry as much as we have about its effect on the Earth, due to the potential protective effects of the clouds, which will cool the atmosphere.[45] According to Lindzen, an opening in the high clouds could act as something of an escape hatch for all of the excess heat that may build up due to global warming. He calls this the "iris effect," to draw an analogy to the iris of the eye, which opens to let in more light. In a similar way, he thinks that the high clouds could open to let out more heat.[46]

This theory, however, has been widely doubted (some would even say discredited) by other scientists, who looked at the same satellite data that Lindzen used for his 2001 paper and could not reproduce his findings. When Lindzen published a 2009 paper to offer more support for his theory, there were more errors. These were freely acknowledged by Lindzen who said that he made "some stupid mistakes" that were "embarrassing." More recently, he has had trouble getting his work published in first-rate peer-reviewed American journals.[47]

Lindzen has nonetheless been treated like a rock star by many global warming deniers, who seem eager to hear a message that confirms their ideology, coming from a respectable source. Lindzen publishes widely in the popular press, including a 2012 editorial entitled "No Need to Panic about Global Warming," which he co-authored with fifteen other climate change dissenters.[48] He has testified at government hearings and spoken at conservative conferences that are dedicated to providing a forum for climate change skeptics. Some of the most notorious such conferences are held by the Heartland Institute, which promotes itself as "the world's most prominent think tank promoting skepticism about man-made climate change."[49]

The Heartland Institute describes its mission as "to discover, develop, and promote free-market solutions to social and economic problems." What requires a bit more digging, however, is to learn that in the 1990s the Heartland Institute worked with Philip Morris to raise doubts over whether second-hand smoking caused lung cancer. Heartland published and distributed research that had been done by Philip Morris, "met with members of Congress on behalf of the tobacco industry, organized 'off the record' briefings, wrote and placed op-eds, and organized radio interviews and letters to editors."[50] One should remember that this lobbying strategy over the health effects of *second-hand* smoke was merely the sequel to an earlier strategy that began in the 1960s *to deny that smoking caused lung cancer even in smokers.* Indeed, Naomi Oreskes and Erik M. Conway make a compelling argument in their book *Merchants of Doubt* that this is when the "manufacturing uncertainty" strategy really began. In a leaked 1969 tobacco company memo, we find the plan laid out rather nakedly: "Doubt is our product, since it is the best means of competing with the 'body of fact' that exists in the mind of the general public. It is also the means of establishing a controversy."[51] Today, Heartland's self-professed number one agenda item is to raise doubts about the truth of global warming.

Between 1998 and 2010, Heartland received over $7.3 million from ExxonMobil. From 1986 to 2010 it received over $14 million from foundations affiliated with the Koch Brothers, whose firm has substantial oil and energy holdings.[52] In 2008, ExxonMobil announced that it would stop all funding of organizations that denied climate change, but Heartland has continued to receive donations from other large corporations, including continued support from "big tobacco" companies. What are we to make of this? Whose agenda is Heartland really serving?

We may never know the full answer to this, but one thing we do know for certain is that the tactic of using private money to fund a think tank that manufactures uncertainty about a scientific matter is not new. In *Merchants of Doubt*,

Naomi Oreskes and Erik M. Conway make the case that this has been the standard playbook for a succession of industry-unfriendly scientific discoveries pertaining to the environment for decades. And, in a chilling similarity to the Discovery Institute, which we met previously ("Creationism in a Cheap Tuxedo," p. 65) in their fight to get intelligent design taught in the public schools, we now understand that the Heartland Institute is pursuing a similar strategy to "undermine the teaching of global warming in public schools [and] promote a curriculum that would cast doubt on the scientific finding that fossil fuel emissions endanger the long-term welfare of the planet."[53] In one leaked document, Heartland's strategy was described as trying to promote the idea that "whether humans are changing the climate is a major scientific controversy." One doesn't know whether to laugh or cry. What's next, a creationist-friendly theory of global warming that school boards will promote as an alternative so that teachers can "teach the controversy"? The topic may be different, but the tactics are the same. "Doubt is our product."

Now, of course these sorts of public relations shenanigans must be separated from the question of whether there is any real scientific dissent over the question of global warming. As we have seen, there is some, but it is small and questionable. We understand that scientific questions are never completely settled. But we now face a complication in that how we handle the problem of scientific uncertainty in this case may have a potentially huge impact on the financial and physical risk to the entire human population. In the face of a minuscule amount of uncertainty, we must consider the risks of waiting. This issue goes beyond science to one of values and policy, but it is inextricably linked with the scientific debate. Public policy officials will face diminished options if they wait until *all* of the scientists are satisfied. Just consider, for instance, what we might face if the theory of evolution by natural selection had some potentially catastrophic consequence for the planet, and we had to wait 150 years for *that* "scientific" debate to be settled!

Naturally, responsible scientists are well aware of these risks and they have made their own recommendations based upon it. One of the earliest and most prominent "whistleblowers" about the threat from global warming came from James Hansen, former head of NASA's Goddard Institute for Space Studies and author of *Storms of My Grandchildren*, who felt that even President Obama does not "get it" and must be woken up to the danger. Another scientist, Kerry Emanuel, who is an MIT colleague and sometime critic of Richard Lindzen, weighed in on the issue of risk this way: "even if there were no political implications, it just seems deeply unprofessional and irresponsible to look at this and say, 'We're sure it's not a problem.' It's a special kind of risk, because it's a risk to the collective civilization."[54] Yet Lindzen, for one, seems willing to take that risk. He contends that there is "groupthink" among other climate scientists and that his strategy of waiting for more evidence so that we don't "overreact" is a wise one. "If I'm right, we'll have saved money. ... If I'm wrong, we'll know it in 50 years and can do something."[55] The problem, of course, is that in fifty years the water may be around our hips and it will be too late.

This is the real debate about global warming. It is not about scientific uncertainty, but about the risks versus rewards of political inaction. But given that this issue is one with such terrible potential consequences, can we really afford to satisfy such a high standard of "proof"? As we saw in the last chapter, truth is one thing, survival is another. Yet it is here that we must stop for a minute, and think about the full import of that sentence for our concern with respecting truth. If what we care about (at least primarily in this book) is the idea of respecting truth, why should we care at all about the risks of waiting until there is scientific "certainty"? Why not let the dissenters do their thing? This is science, not ideology. There are no heretics in science and there should be no purge of skeptics. Respecting truth requires that we take seriously the idea that there might be a challenge to the *truth* of our theory, not that we be forced by an abundance of caution to act before all of the data are in. The *scientific* question about global warming, that is, is not whether we know enough to act, but whether we have enough evidence to say that the theory is true.

At least one extremely prominent scientist thinks that we do not. Freeman Dyson is one of the most famous physicists in the world. Since 1953, he has been a fellow at the Institute for Advanced Study in Princeton, New Jersey, where he has done work on quantum electrodynamics and a range of other topics. And he is a critic of the consensus over global warming. While admitting that global warming is real, and that it is caused by humans burning fossil fuel, Dyson also believes that the current climate models contain far too much error to be predictively accurate.

> The models solve the equations of fluid dynamics, and they do a very good job of describing the fluid motions of the atmosphere and the oceans. They do a very poor job of describing the clouds, the dust, the chemistry and the biology of fields and farms and forests. They do not begin to describe the real world we live in.[56]

His primary objection, however, is not to the "technical facts" about global warming (about which he admits that he "does not know much"), but rather to the perversion of the scientific process which has led to intolerance of criticism and the ostracization of people who dare to question the consensus on global warming.[57] "Heretics who question the dogmas are needed. I am proud to be a heretic. The world always needs heretics to challenge the prevailing orthodoxies."[58] Heretics, he argues, are necessary to the scientific process, because they are sometimes the only ones who lead us to the truth.

But are global warming skeptics motivated by the search for truth? Clearly some are (such as Dyson himself), but one is tempted to wonder if such an in principle defense of skepticism borders on the naive and just gives aid and comfort to those who would just as soon destroy science as respect it. Sadly, Dyson's statements on global warming have been exploited by numerous climate change deniers. Knowing this, what should we say about Dyson's dissent? Is he respecting truth or not? I believe that he is. The price of respecting truth is to champion those methods that lead to truth and one of those is skepticism. Even if we do not always agree with the purpose to which it is put, skepticism, criticism, even "heresy" is one of the most powerful tools that we have for discovering true beliefs. It is directly in the interests of science to allow for the gadflies, who question everything, even if they are inconvenient. Genuine scientific skepticism is something to be protected.

But what, then, of ideological skepticism—the kind of skepticism that is rooted not in any real concerns about truth or the integrity of the scientific process, but instead stems from motivated reasoning? The difference, I think, is one of *attitude*. We must tolerate both, even if we sneer at those whom we suspect of cheating. But we cannot beat ideology by abandoning the principles of science. The best way to fight ignorance and dishonesty is with transparency and better evidence, not by closing ranks and booting out dissenters. No matter the stakes, we should not allow science to become a political process.

What about the threat to our well-being? This is a legitimate concern and it should not be trivialized. Truth is *not* the same as survival, and sometimes survival matters more. But what happens when scientists are tempted to cut this corner? Even if we have the truth on our side, in the long run it may cost us. Just such an instance occurred in the global warming debate when a group of climate scientists' emails were stolen from a server at the University of East Anglia in England, and exposed instances of name-calling, threats to hide data, stonewalling critics, and some private doubts that came to be known as Climategate. In these emails, we saw that scientists too are human and that some of the world's leading climate researchers grew exasperated under the stress of public attention to their work, including relentless freedom of information requests made by climate change skeptics.[59] Although there were also some threats to manipulate data, independent investigations turned up "no evidence of falsification or fabrication of data" and nothing in the emails caused concern over the scientific consensus on the truth of global warming by any of the independent agencies who investigated this matter.[60] But the public relations, of course, were a nightmare, causing climate skeptics to make charges of a conspiracy theory to cover up the "real truth" about climate change which, once it hit the mainstream media, made the general public even more uncertain about whether there really *was* consensus on climate change after all. Few today remember that eight separate government and scientific panels found no evidence of scientific wrongdoing. But they do remember the controversy.

What is a better way to fight ideology? One is by continuing to do science. But one can also expose the cheaters. One finds in Naomi Oreskes's work a tremendous scholarly effort to connect the dots, expose funding sources, and dig up the lies at the heart of so many ideological attacks on science. As a philosopher, I am tempted here also to do my part by exposing the corruption of the word "skepticism."

One suspects that a number of corporate chiefs, governmental officials, lobbyists and others who make their living off fossil fuels are absolutely delighted with Richard Lindzen's (and Freeman Dyson's) "skepticism" about global warming, not because they care a whit about protecting the high standards of scientific truth, but because it suits their interests. At the very least, one worries here about such unconscious mechanisms as denial and motivated reasoning, if not outright dishonesty. As Upton Sinclair so aptly put it, "it is difficult to get a man to understand something when his salary depends upon his not understanding it." But this is just ignorance and political ideology masquerading as scientific skepticism.

And why is it that so many members of Congress who couldn't pass an introductory logic class are so fond of saying that they are "skeptics" about climate change? Refusing to believe something in the face of a landslide of scientific evidence is not skepticism, it is the height of credulity. It is gullible acceptance that it is more likely that there is some kind of wild scientific conspiracy than that the vast majority of scientists have merely reached the same conclusion based on good evidence. The claim, made by Lindzen and others, that climate scientists are hyping the data in order to promote their own careers is ludicrous.[61] Climate change denial is just another example of demanding impossibly high standards of proof for things that one *doesn't* want to believe, alongside complete gullibility in accepting without evidence the plausibility of the most remarkable long shots, just so long as they are congenial to one's political ideology. But there is a distinction between true skepticism ("science doesn't know everything") and posturing for willful ignorance ("how do you know my theory isn't true?").

And, why should we trust the instincts, values, hunches, or even the assessment of facts of those who are so personally motivated to believe something that fits so well with their financial or political interests? One thinks here of the 2012 Presidential-election-night drama on Fox News, where Karl Rove and other conservative commentators just *could not believe* that Obama had won, even though virtually all of the polls in the mainstream media had predicted for weeks that he would. Instead, Rove ignored the data in favor of his own "internal polling," right up to (and past) the time that his own network called the election for Obama.[62] And these are the folks we're supposed to trust on global warming?

But this raises an important question, for was Rove lying to others or to himself? Was he still trying to spin the last few potential voters or did he really believe that Romney could still win in a landslide? The question arises of how to tell the difference between pretending to believe something because it is convenient to your ideology versus really believing it. Are the climate change deniers just being cynical or is this another instance of self-deception?

Until election night, many might have thought that it must be the former; that no one could possibly look at the weight of evidence and miss the truth about global warming. But as one watched Karl Rove sweat, as his ideology blew up in his face on live television, one might become convinced that it was actually the latter. If you tell a lie often enough it is more likely to be believed, even by you. In a fascinating detail of the global warming debate, Chris Mooney cites a study which found that better educated Republicans were *more* likely to have the wrong view on global warming than less educated ones, and to be more sure that they were right![63] This doesn't sound like lying to me. It sounds like delusion.

Perhaps it is a small step from "we aren't going to let our campaign be dictated by fact checkers" to "[you live] in what we call the reality-based community [but] we're an empire now, and when we act, we create our own reality."[64] But does it matter?

I think that it does. Perhaps delusion starts with spin. Perhaps refusing to believe facts begins with cynicism. I therefore maintain that we should seek to prevent cynical, conscious disrespect for the truth before it becomes full-blown self-deception. When data and evidence are so easily obtained, should we really just chalk it up to fate when someone embraces a crackpot ideology and refuses to consider contrary data? Shouldn't we try to intervene in this kind of refusal to look at contradicting evidence before it evolves into a full-blown break with reality?

In fact, I would argue that standing up to disrespect for the truth, when the person is conscious that they are doing it, is the perfect time to intervene. At that point, one can still appeal to logic and reason. One can still refer to data and evidence. It is *good* to get a wake-up call from reality, and the sooner the better. Even if one's political ideology is shattered, it is better to know that right away, so that there is still time to pick up the pieces and embrace a belief system that has a better chance of working in the real world. It is safer for the person who has the false beliefs and it is also safer for the rest of us, who may suffer at the hands of those like the misguided South African President who thought that HIV did not cause AIDS, manifesting that deadly combination of a delusional worldview coupled with great power. As we see with global warming, sometimes our very lives are at stake. And it may already be too late. If we had fought back harder against the cynical doubts of the tobacco industry in maintaining that cigarettes did not cause cancer, perhaps we would not now be facing the challenge of those who have crossed the line into self-deception by rejecting "junk science" about climate change. If we wait until lies become denial, and denial becomes delusion, how can we turn back?

But, as we shall now see, this danger can come from liberal ideology as well.

Is Race a Myth?

The claim that race is a biological myth is not of recent origin. Arguments against the explanatory utility of the concept of race can be traced back at least to Richard Lewontin's 1972 paper "The Apportionment of Human Diversity," in which he argued that most genetic variation was between individuals, not groups.[65] This created a skirmish among academics, but for the most part the push-back didn't bleed over into public consciousness. Probably just as well— some may have thought—for too much attention to this debate might provide fodder for racism and the continued political oppression of minority groups who were just beginning to achieve their civil rights.

This did not stop many on the left from piling on and celebrating Lewontin's finding. Stephen Jay Gould, Steven and Hilary Rose, and a host of other left-wing scientists went on to spend a good deal of their careers decrying racism and the sometimes scientific masks that it could wear. Then came the Human Genome Project (HGP) in 1990 and everyone held their breath. Would it show that there was more variation than had been thought? When the results were announced, the mostly liberal academic community of biologists heaved a collective sigh of relief, for it was learned that humans were 99 percent similar to one another at the genomic level and that we all had our origins in Africa.

This led to a string of over-the-top pronouncements from many scientists, who thought that they now had biological evidence to back up their political convictions. Hadn't science now shown that race wasn't real? On June 26, 2000, J. Craig Ventner, founder of the Institute for Genomic Research and President of Celera Genomics, who had been the government's main competitor in the race to sequence the human genome, said in a press conference alongside President Bill Clinton and Francis S. Collins (the director of the federal effort) that "the concept of race has no genetic or scientific basis."[66] Since then, many have embraced this view as dogma. "The traditional concept of race as a biological fact is a myth," wrote evolutionary biologist Joseph L. Graves, in his influential book *The Race Myth: Why We Pretend Race Exists in America* (Dutton, 2004). Bringing the debate full circle, Richard Lewontin wrote in 2006 that "[a]s a biological rather than a social construct, 'race' has ceased to be seen as a fundamental reality characterizing the human species."[67]

What is the scientific basis for such pronouncements? Curiously, as we have seen, the foundation for this argument reaches back before the HGP results were announced, most articulately stated in a 1998 study by Alan R. Templeton, professor of biology at Washington University in St. Louis, who found that "85 percent of the variation among individuals was due to individual differences, with only 15 percent attributable to 'racial' differences."[68] This led Templeton to remark, even before Ventner, that race is "not a biological concept ... the 15 percent is well below the threshold that is used to recognize race in other species."[69]

So when the HGP results became available, what changed? Essentially nothing, at least as far as the strategy of arguing that race is a myth was concerned. While it was reassuring that the HGP had confirmed the close relationship between individual humans, the real work had already been done, when Lewontin and Templeton argued that the genetic variability within a group was greater than that between groups. Indeed this, as it turns out, is the lynchpin of the argument that race is unreal, which is to say that "there isn't enough variation in humans for our differences to qualify as races."[70]

But the whole thing depends on what you mean by "race."

Now we could stop right here, political suspicions on high alert, and chalk the rest of the debate up to the sometimes strange semantics demanded by political correctness. But I think it is instructive to probe deeper, in order to see that here, no less than in the debate about intelligent design or global warming, political ideology can get in the way of science. What makes one think that the statement that race is a myth is a political rather than a scientific one? And, if it is a matter of ideology, then what is the ideology at stake? In its crassest form, all ideologies may be reduced to the bastard form of "I wish this weren't true, therefore it must not be true." As such, one might be tempted to identify the ideology behind the claim that race is a myth as a simple form of liberal wish-fulfillment: (1) racism is bad, (2) if there are racial differences then racists will use them to discriminate, (3) if there were no racial differences then racists could not use them to discriminate, (4) it would be good if we could show that race is not real, (5) therefore race is not real. Of course, this is too simple. In fact, it is insulting. But the question so framed leads us to wonder whether perhaps a slightly more sophisticated political motivation might be behind the "scientific" arguments of such biologists as Lewtontin, Templeton, and Graves.

(1)   In order for a biological difference (in plants or animals) to qualify as one of race, "the genetic distance between one population and another has to be significantly greater than the genetic variability that exists within the populations themselves."[71]

(2)   As we have seen in scientific work, from the HGP and before, the variation *within* any population of humans is about 85 percent, whereas the variations *between* populations are no more than 15 percent.

(3)   This is too small to qualify as a "racial" difference.

(4)   Therefore, there are no racial differences between humans.

Now it is important to note here that although this argument may look scientific, it is really semantic. And its motivation is purely ideological. No one is denying the empirical reality that there are differences between populations of individuals. The only disagreement is a taxonomic one—whether we are willing to call these differences "racial." Why shouldn't we? Well, for one thing, we have largely given up on the concept of "race" in classifying plants and other animals. As Lewontin wrote in 2006, "the classification of animal and plant species into named races was at all times an ill-defined and idiosyncratic practice. There was no clear criterion of what constituted a race of animals or plants. ... every population is a separate 'geographic race' and it was realized that nothing was added by the racial category."[72] The same logic might now reasonably be adopted, he feels, in human biology as well. But should it? What explanatory or scientific goal would that serve? Is the argument that there are no racial differences in humans (and therefore that we should stop talking about them) intended to make our biological explanations sharper or more penetrating? Or is the goal to stop discrimination?

To a certain extent, it is instructive to understand this debate as part of the larger one over nature versus nurture that has raged for more than a century in human biology. Here the fault lines are clear. Among a certain camp, there is strong intellectual resistance to the idea that *any* human difference—especially a behavioral one—can be chalked up to nature. In his book *The Blank Slate: The Modern Denial of Human Nature*, Steven Pinker makes a compelling case that a good deal of modern prejudice in favor of "environmental" explanations for human action is ideological, rather than scientific. While it may make us feel good to think that we can, through free will or the right environment, change anything about our behavior, this just is not borne out by the scientific facts. Neither, as Pinker admits, can the case be made that genes are destiny, but he is at pains to point out that this is *not* what he is arguing for in his book; he never said that nature explained everything. Instead, he merely seeks to make the *negative* case, that the folks who think that every human difference can be explained by nurture are simply wrong.

This framework helps to make clear the stakes of the debate over whether race is a biological myth.[73] For, if it is not, then what is to stop someone from making the transition from talking about how racial differences influence our physical characteristics to making the point that they might also affect our behavioral ones? For most liberals, this is plutonium. In fact, the modern field of behavioral genetics, which studies the above effects, has met with stiff resistance over whether science should even be studying this stuff.

As liberals, most academics do not like the idea that there might be fixed genetic influences on our behavior, let alone that these could be studied by science. And, when the topic turns to the study of racial differences, it is not uncommon to find political criticisms taking precedence over scientific ones. Just such a phenomenon occurred following the publication of *The Bell Curve* in 1994, in which Richard Herrnstein and Charles Murray argued that there were demonstrable ethnic differences in IQ scores. Despite obvious methodological flaws in their analysis, the book was initially attacked *even by scientists* for its political implications.[74] This has always seemed to me a deplorable intrusion of ideology into science, for if the work was flawed what could make shorter work of it than to reveal its scientific shortcomings?

But what is the use of respecting truth, some might argue, if it might be used for nefarious purposes? Don't we bear some responsibility for how science is used? Perhaps it is better to deny that such study is even possible than to see it exploited, and the best way to guarantee *that* is by denying that race is a valid scientific concept. As a liberal myself (and the spouse of a woman of color), I understand such normative concerns and wish that there were some way to stand up for the study of truth while knowing in advance that it would never be misused. But I cannot guarantee this. Science never can. So what should we do? I submit that trying to block the study of topics that we find politically offensive is no way to deal with the problem. The truth will eventually come out. The claim that race is not real—that it has no biological or genetic basis—is just the latest flashpoint in the debate over facts versus values. But redefining the word "race" so that it is safe from scientific investigation is not going to protect us. For to say that the concept of race is a "cultural construction" does not change the biological facts.

The claim that race is "socially constructed" is superficially true, but hardly definitive. Words are social. As we see with President Obama, there is a social component to whether we are willing to "call" someone black, even though he may have one white parent. The use of language is culturally influenced and may vary from society to society. But this does not mean that "race" has no biological correlate. Whether we are willing to use the word "race" or not, there is *something* that constitutes the set of group differences between human populations based on their geographic ancestry (even if it is only 15 percent) and that is real and worthy of scientific investigation. We do not respect truth by trying to define it out of existence.

By analogy, consider the question of whether we are willing to *call* someone "tall" or "short." These are socially constructed terms and they may be relative to one's culture. What is considered "tall" in one community may be considered "short" in another. Also, the valence of the terms may vary, depending on the social context in which they are used. It may be considered discriminatory to call someone "tall" or "short" in certain societies. So should we abandon the usage of these words? (Are there, perhaps, some societies that do not even *have* a word for these concepts?)

But, even if we do abandon these words, this does not change the fact that one's height is influenced by one's genotype. Perhaps this provides a useful analogy for how we might think about the concept of race. At this time in American society, we are socialized to think that it is a bad thing to identify someone by their race—or refer to their racial characteristics—because this may be used to discriminate against them. It is not politically correct. Consequently, many people may wish that racial differences were not real and encourage us to jettison the word "race" from our vocabulary.[75] But, even if we do this, note that this is an ideological and linguistic—not scientific or biological—decision. Race and racial differences are just as real whether we choose to identify them or not, just as height is real whether we eschew "heightist" vocabulary or not.

As noted, many scientists have found solace in the results of the HGP, which show that humans share 99 percent of our DNA with one another and that we have a common ancestry. This is a cheering result for our common humanity in that it reinforces the fact that at some level we are all related. But does this in and of itself show that race is not "real"? Absolutely not. First, it is important to dismiss the vacuous statement one sometimes hears that just because you cannot tell by looking at someone's genotype what race they are, this means that race is a fiction. One may not be able to discern someone's height merely by looking at their genotype either, but this does not mean that height is not biologically influenced. Similarly, it is highly misleading to celebrate the statistic that we are 99 percent similar in our genotype. As Michael Specter points out in his book *Denialism*, "we share 98.4% of our genes with chimpanzees [but] few would argue that makes us nearly identical to them."[76] We share approximately 85 percent of our genes with mice and 60 percent with the fruit fly. Due to evolution, it is not surprising that all life has a common ancestral history. But does this mean that the concept of "species" too is a cultural creation? We may only be 1 percent different from one another, but shouldn't science study that 1 percent?

Now in some sense, all of this talk about percentages of similarity is just ridiculous and critics of the concept of "race" are right about one important thing: the word "race" is just a proxy for one's individual genotype. Of course, there is some slippage between the terms (although one study found a 99.86 percent correlation between subjects' self-identified race and their genetic cluster)[77] and it is more accurate to make predictions based on our individual genotypes than on our "race." Ultimately, all of the differences between us are individual and, given the growth of personal genomics, the day might not be too far off when instead of talking about the broad categories of race, or even family, we will instead talk about our individual genomes. As Lewontin found with plants, aren't we all, in some sense, a category of one?

Yet even if this is true, it does not mean that there are no meaningful things to learn about us, based on the ancestry of our forebears, whether we choose to call these differences "racial" or not. As much as the "race is a myth" crowd would like to discount such differences by redefining the meaning of the word "race," it is well known that certain diseases such as sickle cell anemia and thalassemia have different rates of racial susceptibility. Shall we call this something other than race? The disease patterns are nonetheless real. And despite the absurd statement that "racially based medical differences just do not exist,"[78] we now have concrete evidence that this view is wrong. While the higher rates of hypertension, prostate cancer, and other diseases in black patients may potentially be explicable by environmental differences, what might one say about recent discoveries in pharmacology, which have found differential effects of some medicines in those who self-identify as African American?

BiDil was approved by the FDA in 2005 as the first "race-based" medicine, specifically to treat blacks who suffer from congestive heart failure. It is surely not cultural construction, but a fact of biology, that BiDil relieved hypertension in those who self-identify as African American, but not other ethnic groups.[79] Is this a myth? It is hard to see how it could be. One notes also that the discovery of BiDil opened the door for more "race-based" medical treatments. A study in *The Pharmacogenomics Journal* has reported nine clinical trials that were studying diseases or treatments in groups that were defined by race, including chronic hepatitis B in blacks and Hispanics and respiratory syncytial virus in Native American infants.[80] Should we eschew this kind of medicine, because we do not like to use such racial definitions and remember all too well the troubled history of "racial" medicine at the Tuskegee Institute? But whom would we really be serving if we did that?[81]

Now let me be clear about something. I am not saying that there are no potential dangers in this line of research, nor that we should ignore them. In medicine in particular we should remember the admonition that individual differences *are always* greater than group ones. And there is no excuse for discrimination. Even when we recognize group differences this does not mean that we should use these to judge one group inferior. The fact/value distinction must be just as stringent in medicine as it is in any other type of science (subject to the caveat that in medicine our goals are normative, in that we seek health for the patient, rather than knowledge per se). But none of this means that we should not care about values or how our research is used. No matter what science finds, it is up to us as human beings to make the moral decision how to use it. How any racial differences between us should be used is a moral question, not a scientific one. Indeed recognizing this distinction—where we do not let science make moral decisions, but we also do not allow our values to intrude upon science—is the best path to follow. As we may see from the history of science, we should not allow our morality to hinge on the discoveries of science, for what if science someday comes up with a finding that we think is awful? Resisting unsavory truths cannot save us. Science will eventually eclipse our ideologies. And certainly we do not want to be put in the same position as intelligent design theorists or global warming deniers. But, despite the inevitable moral decisions over how to use scientific knowledge, this does not mean that there is no possible difference that one's biology could make (at the individual or the group level) for our physiology, our propensity to contract certain diseases, or ultimately—if the behavioral geneticists are right—perhaps even for our behavior.

It is conveniently overlooked by many critics of behavioral genetics that an important part of the HGP facilitated the study of the effect that genes might have on behavior. Indeed it may come as a shock to learn that there is an entire web page, hosted by the Oak Ridge National Laboratories and sponsored by the US Department of Energy, that is devoted to this research.[82] Here one learns of ongoing efforts to use results from the HGP to study such behavioral traits as stuttering, perfect musical pitch, arm-folding preference, and the ability to curl one's tongue or move one's ears. But one also finds links to research on much more incendiary topics, such as whether there is a genetic component to alcoholism or homosexuality. One should not, of course, prejudge what such research will conclude merely because scientists are investigating these topics; there may or may not be a genetic component to any one of thousands of human behaviors, but the results so far are there for anyone to see and the point for respecting truth seems clear: these are scientific debates, not ideological ones.

One of the most provocative studies in behavioral genetics—which predated the HGP—was done on a Dutch family, whose male members seemed to have a history of aggression.[83] Could there be a genetic explanation? Researchers believe that they found one in this case which, even though it was limited to a rare genetic disorder, drew one of the first links between genes and aggressive behavior. There are even some studies of biological twins reared apart, which suggest that one's political ideology itself may be linked to inborn temperament.[84] Work on these topics is still in its infancy, at least in part due to inadequate funding as a result of concerns over whether anyone should even be doing this kind of research. Will it find things that we deem to be repugnant? Perhaps so, but if we care about respecting truth, our objections should be to flaws in the research not to its alleged political values.

Behavioral genetics is founded on the hypothesis that genetics may someday explain not just our physical characteristics but also our behavioral ones. Perhaps this view is mistaken. If so, nothing will make shorter work of it than empirical results which contradict the original finding. But, until we find them, it seems unwise to let political ideology intrude into our scientific investigations any more than we would counsel letting religious ideology decide what gets taught in biology class. We may not like the results. Who would want to learn from a genomic test that they have a family history of aggression any more than that they carry the gene for prostate cancer? But respecting truth means having the courage to investigate dangerous and unsavory truths as well as pleasant ones. And, in the long run, many believe that we are better served by allowing science to roam wherever our curiosity may take us, instead of putting ideological blinders on the types of knowledge that we will allow it to find.

Indeed, in a curious twist, we may even someday find that the study of genetics itself can help us to overcome racism. It has been widely hypothesized in sociology that hatred and suspicion of those whom we deem to be members of an "out-group" is a part of our evolutionary heritage. When we see a stranger, it is in our evolutionary interest to mount a sufficiently aggressive—or at least hostile—response, in order to defend ourselves against a potential threat. Anthropologists have never found a human population that did not have some racial stereotypes and psychologists have found that children start to learn these from infancy.[85] But, in a fascinating study, scientists have recently learned that children with a rare genetic disorder called Williams syndrome have no racial biases whatsoever.[86] Those with Williams syndrome are "hypersocial" and exhibit no social anxiety of any kind. Quite simply, they exhibit the polar opposite of xenophobia: they have no social fear. Due to this, they are at increased risk for being victimized and must be protected for their willingness to trust. In a telling detail, these children *do* exhibit gender stereotypes, of unknown origin, which has led scientists to speculate that while social fear may be a part of forming racial stereotypes, it is perhaps not one for those based on gender.

Even if all of this is due to a genetic deficiency, might it still hold a lesson for how to avoid racial bias? "If social fear was culturally reduced, racial stereotypes could also be reduced," speculates the author of the study, Andreas Meyer-Lindenberg. If we, as a society, could find ways to have less fear of one another and create more opportunities for social interaction, might we also be able to diminish racism?[87] Surely those who are racists do not form their beliefs after consulting their genotypes. And those with Williams syndrome are nonetheless capable of identifying race—they just do not care about it. For both groups, environment surely plays a role.[88] Thus critics of the concept of race seem right that, in some sense, the way that we use "race" does have an important social and cultural component. Perhaps if we change our environment, we will discover ways to overcome any built-in propensities for racism.[89] This is a social and political value that seems worth pursuing, but it does not mean that there is no biological basis for race. In the meantime, may we learn from the children with Williams syndrome that although race may not be a myth, it is a superficial and asinine way to choose your friends?

Conclusion

The problem with ideology is not that it is based on ignorance (though in specific cases that may be true), but instead that it tempts us to reject knowledge that contradicts what we want to believe. As opposed to the irrational rejection of truth that can occur due to mistakes in our reasoning (which we explored in Chapter 3), with ideology we at some level seem conscious of our decision to insulate our beliefs from refutation.

But why? How can anyone reasonably expect lies and willful ignorance to flourish in an environment that, in the long run, seems to reward truth? Resistance to scientific knowledge (either by politics or by religion) does not have a good track record. Eventually we figure out that the Earth moves. Or that Lysenko was wrong. Or that the Earth's temperature is rising. The advantages of ideology are short lived, though sometimes brutal (just ask Giordano Bruno). But in the long run they are swamped by science. It took the Catholic Church 350 years to apologize to Galileo, but apologize they did. Science cannot be turned back indefinitely. In the short run, ideology may tell us that certain truths are "dangerous" and counsel us to avoid them. In the long run, however, ideology can be defended only by the "pitiful rearguard actions" pointed out by Freud. Perhaps it is better to face the truth right away—no matter how horrible it may seem—than to run from it. So why cling to fantasies?

One recalls here Robert Trivers and his insights on self-deception. Are we actually conscious of our ideological resistance, at least when we are already well into the fight and our back is up over some belief that is threatening our ideology? Trivers observed that the best way to fool others is first to fool ourselves. We have already seen how this played out, in the last chapter, with unconscious cognitive bias. But maybe the same mechanism is at work too with ideology. When we are conscious of a threat to our treasured beliefs, how long does it take before motivated reasoning kicks in and we allow the unconscious part of our brain to do the bidding of whatever we have *chosen* to believe? Do global warming deniers really believe what they are saying? Did they always? Was there once a time when we might have reached them?

Whatever mechanism is at work, the remedy is the same. If we want to respect truth, we must root out bias, and the quicker the better. If we are conscious of it, the challenge is to be honest with ourselves. We should actively test our favored beliefs against reality (just as scientists do) and change them accordingly. But if our biases are *unconscious*, we should be no less vigilant. How so? By not giving in to the easy belief that while *others* may suffer from cognitive biases, we ourselves are surely immune. We should *assume* that we are biased and be on the lookout for how. The scientific attitude of constantly comparing one's beliefs against empirical evidence is an ideal way to keep from fooling ourselves. This, at base, is what respecting truth demands: that we not be easy on our own beliefs. That we always assume that we could be wrong, especially when we most desperately hope that we are right. If we respect truth, we should embrace critical thinking and care about the methods of science and reason, even if the truths that they discover make us uncomfortable.

Recently in the USA, we seem to be backsliding. In the last decade, disrespect for truth has become so pervasive that it has filtered over into our public institutions, even those that—in the past—have professed to be guardians of the truth. We are not talking about just a few crackpots anymore. We see it in speeches in the US Senate. We see it on the news and in our classrooms. Hostility toward facts that clash with our worldview happens first. Next comes contempt for the mechanisms of *finding* truth (and perhaps even for the notion of truth itself), when it conflicts with what we hope is true. Finally, distrust of those who claim to *uphold* the truth arrives and we find ourselves unsure whom to believe anymore. In the absence of trusted sources and respect for truth-producing mechanisms, isn't one belief just as good as another? Ideology happens when desire seduces us into denial. But if our denial is shared by others—who reinforce our fallacies—the danger for truth multiplies. What can be done when disrespect for truth transcends the individual and goes viral, while those whom we have trusted to guard the truth fail in their responsibilities to uphold it?

Notes

1 Though perhaps this isn't such a clear line over time. Does lying to others over a long enough period of time lead to a mindset where we become prone to believe our own lies?
2 China by far has the most atheists; the USA is at around the same level as Saudi Arabia (which, it should be remembered, has religious police). See the most recent "Global Index of Religiosity and Atheism," 2012, <www.wingia.com/web/files/news/14/file/14.pdf>.
3 Christopher Hitchens, *god is not Great: How Religion Poisons Everything* (New York: Twelve, 2007), 150.

4 Ibid., 11.

5 On p. 361 of *The God Delusion* (New York: Houghton Mifflin, 2006), Dawkins says "as many atheists have said better than me, the knowledge that we have only one life should make it all the more precious." But on what basis does Dawkins claim to know that we have only one life? Note that such a claim is even stronger than atheism! An atheist would never say that he *knows* God doesn't exist. That would be ludicrously strong, unnecessary, and parallel to the irrationality of the theist saying he *knows* that God *does* exist. On the subject of God's existence, Dawkins recognizes that it is sufficient merely to declare one's disbelief: one's atheism. But on the subject of life after death, Dawkins seems tempted into taking the unnecessary step of saying he "knows" that there is no afterlife. Why? Whether God exists or not, it is still possible for there to be an afterlife. And, unlike theistic claims about God, which tend to be faith-based rather than evidential, the claim that there is an afterlife could well be one where evidence is relevant, but it is just inconveniently unavailable. Thus, in this case, I think that Dawkins's response is too strong and should be parallel to the case for agnosticism that he makes about the possibility of extraterrestrial life.

6 Karl Jansen, "The Ketamine Model of the Near-Death Experience: A Central Role for the N-Methyl-D-Aspartate Receptor," *Journal of Near-Death Studies* 16, no. 1 (1997): 5–26; Zalika Klemenc-Ketis *et al.*, "Carbon Dioxide May Explain 'Near Death Experiences,'" *Critical Care* 14, no. 2 (2010), <www.ncbi.nlm.nih.gov/pmc/articles/PMC2887177/>.

7 In his book *Erasing Death* (New York: HarperCollins, 2013), Sam Parnia explores the various clinical criteria for death and discusses several cases where patients had no heartbeat, no lung function, and had fixed and dilated pupils *for hours*, and nonetheless were resuscitated and regained full cognitive function. Some of these patients reported an experience of bright lights, a tunnel, and welcoming spirit that are the hallmark of near-death experiences. In these cases, however, Parnia argues that by any reasonable definition these are *actual* death experiences, and one needs to contend with the fact that their disembodied consciousness survived physical death.

8 Mario Beauregard, *Brain Wars* (New York: HarperColllins, 2012), 171–72.

9 "Maria's near-death experience: Waiting for the other shoe to drop," *Skeptical Inquirer* 20, no. 4 (July/August 1996).

10 For more information on the AWAreness during REsuscitation (AWARE) study, see Parnia's book, *Erasing Death.*

11 Parnia reports that there have been two near-death experiences involving claims of out-of-body experience in the study so far, but since they occurred in rooms without the picture shelves they must be considered anecdotal.

12 Although, following Sam Harris, one might still wish to reserve the moral right to challenge such religiously inspired values as advocacy for stoning and clitorectomy.

13 There also must be some attempt to be honest about the equal counting of "evidence." If allegations about "complexity" are to be counted on the positive side of the ledger, surely the existence of evil must be counted on the other.

14 The full text of Act 590 can be found in M. Ruse (ed.), *But Is It Science? The Philosophical Question in the Creation/Evolution Controversy* (Amherst, NY: Prometheus Books, 1996), 283–86.

15 This quotation is taken from Judge Overton's decision in *McLean v. Arkansas*, reprinted in full in Ruse, *But Is It Science*, 307–31. The quotation is on p. 320.

16 *Edwards v. Aguillard*, 482 U.S. 578 (1987).

17 They can, however, be proven false, which is the basis for Karl Popper's idea that science proceeds not by verification but by falsification.

18 Dawkins, *The God Delusion*, 124.

19 Ibid., 127.

20 Ibid.

21 Ibid.
22 Ibid., 128.
23 Hitchens, *god is not Great*, 281–82. Also, see Joe Palca, "Finding our inner fish," *NPR*, July 5, 2010.
24 Dawkins, *The God Delusion*, 121.
25 Church of the Flying Spaghetti Monster website, <www.venganza.org/>.
26 National Center for Science Education, "Anti-evolution and Anti-climate Science Legislation Scoreboard," <http://ncse.com/evolution/anti-evolution-anti-climate-science-legislation-scorecard-2012>.
27 This bill borrows substantially from the original Louisiana Academic Freedom Act, not only in intent but in language. It is ironic to note that this whole debate got its start in Tennessee in 1925 with the Scopes Monkey Trial, in which a public school teacher was arrested for teaching evolution.
28 Paul Harris, "Four US states considering laws that challenge teaching of evolution," January 31, 2013, <www.guardian.co.uk/world/2013/jan/31/states-laws-challenge-teaching-evolution>.
29 "Review of *Blueprints: Solving the Mystery of Evolution*," *New York Times*, April 9, 1989.
30 "Nothing in Biology Makes Sense Except in Light of Evolution," *American Biology Teacher* 35 (March 1973): 125–29.
31 For more on this see the October 15, 2012, cover story in *Time* magazine entitled "Who is telling the truth? The fact wars," in which the reporter seems obsessed with digging up exactly ten lies on each side, so that he can then declare a pox on *both* their campaigns. Those who were paying attention during the 2012 Presidential campaign, however, will remember that the enormous distortions and outright lies told by the Romney campaign were far more numerous (and arguably worse) than those told by Obama. See here "The real loser: The truth," *New York Times*, November 5, 2012, which points out that *PolitiFact* chronicled nineteen "pants on fire" lies told by Mr. Romney since 2007, compared to seven by Obama.
32 For more on the media's role in disrespecting truth by adhering to an ill-advised "objectivity" bias see Chapter 5.
33 Mooney, *The Republican War on Science* (New York: Basic Books, 2005), 81.
34 Frank Newport, "Americans' global warming concerns continue to drop," *Politics*, Gallup, December 17, 2009, <www.gallup.com/poll/126560/americans-global-warming-concerns-continue-drop.aspx>.
    Note that by 2010 the same poll question showed that the number of Americans who thought that the threat of global warming had been exaggerated had *increased* to 48 percent!
35 Mooney, *Republican War on Science*, 79.
36 "More say there is solid evidence of global warming," *PewResearch*, October 15, 2012, <www.people-press.org/2012/10/15/more-say-there-is-solid-evidence-of-global-warming>. Note the widespread confusion over whether scientists are divided, within *both* political parties.
37 Mooney, *Republican War on Science*, 84.
38 Peter T. Doran and Maggie Kendall Zimmerman, "Examining the Scientific Consensus on Climate Change," *EOS*, 90, no. 3 (January 20, 2009): 22–23, <http://tigger.uic.edu/~pdoran/012009_Doran_final.pdf>. Note that unlike Naomi Oreskes's earlier review, this survey included *all* Earth scientists listed in a database of geoscience faculty, whether they had published any work in climate science or not.
39 It is instructive to note here that until very recently, the number of people who believed in the seriousness of global warming *dropped* from a peak in 2004 until about 2009, even as scientific consensus grew. See Naomi Oreskes and Erik M. Conway, *Merchants of Doubt: How a Handful of Scientists Obscured the Truth on Issues from Tobacco Smoke to Global Warming* (New York: Bloomsbury Press, 2010), 170, but also take a

look at the Gallup poll, Newport, "Americans' global warming concerns continue to drop," <www.gallup.com/poll/126560/americans-global-warming-concerns-continue-drop.aspx>, which tracks the period from 1998 to 2010. Only recently (since about 2009) have things begun to turn: "AP-GfK Poll: Science doubters say world is warming," <http://news.yahoo.com/ap-gfk-poll-science-doubters-world-warming-080143113.html>.

Indeed, since 2009, even some Republicans have begun to come around, with half now believing: Jason Koebler, "Poll: Half of Republicans believe in global warming," *U.S.News*, October 15, 2012, <www.usnews.com/news/articles/2012/10/15/poll-half-of-republicans-believe-in-global-warming>.

For over a decade, the doubts raised by partisan ideologues *who were not experts in climate science* filtered their way into public consciousness, fulfilling the dream outlined in a 1998 memo from the American Petroleum Institute which outlined a strategy for spending millions of dollars to spin Congress, the media, and the public over to their point of view. "Victory will be achieved when recognition of uncertainties becomes part of the 'conventional wisdom.'"

40 See not only Chris Mooney's *The Republican War on Science*, but also Naomi Oreskes and Erik M. Conway's excellent *Merchants of Doubt*.

41 James Hansen, *Storms of My Grandchildren* (New York: Bloomsbury, 2009); James Hoggan and Richard Littlemore, *Climate Cover-Up: The Crusade to Deny Global Warming* (Vancouver: Greystone Books, 2009).

42 James Lawrence Powell, "Why climate deniers have no scientific credibility," *DeSmogBlog.com*, November 15, 2012, <www.desmogblog.com/2012/11/15/why-climate-deniers-have-no-credibility-science-one-pie-chart>.

43 "More say there is solid evidence of global warming."

44 Indeed, recent reporting has shown that even while ExxonMobil was spending money to obfuscate the facts about global warming it was simultaneously pursuing new opportunities for drilling in Arctic areas that had previously been inaccessible until global warming. See Steve Coll, *Private Empire: ExxonMobil and American Power* (New York: Penguin Press, 2012), and "ExxonMobil: A 'private empire' on the world stage," *NPR*, May 2, 2012, <www.npr.org/2012/05/02/151842205/exxonmobil-a-private-empire-on-the-world-stage>.

45 I do not believe it is entirely ad hominem to note here that Lindzen is also a skeptic about the link between smoking and lung cancer, since it bears on his propensity to be skeptical about well-accepted scientific truths on other topics as well. See Hansen, *Storms of My Grandchildren*, 15–16.

46 Justin Gillis, "Clouds' effect on climate change is last bastion for dissenters," *New York Times*, April 30, 2012.

47 Ibid.

48 Claude Allegre *et al.*, "No need to panic about global warming," *Wall Street Journal*, January 27, 2012, <www.wsj.com/articles/SB10001424052970204301404577171531838421366>.

49 "Toxic shock: A climate-change sceptic is melting," *Economist*, May 26, 2012, <www.economist.com/node/21555894>.

50 Oreskes and Conway, *Merchants of Doubt*, 234.

51 Mooney, *Republican War on Science*, 67.

52 Andrew Revkin, "Skeptics dispute climate worries and each other," *New York Times*, March 8, 2009, and Juliet Eilperin, "Climate skeptics seek to roll back state laws on renewable energy," *Washington Post*, November 25, 2012.

53 Justin Gillis and Leslie Kaufman, "Leak offers glimpse of campaign against climate science," *New York Times*, February 15, 2012.

54 Gillis, "Clouds' effect on climate change is last bastion for dissenters."

55 Ibid.

56 Freeman Dyson, "Heretical thoughts about science and society," *Edge.org*, August 8, 2007, <https://edge.org/conversation/heretical-thoughts-about-science-and-society>.

57 "Freeman Dyson takes on the climate establishment," interview by Michael D. Lemonick, Yale University's *environment360*, June 2, 2009, <http://e360.yale.edu/feature/free man_dyson_takes_on_the_climate_establishment/2151/>.

58 Dyson, "Heretical thoughts about science and society."

59 Seth Borenstein and Raphael Satter, "Emails suggest science not faked, but doubt lingered," *HighBeam Research*, December 12, 2009, <www.highbeam.com/doc/1P2-21014524.html>.

60 David Biello, "Negating 'Climategate,'" *Scientific American* 302 (February 2010).

61 "Alarmism over climate is of great benefit to many, providing government funding for academic research and a reason for government bureaucracies to grow. Alarmism also offers an excuse for governments to raise taxes" (Allegre *et al.*, "No need to panic about global warming").

62 Jeremy W. Peters, "Rove's on-air rebuttal of Fox's Ohio vote call raises questions about his role," *New York Times*, November 7, 2012, <www.nytimes.com/2012/11/08/us/politics/roves-on-air-rebuttal-of-foxs-ohio-vote-call-raises-questions-about-his-role.html?_r=0>.

63 Mooney, *The Republican Brain: The Science of Why They Deny Science—and Reality* (Hoboken, NJ: John Wiley & Sons, 2012), 48.

64 Ron Suskind, "Faith, certainty and the presidency of George W. Bush," *New York Times Magazine*, October 17, 2004.

65 Richard Lewontin, "The Apportionment of Human Diversity," *Evolutionary Biology* 6 (1972): 391–98.

66 Michael Specter, *Denialism: How Irrational Thinking Hinders Scientific Progress, Harms the Planet, and Threatens Our Lives* (New York: Penguin Press, 2009), 196. Note, however, that one of the men standing next to him when he said this later wrote, "Well-intentioned statements over the past few years, some coming from geneticists, might lead one to believe there is no connection whatsoever between self-identified race or ethnicity and the frequency of particular genetic variants ... [But] it is not strictly true that race or ethnicity has no biological connection"; Francis Collins, "What We Do and Don't Know about 'Race,' 'Ethnicity,' Genetics and Health at the Dawn of the Genome Era," *Nature Genetics* (suppl.) 36, no. 11 (2004): S13–S15.

67 R. C. Lewontin, "Confusions about human races," *Is Race "Real"?*, Social Science Research Council, June 7, 2006, <http://raceandgenomics.ssrc.org/Lewontin/>.

68 *Chronicle of Higher Education*, October 30, 1998, A19.

69 Ibid.

70 Joseph Graves, *The Race Myth: Why We Pretend Race Exists in America* (New York: Dutton, 2004), 5.

71 Ibid., 5.

72 Lewontin, "Confusion about human races."

73 In fact, some of the players are even the same. See Leon Kamin, R. C. Lewontin, and Steven Rose's book, *Not in Our Genes* (New York: Pantheon, 1985), in which they make the case against Pinker, Dawkins, and the entire field of evolutionary psychology in general.

74 For an excellent critique of *The Bell Curve* see Thomas Sowell, "Ethnicity and IQ," in *The Bell Curve Wars: Race, Intelligence, and the Future of America*, ed. S. Fraser, 70–79 (New York: Basic Books, 1995).

75 A common example seen these days is police bulletins that include detailed physical descriptions of a suspect, but are not allowed to make any reference to race.

76 Specter, *Denialism*, 198.

77 Neil Risch, *et al.*, "Genetic Structure, Self-Identified Race/Ethnicity and Confounding in Case-Control Association Studies," *American Journal of Human Genetics* 76, no. 2 (2005): 268–75.

78 Graves, *Race Myth*, 111.
79 Specter, *Denialism*, 195. Also, Jerry Adler "What's race got to do with it?" *Newsweek*, January 12, 2009.
80 Adler, "What's race got to do with it?"
81 It has been estimated that BiDil will prolong the lives of 750,000 African Americans.
82 Human Genome Project Information Archive [cited page no longer available], <http://web.ornl.gov/sci/techresources/Human_Genome/index.shtml>.
83 H. G. Brunner, M. Nelen, X. O. Breakefield, H. H. Ropers, and B. A. van Oost, "Abnormal Behavior Associated with a Point Mutation in the Structural Gene for Monoamine Oxidase A," *Science* 262, no. 5133 (1993): 578–80.
84 J. Alford, C. Funk, and J. Hibbing, "Are Political Orientations Genetically Transmitted?" *American Political Science Review* 99, no. 2 (2005): 153–67. See also John Jost, "The End of the End of Ideology," *American Psychologist* 61, no. 7 (2006): 651–70.
85 There are numerous studies which have found that children notice race from infancy and begin to internalize racial stereotypes as early as three years old. See D. van Ausdale and J. R. Feagin, *The First R: How Children Learn Race and Racism* (Lanham, MD: Rowman & Littlefield, 2001); see also P. A. Katz, "Racists or Tolerant Multiculturalists? How Do They Begin?" *American Psychologist* 58, no. 11 (2003): 897–909.
86 Robin Nixon, "Individuals with rare disorder have no racial biases," *LiveScience* [blog], April 12, 2010, <www.livescience.com/8189-individuals-rare-disorder-racial-biases.html>.
87 One recent study found that having a different race room-mate in college did in fact appear to change white students' attitudes. S. Gaither and S. Sommers, "Living with an Other-Race Roommate Shapes Whites' Behavior in Subsequent Diverse Settings," *Journal of Experimental Social Psychology* 49 (2013): 272–76.
88 Although the lack of racial bias has only been studied so far in children with Williams syndrome, one anticipates the results of follow-up studies that try to measure this in adults, thus shedding further light on environmental influences.
89 Though we still do not know whether they are at all in-built, or learned. For all the robustness of the IAT (Implicit Association Test) results, it cannot tell us where our biases come from.

5

SOURCES OF (MIS)INFORMATION

Why the Media Worship Objectivity but the Ivory Tower Rejects Truth

> If you tell the same story five times, it's true.
>
> Larry Speakes, Press Secretary to Ronald Reagan

As we try to make our way through the thicket of deception, spin, and misinformation that comes to us from those who disrespect truth in service of their own ideology, it is disappointing to realize that some of the biggest failures arise from those who profess fidelity to a standard of objectivity that is meant to safeguard the search for truth: the media and academics. Of course, the most blatant threat to truth comes from those who cynically exploit our desire for information and education (and play on our propensity for confirmation bias) such that they either feed us exactly what we want to hear or spin us so that we hear only what they want us to believe. Here some of the worst offenders are those organizations that mimic the media and academics as a cloak for their own ideology. Within this category we find various cable news channels, advocacy groups, think tanks, political campaigns, and industry research groups that have a vested interest in distorting the truth so that it matches their self-interested agenda. It is heartbreaking that in recent years even the real media and legitimate academics themselves have sometimes devolved to this level, so that we cannot always tell anymore when we are learning and when we are being spun. But, before we begin to examine the failures of those who at least take themselves to be educating and informing us, it is worth a look at those who are only pretending.

Lobbying for Truth

If there is one thing you can be certain of, it is that the results of a non-scientific study will miraculously match the ideology of the group that sponsored it.

Whether one is looking at "internal polling" done by political campaigns, "industry research" on the safety of a product that they themselves manufacture, or even faux-scientific studies on immigration, guns, or welfare done by advocacy groups masquerading as "think tanks," there is no more obvious mark of a biased source of information than that they already know the desired outcome before the research has even begun. But it does not have to be this way. Even when investigators have a vested interest in things coming out a certain way, if we care about truth there are several protocols that can be put in place to protect objectivity.

Look, for example, at the field of medicine. It is well known that health care is not value neutral. Obviously, the field of medicine is not indifferent in favoring the promotion of health over death and disease. Most research studies on a new drug or treatment are performed primarily for the goal of using them to treat illness, rather than merely for the sake of academic curiosity. But it is also widely recognized that the goal of promoting health would be poorly served by not allowing truth to determine what works and what doesn't. Although medicine has a normative goal, this does not mean that it must be subjective. With the institution of such safeguards as double-blind controlled experiments (where neither the researcher nor the subject knows whether he or she is getting the actual treatment or a placebo) one is safeguarding against the sort of wish-fulfillment, motivated reasoning, confirmation bias, and other irrationalities that may foul up the results of clinical trials. In some cases, of course, researchers may make a mistake or cheat, so we must insist that their data be shared, so that it can be reviewed by independent researchers and/or government agencies (such as the FDA) before it is approved for use on patients. As a final check on the baser motives that might influence medical research, journals normally require authors to make full disclosure of funding sources and other possible conflicts of interest as well. In medicine, we recognize that human oversight and weakness can get in the way of the search for truth, but this doesn't mean that we must give up objectivity. The sort of controls that scientific research uses—double-blind trials, sharing data, disclosure of funding sources and conflicts of interest, and insistence on replication of novel findings—enables us to do our best to maintain objectivity, so that we may learn the truth *despite* human bias. Even if we may hope that a drug will work or that a treatment will be effective, we do no one a favor to deny reality.

Of course, it does not always work this way, even in medicine. Despite our vigilance, there are occasional instances of outright fraud—whether motivated by ego or by greed—that may confound the scientific process, such as the example explored in the last chapter concerning the alleged link between childhood vaccines and autism. Indeed, in one study, researchers learned that even when scientists are following good protocols, the presence of external funding alone can subtly influence study design and introduce bias.[1] One applauds the scrutiny that comes from such publicity and trusts that over time these sorts of errors may diminish as further researchers shine a light on them. Yet it is also possible for entire groups of researchers sometimes to be duped by self-deception or wishful thinking.

The best instance of the latter comes to us not from medicine, but from aerospace, where the world witnessed one of NASA's most sophisticated pieces of engineering blow up just after take-off in the *Challenger* space shuttle disaster of 1986. What caused this? A government panel of experts determined the proximate cause to be a defect in the rubber O-rings that were used on the shuttle, which could fail at cold temperatures. Surprisingly, this weakness had been known by various NASA engineers and contractors as far back as 1977, but the potential safety risk for the shuttle was downplayed for years, most tragically on the morning of *Challenger*'s fateful launch, when unseasonably cold temperatures in Florida caused a key manufacturer to recommend against launch, only to change its recommendation after being bullied by NASA managers.

The likely role of the rubber O-ring was identified and dramatically demonstrated by the world-famous physicist Richard Feynman, who dunked a sample O-ring into a pitcher of ice water at a televised hearing, to show how it would deform at cold temperatures. It was also Feynman, many felt, who later identified the *real* cause of the *Challenger* disaster, which was a breakdown in communication between NASA contractors and managers, the presence of a culture of group-think at NASA, and an overly ambitious launch schedule. Despite housing some of the best scientific minds in the country, Feynman argued that NASA's decision about the shuttle's launch schedule was dictated more by politics than by science. As Feynman put it "for a successful technology, reality must take precedence over public relations, for nature cannot be fooled."

Although this sort of failure is potentially catastrophic when it occurs, it is also rare. And, although it may not work quickly enough to prevent every tragedy, it is reassuring that science has a built-in mechanism of criticism and revision that is intended to root out this kind of error before it becomes systemic, thus preserving the notion of objectivity as the best means of discovering truth. Contrast this, however, with the sort of outright deception that is customary in partisan polling, industry research, and policy recommendations produced by advocacy think tanks, where the overriding interest is in getting us to vote a certain way, buy a certain product, or believe that something is true (even when it isn't). Here one wonders whether the entire point *is* for reality to take a back seat to public relations. For example, the reader may once again turn to the path-breaking work of Naomi Oreskes and Erik M. Conway, who have unmasked the corruption of tobacco industry research on the dangers of smoking, along with numerous other examples of the corporate manipulation of science, in their book *Merchants of Doubt*. For discussion of the problems with partisan polling, one might turn to Nate Silver's *The Signal and the Noise*, which highlights the dangers of self-deception and the virtues of "reality-based" polling. And, for a more thorough examination of the problem with ideologically influenced social research done at partisan think tanks, one might see my own *Dark Ages: The Case for a Science of Human Behavior*.[2] Need we do more here than stipulate that there are liars aplenty, who seek to manipulate public opinion for their own benefit, rather than tell the truth? But that is only part of the problem—and not even the most important part—for what to say about those institutions such as universities and the mainstream media that *do* take themselves to be guardians of the truth, but have grown increasingly complicit over the years, instead, in disrespecting it?

Media Bias

The problem of media bias is often mentioned within the context of left- and right-wing ideologies that are allegedly held by reporters and publishers, but that is hardly exhaustive of the subject, nor even perhaps the main threat to respecting truth. Of course, *any* journalistic bias should dismay us. We may expect bias from industry or politics, but many still subscribe to the old-fashioned view that the media should be bound by strict standards of objectivity, multiple sourcing, disclosure of conflicts of interest, and other safeguards that may help them to discover the truth. Of course, it is naive to suppose that all journalists these days even strive to live up to this standard, for today we have unabashedly partisan news sources that make no bones about defending their point of view. But it is nonetheless important to point out that even before the recent explosion of partisan cable TV and radio in the last few decades, there were rumors of media bias over the years at the "big three" television news organizations and the "prestige press" newspapers, normally involving the way that a story was reported or complaints about how many liberals worked for those news organizations. Of course, some would claim that these historical complaints were just a function of journalists digging up truths that conservatives would rather ignore. (As Steven Colbert once quipped, "reality has a well known liberal bias.") But claims of journalistic bias have never been as bad—or probably as warranted—as they have in recent years.

Today we have a 24-hour news cycle and the rise of media that are meant to exploit their own niche in this market. We have Fox News on the right and MSNBC on the left, along with a smattering of partisan radio talk-show hosts such as Rush Limbaugh, who make no apology for engaging in overt advocacy for their ideological views. Of course, few would admit to outright bias; perhaps they even think they are telling the truth. Still, there is little pretense that these cable "news" or radio shows are doing anything other than presenting the news of the day from their own partisan point of view and—despite the Fox News slogan of "fair and balanced" coverage—few can say this without an ironic smirk.

Ted Koppel, perhaps the staunchest of the "old media" supporters, has put it this way:

> Beginning, perhaps, from the reasonable perspective that absolute objectivity is unattainable, Fox News and MSNBC no longer even attempt it. They show us the world not as it is, but as partisans (and loyal viewers) at either end of the political spectrum would like it to be. This is to journalism

what Bernie Madoff was to investment: He told his customers what they wanted to hear, and by the time they learned the truth, their money was gone.[3]

But there is another kind of media bias, that is perhaps even more damaging to the idea that journalism is meant to safeguard truth, that has infected the mainstream "non-partisan" media in recent years, which I will call "objectivity bias." Perhaps due to the rise of so many hyper-partisan media outlets these days, many in the mainstream media are sensitive to criticism that they too are biased. At all costs, they do not want to be considered just another MSNBC or Fox News. This has led to an overreaction of "faux-objectivity," where the non-partisan news outlets profess (really) to be fair and balanced, and try to demonstrate this by relentlessly presenting both sides of any "controversial" issue.[4] They pursue "balance" by presenting two sides to every issue (even when there really aren't two credible sides) and "fairness" by refusing to adjudicate between them, suggesting that the truth may be "somewhere in between."[5] But this isn't objectivity. True objectivity in journalism should be the same as it is in science: where one refuses to allow prejudice or bias—either your own or others'—to interfere with the discovery of truth. Journalism is about truth, not arbitration.

The issue of how best to pursue objectivity is a topic of current debate in journalism, and it is beginning to be recognized by some that it can be quite tricky:

> our pursuit of objectivity can screw us up on the way to 'truth.' Objectivity excuses lazy reporting. If you're on deadline and all you have is 'both sides of the story,' that's often good enough. It's not that such stories laying out the parameters of a debate have no value for our readers, but too often, in our obsession with ... "the latest," we fail to push the story, incrementally, toward a deeper understanding of what is true and what is false.[6]

We already got a taste of this in Chapter 4 of this book, where we saw that some media stories in the 2012 Presidential campaign seemed obsessed with counting an equal number of "lies" told by both the Obama and Romney political campaigns, despite objective evidence that Romney had been much more deceptive.[7] Such "balance" must seem tempting to journalists who are afraid of being accused of political bias, for it enables them to say "a pox on both your houses" and never get to the bottom of the real story about which campaign was more deeply engaged in prevarication. But the lies in the 2012 political campaign *weren't* equal, even if "faux-objective" journalists wanted to pretend so. Drawing a false equivalency doesn't show objectivity.

A better example of the problem with objectivity bias can be seen in the last few years of news coverage on the issue of global warming. As we saw in Chapter 4, there is a deeply entrenched, well-organized, and well-funded lobby against the truth about global warming. Part of their strategy is to try to bully media outlets into presenting "both sides" of the issue. In this, one recognizes a similarity with the "teach the controversy" strategy that intelligent design theorists exploit against evolution. But, as with critics of the scientific evidence for evolution, we should recognize that it is dishonest to insist that news organizations give equal time to critics of the scientific evidence for global warming, because there is virtually no scientific dissent on the subject. The format is a familiar one on television. The host presents an eminent climate scientist on one side of a split screen and a "skeptic" (who may or may not have any scientific credentials) on the other, and gives them equal time to "make their case." The skeptic is allowed to get away with saying that some of the scientific evidence is "unproven" and the scientist is normally asked to respond to the most ludicrous claims of conspiracy and malfeasance leveled by the skeptic. After they've each had a turn to speak, the host normally pronounces the issue "controversial," then turns to the audience as if to say "you decide."

Naturally, the leading critic of this practice, Arianna Huffington, has herself been dogged by claims of partisanship for taking a stand on the truth of global warming. She writes:

> In the pursuit of "balance," many in the media have forgotten that the highest calling of journalists is to ferret out the truth. Instead, far too many reporters, like Pontius Pilate, wash their hands of finding the truth and consider presenting two sides of the climate change story proof of their "objectivity." [But] not every story has two sides, and the truth is, in fact, often found solidly on one side or the other. The earth is not flat. Evolution is a fact. Global warming is real.[8]

The consequence of this "balanced" practice is confusion by the public over whether the scientific issue has actually been settled. For if the media refuses to call a charlatan a charlatan, perhaps there really might be something to the skeptics' case? We have already seen the fallout from irresponsible journalism on the vaccines and autism debate, where the media pushed the "controversy" long past the point where the original research had been discredited. And the impact was real. How many families saw their children suffer from preventable diseases because they were confused by media stories over the risks of vaccination? And we risk the same thing now—on a much larger scale—with global warming.

There has actually been some scientific work on the question of how the quest for journalistic "balance" can lead to biased (inaccurate) coverage on the issue of global warming by the "prestige press" in America. ("Bias" here is used not in the ideological sense, but instead to mean "information bias," where press coverage diverges from the general scientific consensus; "prestige press" is defined in the study as *The New York Times*, *The Washington Post*, *The Los Angeles Times*, and *The Wall Street Journal*).[9] In one study it was found that:

[I]n the majority (52.6%) of coverage in the US prestige press, balanced accounts prevailed; these accounts gave "roughly equal attention" to the view that humans were contributing to global warming, and the other view that exclusively natural fluctuations could explain the earth's temperature increase. ... This bias, hidden behind the veil of journalistic balance, creates both discursive and real political space for the US government to shirk responsibility and delay action regarding global warming.[10]

One first-hand account of this sort of bias in action was experienced by James Hansen, whom we discussed earlier as the former director of NASA's Goddard Institute for Space Studies, who writes:

I used to spread the blame uniformly until, when I was about to appear on public television, the producer informed me that the program "must" also include a "contrarian" who would take issue with claims of global warming. Presenting such a view, he told me, was a common practice in commercial television as well as radio and newspapers. Supporters of public TV or advertisers, with their own special interests, require "balance" as a price for their continued financial support. Gore's book reveals that while more than half of the recent newspaper articles on climate change have given equal weight to such contrarian views, virtually none of the scientific articles in peer-reviewed journals have questioned the consensus that emissions from human activities cause global warming. As a result, even when the scientific evidence is clear, technical nitpicking by contrarians leaves the public with the false impression that there is still great scientific uncertainty about the reality and causes of climate change.[11]

The upshot of all this is that a good deal of the mainstream media—and not just partisan media—has abdicated its responsibility to tell the truth. Objectivity is an important ideal and it should be respected and protected (because it can lead us to truth), but the false worship of objectivity *for its own sake*—as if it could some-how only be served by refusing to intervene even when a lie is afoot—is a danger to the truth-telling mission of journalism. Objectivity counsels a commitment to the facts, not empty impartiality. But when it comes to science, the media often gets this wrong and the public is misled.

Naomi Oreskes and Erik M. Conway write:

[N]ot every "side" is right or true; opinions sometimes express ill-informed beliefs, not reliable knowledge. ... Some sides represent deliberate disin-formation spread by well-organized and well-funded vested interests, or ideologically driven denial of the facts. Even honest people may be confused or mistaken about an issue. When every voice is given equal time—and equal weight—the result does not necessarily serve us well.[12]

In a heartbreaking passage, Oreskes and Conway go on to trace the tragic consequences of this for the issue of global warming:

> Until recently the mass media presented global warming as a raging debate—twelve years after President George H.W. Bush had signed the U.N. Framework Convention on Climate Change, and *twenty-five years* after the U.S. National Academy of Sciences first announced that there was no reason to doubt that global warming would occur from man's use of fossil fuels. "Balance" had become a form of bias, whereby the media coverage was biased in favor of minority—in some cases extreme minority—views. In principle, the media could act as gatekeepers, ignoring the charlatans and snake oil salesmen, but if they have tried, our story shows that at least where it comes to science they have failed. As we have seen, it wasn't just obviously right-wing outlets that reported false claims about tobacco and … other subjects; it was the "prestige press"—indeed, the allegedly liberal press—as well.[13]

Add in the problem of human susceptibility to some of the cognitive irrationalities that we explored in Chapter 3, and it amounts to almost a "perfect storm" (pardon the pun) against the truth on global warming. Remember:

- Confirmation bias: where we are more likely to seek out and remember evidence that supports our views.
- Motivated reasoning: where we are motivated to defend our views rather than look for reasons why they might be wrong.
- The reiteration effect: where an often repeated message is more likely to be believed (even if it is untrue).
- Source amnesia: where we remember the information, but forget where we heard it or whether the source was credible.
- The backfire effect: where exposure to contrary information does not necessarily convince hardcore partisans to change their views, but can instead harden them.

With the easy availability of blatantly *non-objective* partisan media—and the cowardice of the nominally objective non-partisan mainstream media to defend the truths of science—is it any wonder that such a large percentage of the American public feels justified in their erroneous belief that there is a scientific controversy over global warming? When those who are supposedly objective seem so tentative, and those who tell us exactly what we want to hear seem so certain, we quickly approach the point of de facto manipulation of the American public by the entire media: partisan and mainstream. In such an environment, one could almost make out a case of professional malpractice against those who profess to safeguard the truth. The blame, of course, lies primarily with media outlets like Fox News that lie to their viewers on the subject of global warming. But hasn't the mainstream media at least been a willing accomplice?

The problem with all of this media mayhem is that it creates an environment in which liars prosper: where an American president can start a war over an outright lie which, even after it is exposed, is still believed by many. In a world in which one can do that, lying about global warming is comparatively easy. The mainstream media, if it wishes to fulfill its foremost obligation to discover and tell the truth, must at the very least be prepared to challenge those who lie or pretend to care about the truth when they don't. Digging up the truth may be hard, but asking critical questions of those whom we know to be spinning or lying should be the minimum responsibility of credible journalism. It should go without saying that failure to do so is highly disrespectful of truth. For in order to tell the truth, one must first have the courage to defend it.

The Ivory Tower

It is now time to look at another institution that has offered itself as a guardian of truth: the university. Of course, universities are pretty diverse places and are normally broken into separate faculties for natural science, social science, and the humanities, which are customarily further divided into separate departments. Among these, there are probably as many views about truth as there are professors. Yet it is interesting to note that there are some trends and clusters of opinion on the subject.

As I have argued throughout this book, natural science on the whole does a pretty good job of respecting truth. The values of the disciplines of physics, chemistry, and biology tend to favor questioning one another's theories *not* because one feels that truth is unreachable, but because one believes that truth is out there, but the theory at hand just has not reached it yet. Various procedures and protocols are therefore put in place—such as peer review and the replication of experiments—to keep us from fooling ourselves about whether we have found truth. And some social scientists (and even the occasional humanist) have followed suit.[14]

But there are others within the academy who question the very notion of truth itself and, through their academic work, have done everything they can to undermine it.[15] Here the idea put forth is that all knowledge—even scientific knowledge—is a social construction of reality and not based on any sort of real facts or evidence, precisely because facts and evidence themselves are social creations. If this sounds odd, it is because it is. The best way of putting it, I think, is to understand this claim as contending that there is no objective "God's-eye" viewpoint from which one can determine the brute facts about reality. So what we call "the truth" is merely a fiction created by human beings who mistake their own limited perspective for an objective one. But another angle here is political, which is the claim that knowledge is power and that any claims about "expertise" are fundamentally authoritarian, leaving scientific pronouncements about "truth" to sound vaguely fascist.

Here we have veered deeply into "relativism" and "postmodernism," which are very difficult terms to define, let alone understand. "Relativism" is normally understood (at least by philosophers) to be a claim that there is no such thing as absolute truth: that any truth is relative to one's point of view. This idea is originally attributed to the ancient Greek philosopher Protagoras, who famously said that "man is the measure of all things." Close behind is the cluster of ideas known as "postmodernism," which grew out of literary critics' and artists' reaction to "modernism" in the late nineteenth century. The epistemologist Michael Lynch tells us that postmodernism is "impossible to define" and that part of the popularity of the term is that it is obscure.[16] He goes on to say that the best way of understanding it is as a claim about the importance of "context" in framing human knowledge, but others have interpreted it more radically as a claim not just about the impossibility of objective knowledge, but a denial of independent reality itself. Thus there is no truth, because there is no objective fact or reality to which it could correspond. Why then would anyone insist that they know the truth? In order to assert their power.

This latter formulation—especially the insistence on the political problems of "expertise" and "authority"—have been used by some scholars on the left to criticize that most stalwart defender of truth: science. Bruno Latour and others embarked on the "social study of science" in order to show how scientific knowledge—like all knowledge—was a mere "social construction" created by the people who *did* science rather than by reality itself. As such, they contend, it said more about the power relationships of scientists than it did about the reality that they allegedly investigated. Feminist critics of science, such as Sandra Harding, took this argument one step further and made the claim that science was sexist, in that, as Ophelia Benson and Jeremy Stangroom explain it: "to be scientific is to be dispassionate, impartial, disinterested, whereas to be a woman is to be emotional and interested in the wellbeing of friends and family."[17] To insist that the secrets of nature would yield to the assault of scientific method was just too much for Harding. At one point, she claimed in print that Isacc Newton's classic *Principia Mathematica* was a "rape manual."

We arrive here at the door of what is politely referred to as the "Science Wars," where an assortment of sociologists, historians, philosophers, and cultural and literary critics unleashed a barrage of invective against the natural sciences, meant to show not only that they were wrong to believe in truth but also that they were fascists. Apparently convinced that this attack would somehow defend the interests of minorities, women, and the poor, all of science was dismissed by these theorists as an apology for conservative values. Of course, the natural scientists (abetted by empiricist philosophers and historians of science) fought back, at least in part by suggesting that their critics were obscure, incoherent, and sometimes even "unzipped." This reached fruition when a group of prominent scientists and science scholars produced two volumes that made a case for the objectivity and value of science.[18] Mostly, however, scientists ignored them.

Should we? Here I think it is important to point out that it is not necessarily disrespectful of truth to question whether truth exists or to suggest that we are somehow barred from knowing it. Merely raising questions and pursuing lines of inquiry is what the university is all about. One might even say that criticism is one way of showing respect. And, as we've already seen in this book, science is not perfect and it can sometimes lead to problems of bias and even outright fraud (and surely sometimes also discrimination and oppression), even when scientific protocols are in place. It is important to examine science and keep its practices honest.

But one should face squarely here the concern that while *some* of the relativist and postmodernist criticisms of science *might* have some merit, we are at least owed a coherent argument to assess whether they are true. Accusations are one thing; proof is another. But there's the rub. How can one hope to engage in rational argument over the truth of the "social construction of knowledge" claim against science when it is a fundamental truism of relativism and postmodernism that there is no such thing as truth? While this observation might seem to leave science fighting a ghost, I think that in fact it is much more embarrassing for the other side, which is put in the position of figuring out how to convince someone who does not already agree with their ideology that they should be taken seriously. Much like those who use intelligent design to attack evolution by natural selection, the burden of proof ought to be on those who would *attack* science, not those who defend it. Extraordinary claims require extraordinary evidence, remember? Without this, one is left to conclude that the relativist and postmodernist criticisms of science are based on *terrible arguments* and that anyone who doesn't already buy into their politics will not buy their criticisms either. This level of weakness probably *does* at some level show disrespect for truth (or, if you prefer, at least some level of professional incompetence), in that it is normally the mark of a weak theory that one must be an advocate in order to understand it.

But there are also some devastating criticisms of the theory itself.

First, there is the irony just noted that one of the first things relativists do is try to convince you that it is *true* that there is no such thing as truth! What can they do if you reply "well that's true for you, not for me."

Second, in order to be taken seriously, social construction theory's criticism of science must address the issue of the success of science. If there is no such thing as truth, then why has science and technology been as successful as it has? If knowledge is just a social creation, why do we have antibiotics and space flight? If facts are so unknowable, why do we use road maps and airplanes?

Third, it feels deliciously appropriate to question whether relativism and postmodernism are themselves just a hoax. In 1996, Alan Sokal, a physics professor at NYU, submitted an article entitled "Transgressing the Boundaries: Towards a Transformative Hermeneutics of Quantum Gravity" to the journal *Social Text*, an academic journal of postmodern cultural studies. Without submitting it for peer review by another physicist (for if facts are relative why bother to consult with "experts"), the piece was soon published in an issue devoted, ironically enough, to the "Science Wars." But this was no ordinary article, for the whole thing was cooked up as a sham by Sokal himself, who was inspired after reading Gross and Levitt's *Higher Superstition*, to see how far he could push things. By his own admission, his article was "a pastiche of Left-wing cant, fawning references, grandiose quotations, and outright nonsense ... structured around the silliest quotations [by postmodernists] ... about mathematics and physics."[19] After a little Bohr and a bit of Heisenberg, he was suddenly questioning the existence of physical reality and making all sorts of "questionable-to-insane propositions about the nature of the physical world."[20] When his "gotcha" essay appeared soon after, the lion's share of observers concluded that postmodernism had now been revealed for what it was: a melange of poseurs and know-nothings who, "really didn't know squat about science and [were] devoted to the project of making shit up and festooning it with flattering citations to one another's work."[21]

Of course, none of my observations so far rise to the level of refuting relativism or postmodernism, or even of meeting argument with argument. There are numerous other books out there that do a masterful job of demonstrating the follies of the politicization of truth that has occurred at the hands of relativism and postmodernism. In chapter 3 of his book *True to Life: Why Truth Matters* (MIT Press, 2004), Michael Lynch does a tremendous job of discombobulating relativism and postmodernism point by point. In their book *Why Truth Matters*, Ophelia Benson and Jeremy Stangroom do a similarly laudable job of showing the weaknesses of these arguments. I take both of these books to offer a definitive rendering of the intellectual bankruptcy and dangers of relativism and postmodernism, and the notion of the social construction of truth that was fashioned out of them. What I offer here instead is my contention that these ideas have been used to damage the very political goals that their defenders profess to uphold. If the whole point of politicizing truth was to seek liberation and break up the hierarchy, then it is at least ironic that in undermining the foundations for truth—in science, in respect for objectivity, in deference to the idea that facts should matter to public policy—these critics of science have ended up hurting the "little people" most, whom the "truth radicals" were trying to defend in the first place.

Of course, it is reasonable to ask how this could possibly be the case. Given the weakness of the social critics' arguments, one wonders who would take them seriously and how much of a threat they could possibly pose to the idea of truth. But while these theories were widely reviled outside the academy, and often even by many academics within it, they also proved to be incredibly influential when it came time for conservative critics of science to seek intellectual cover for their attacks on evolution and global warming. By questioning the objectivity of science and its ability to discover the truth—insisting that science was "just another ideology" and that scientists were doing their work only to sustain their own partisan interests—the cultural critics of science on the left handed a valuable gift to the evangelical right-wing critics of science, who wished to question truths that they did not like.

This is certainly a case of strange bedfellows, for it puts the mostly liberal academics in the humanities who promoted relativism and postmodernism in bed with the conservatives who wanted to deny the truth of evolution and global warming. Remember "doubt is our product"? The literary critics gave them a fig leaf of doubt. Relativism about truth is sometimes now used by conservatives to question whether scientists can ever be certain, and use this to suggest that—in the absence of proof—all we have is ideology, and one might be just as true as another. Thus have liberal academics unwittingly given aid and comfort to a conservative agenda that they probably despise.

This does not necessarily make their views wrong, but it does suggest that promoting fashionable academic notions, even though the arguments for them are weak, is playing with fire and can cause real damage. We sorely need some social responsibility here; journalists are not the only guardians who can be accused of disrespecting truth. If one is just playing around with language, at least understand that your ideas will be taken seriously by someone who may use them to destroy something that you care about. And in fact this is precisely what happened in the field of the "social construction of knowledge" in the humanities, when the conservatives used relativism and postmodernism to attack the scientific evidence for global warming.

In recent years there has been some soul searching and regret *even by some of those who launched the "Science Wars"* as they recoil in horror to see how their ideas have been used by conservatives.[22]

Literary critic and humanist Michael Berube writes:

> But now the climate-change deniers and the young-Earth creationists are coming after the natural scientists. ... and they're using some of the very arguments developed by an academic left that thought it was speaking only to people of like mind. Some standard left arguments, combined with the left-populist distrust of "experts" and "professionals" ... who think they're the boss of us, were fashioned by the right into a powerful device for delegitimating scientific research.[23]

Indeed some of this "fashioning" has proceeded *with the direct assistance* of the social critics of science, such as philosopher Steve Fuller, who testified in the *Kitzmiller v. Dover Area School District* decision over whether intelligent design should be taught in science classrooms, *on the side of the intelligent design theorists!* Compare this to the judge in this case, who—in the eyes of one commentator—showed great respect for science:

> One of the great gestures of respect for one's fellow Americans is to tell them the truth. To do otherwise is the height of disrespect. In Kitzmiller

et al. v. Dover Area School District, Judge John E. Jones III demonstrated his respect for his fellow Americans and the Constitution by being receptive to the truth of the plaintiffs presented to him and then making that truth the foundation of his written opinion.[24]

The idea of giving aid and comfort to the enemy apparently has caused Berube to have second thoughts. As it turns out, his primary allegiance seems not to have been to postmodernism or relativism at all, but to the liberal politics that he and others thought that these notions were advancing. Near the end of his piece, he is in a mood to bargain:

> I'll admit that you were right about the potential for science studies to go horribly wrong and give fuel to deeply ignorant and/or reactionary people. And in return, you'll admit that I was right ... that the natural sciences would not be held harmless from the right-wing noise machine. And if you'll go further, and acknowledge that some circumspect, well-informed critiques of actually existing science have merit ... [I will] acknowledge that many humanists' critiques of science and reason are neither circumspect nor well-informed.[25]

An even more surprising recantation (though he almost certainly would not call it that) was written by none other than Bruno Latour, who was himself one of the *founders* of science studies and the theory of the social construction of knowledge.[26] Early in his piece, Latour identifies the sort of problem that troubles him, when he notes a 2003 editorial in the *New York Times* that emphasizes the strategic role that "lack of scientific certainty" can take in the Republican case against the truth of global warming. This worries him into a full-fledged identity crisis over the role he might have played in this:

> Do you see why I am worried? I myself have spent some time in the past trying to show *"the lack of scientific certainty"* inherent in the construction of facts. ... But I did not exactly aim at fooling the public by obscuring the certainty of a closed argument—or did I? After all, I have been accused of just that sin. Still, I'd like to believe that, on the contrary, I intended to *emancipate* the public from prematurely naturalized objectified facts. Was I foolishly mistaken? Have things changed so fast?[27]

Apparently it is all right to undermine scientific certainty, so long as it serves the purposes only of the political left.

Latour goes on to lament that:

> [E]ntire PhD programs are still running to make sure that good American kids are learning the hard way that facts are made up, that there is no such

thing as natural, unmediated, unbiased access to truth, that we are always prisoners of language, that we always speak from a particular standpoint, and so on, while dangerous extremists are using the very same argument of social construction to destroy hard-won evidence that could save lives. Was I wrong to participate in the invention of this field known as science studies? Is it enough to say that we did not really mean what we said? Why does it burn my tongue to say that global warming is a fact whether you like it or not? Why can't I simply say that the argument is closed for good?[28]

Indeed, Latour is troubled to find the fingerprints of social critique in *many* of the right's wildest conspiracy theories:

> Maybe I am taking conspiracy theories too seriously, but it worries me to detect, in those mad mixtures of knee-jerk disbelief, punctilious demands for proofs, and free use of powerful explanation from the social neverland, many of the weapons of social critique.[29]

At the denouement, however, Latour refuses to recant completely, saying " ... in spite of my tone, I am not trying to reverse course, to become reactionary, to regret what I have done, to swear that I will never be a constructivist any more."[30] He tells us that he merely wants to "retest the linkages" of his views and submit them to newly informed critical scrutiny. Near the end of his piece, however, Latour does ask for some sort of forgiveness and credit at least for having good intentions:

> My argument is that a certain form of critical spirit has sent us down the wrong path, encouraging us to fight the wrong enemies and, worst of all, to be considered as friends by the wrong sort of allies because of a little mistake in the definition of its main target. The question was never to get *away* from facts but *closer* to them, not fighting empiricism but, on the contrary, renewing empiricism.[31]

Yet many would feel it is too late for that. The damage has been done and he knew darned well what the target was. He never intended to defend empiricism. What we witness here is not the genuine remorse of someone who has spent most of his career undermining the best tools that we have for discovering truth, but the feeble bargaining of a thoughtless bully who has gone too far and now wants us to believe that he never intended to hurt anyone.

Whether it is journalists who betray the truth for ideology (or for fear of being *accused* of being ideological) or those academics who want to play with ideas as if they had no real-world consequences, I believe that there is such a thing as professional malpractice against the concept of truth. Indeed it is curious to note here a confluence in outcome between those who—like the mainstream media—*embrace* objectivity (but betray it by pretending that there are two sides to every issue or that we can't tell what is true), and those who *reject* objectivity—like the relativists (who deny absolute truth all together). In some ways, it doesn't matter whether there *is* no truth or we have just given up on finding it. The result is the same. In the absence of agreed upon standards and methods of inquiry, truth becomes a matter of opinion instead of discovery. Argument instead of fact. Why *not* believe that cigarettes don't cause cancer? That evolution is false? That the Earth is not warming?

A good deal of social science has unfortunately picked up on this line of argument and, instead of emulating the standards of good science from natural science and medicine, has questioned whether a science of human behavior is even possible.[32] Some, worried about the potential consequences that scientific notions of causation might have for the notion of free will, have chosen to emphasize the uniqueness of human affairs, and embraced a spurious set of arguments which purport to show that complexity and subjectivity must condemn the social sciences to a series of stories, anecdotes, and case studies. Others have chosen to emphasize the importance of political values in social scientific work and have embraced a set of shoddy standards that provide only a veneer of scientific respectability. Here one finds the common methodological sins of cherry-picking data, refusing to make precise predictions, not offering data for other investigators to test, and a host of other offenses against good scientific protocol.

Conclusion

The upshot of all this is that a shockingly high percentage of the media and academics disrespect truth by refusing to stand up for it. In both cases, we find institutions of public trust who take themselves to be safeguards of truth, but fall down on the job. As if the lies of the political ideologues were not obvious and had no detrimental effect on public welfare. As if natural scientific methods were not obviously responsible for the bounty of technology that we enjoy in the modern era.

Yet the truth is that there *is* a way to find truth, and that way is through science and reason. I do not claim that one disrespects truth merely by criticizing science. There is a role for philosophers and sociologists of science to play in keeping scientists honest. But if one is committed to the idea of truth, then the critic of science must offer more than the high rhetoric of literary theory to explain how it is that science has had the success it has, if it is not actually discovering truth.

It is regrettable that we as individuals suffer from cognitive irrationalities that prevent us from finding or recognizing the truth. It is deplorable that so many ideologues choose to exploit this weakness by lying about the truth in their own self-interest. Yet it is almost *criminal* that so many in the media and academics—who are in a position to see what is going on and to stop it—have done so little to counter those weaknesses and lies by standing up for truth. It is one thing to overlook the truth. It is worse to obfuscate it. But almost as bad is to remain complicit when those methods that lead to truth are being attacked. Science may not be perfect, but it is arguably the best method that we have for the discovery of truth.

Notes

1 Paul Ridker and Jose Torres, "Reported Outcomes in Major Cardiovascular Clinical Trials Funded by For-Profit and Not-for-Profit Organizations: 2000–2005," *Journal of the American Medical Association* 295, no. 19 (2006): 2270–74.

2 *Dark Ages: The Case for a Science of Human Behavior* (Cambridge: MIT Press, 2006). For a discussion of the debate over whether immigrants "pay their own way" in the American economy, see pp. 22–24.

3 Ted Koppel, "Olbermann, O'Reilly and the death of real news," *Washington Post*, November 4, 2010.

4 For one recent example see Joe Romm, "CNN still gives equal time to anti-science disinformation," *Climate Progress*, December 6, 2012, <www.thinkprogress.org/cli mate/2012/12/05/1288011/cnn-still-gives-equal-time-to-anti-science-disinformation/ mobile=nc>.

5 Some have called the latter "moderation bias." See James Poniewozik, "Moderation in excess," *Time*, November 16, 2009.

6 Brent Cunningham, "Re-thinking Objectivity," *Columbia Journalism Review*, no. 4 (July/August, 2003).

7 See note 31, p. 91.

8 Arianna Huffington, "Flat Earth thinkers complicate fight for environment," *Sun-Sentinel.com*, November 22, 2011, <http://articles.sun-sentinel.com/2011-11-22/ news/fl-ahcol-flat-earth-huffington-1122-20111122_1_nrdc-global-warming-huffpost>.

9 M. Boykoff and J. Boykoff, "Balance as Bias: Global Warming and the US Prestige Press," *Global Environmental Change* 14 (2004): 125–36.

10 Ibid.

11 "The threat to the planet," *New York Review of Books* 53, no. 12 (July 13, 2006). See also his earlier-cited book *Storms of My Grandchildren* (New York: Bloomsbury, 2009).

12 Naomi Oreskes and Erik M. Conway, *Merchants of Doubt: How a Handful of Scientists Obscured the Truth on Issues from Tobacco Smoke to Global Warming* (New York: Bloomsbury Press, 2010), 240.

13 Ibid., 242–43.

14 There are of course disciplinary factions, but on the whole economists, quantitative political scientists, and experimental psychologists tend to think of themselves as the most "scientific" of the social sciences, with sociology and anthropology the customary outcasts to "qualitative" methods.

15 Here one finds the bulk of the work being done by faculty in the literary criticism and continental philosophy wing of the humanities.

16 Michael Lynch, *True to Life: Why Truth Matters* (Cambridge: MIT Press, 2004), 35.

17 Ophelia Benson and Jeremy Stangroom, *Why Truth Matters* (London: Continuum, 2006), 51.

18 Paul Gross and Norman Levitt, *Higher Superstition: The Academic Left and Its Quarrels with Science* (Baltimore: Johns Hopkins University Press, 1994) and Paul Gross, Norman Levitt, and Martin Lewis, eds., *The Flight from Science and Reason* (New York: New York Academy of Sciences, 1996).

19 Alan Sokal, "A physicist experiments with cultural studies," *Lingua Franca* 4 (May 1996).

20 Michael Berube, "The science wars redux," *Democracy* 19 (Winter, 2011), <www. democracyjournal.org/19/6789.php?page=all>.

21 Ibid.
22 Judith Warner, "Fact free science," *New York Times Magazine*, February 25, 2011.
23 Berube, "Science wars redux."
24 Barbara Forrest quoted from Benson and Stangroom, *Why Truth Matters*, x.
25 Berube, "Science wars redux."
26 Bruno Latour, "Why Has Critique Run Out of Steam? From Matters of Fact to Matters of Concern," *Critical Inquiry* 30 (Winter 2004): 225–48.
27 Ibid., 227.
28 Ibid.
29 Ibid., 230.
30 Ibid., 231.
31 Ibid.
32 For a good example of this see Bent Flyvbjerg, *Making Social Science Matter: Why Social Inquiry Fails and How It Can Succeed Again* (Cambridge: Cambridge University Press, 2001).

6

SOURCES OF HOPE

The Wisdom of Crowds, Group Benefits, and Why *Wikipedia* is More Reliable than You Think

> The sordid and savage story of history has been written by man's irrationality, and the thin precarious crust of civilization which has from time to time been built over the bloody mess has always been built on reason.
>
> Leonard Woolf

When we look out over the landscape of deceit, lies, spin, bullshit, ignorance, and indifference that sometimes defines the human relationship with truth, it is easy to give up hope. After all these centuries, why aren't we better at using reason? Haven't we been fighting roughly the same battle against ideology and ignorance (though cloaked in different forms) since the Enlightenment?[1]

But I believe that there are also sources of great hope on the horizon. These can be seen not just by reflecting on the achievements that respect for reason has produced in finding truth over the centuries—particle physics, a moon landing or two, modern medicine—but also in the promise that reason holds for the future (seen today in venues that it is easy to take for granted when we are focused on the latest outrage in politics or some depressing statistic about human ignorance headlined by the media). Some of these sources of hope are old (science and logic) and some of them are new (the benefits of crowd sourcing and the resistance to censorship that is enabled by widespread access to social media). But all are important to the future progress of reason and give us hope that we have tools—both old and new—that can help us to fight against the conscious and unconscious biases and mistakes that can undermine even the most solid commitment to respecting truth.

The Best Disinfectant

In his book *Infotopia: How Many Minds Produce Knowledge,*[2] Cass Sunstein explores some fascinating research which purports to show that, under certain circumstances, group reasoning is more likely to lead to truth than individual reasoning. But how could this be? As we have seen, groups introduce the possibility for correction of individual errors, but they can also introduce potential problems too, such as "group think" (where individual opinions are unduly influenced by others) or spin doctors and charlatans (who are purposely trying to lead everyone else astray). And, if there are errors in individual reasoning (as we discussed in Chapter 2), why wouldn't these just be amplified in a group setting?

But the remarkable thing is that even though all of these problems can potentially happen, they usually don't. On the whole, good information is more likely to be produced by groups than by individuals. As Sunstein writes, "the great advantage of aggregated information is that, most of the time, it is stunningly accurate."[3]

Of course, certain conditions apply. *If* we use majority rule and *if* the individuals in the group are likely to get the right answer at least 51 percent of the time, then groups can be relied upon to converge on the truth. The miracle that coordinates this is called the Condorcet Jury Theorem and, even though many people find it confusing, it is actually based on a fairly simple insight from statistics.

> Suppose ... that there is a three-person group in which each member has a 67 percent probability of being right. The probability that a majority vote will produce the correct answer is 74 percent. As the size of the group increases, this probability increases too. ... If group members are 80 percent likely to be right individually, and if the group contains ten or more people, the probability of a correct answer by the majority is overwhelmingly high—very close to 100 percent.[4]

Such an effect is quite common, with perhaps the most accessible example being the "ask the audience" lifeline on the TV show "Who Wants to Be a Millionaire?" If the question at issue is something that the average person would probably know—even though the contestant may not—it is highly likely that a poll of the audience will reveal the correct answer. In fact (as anyone who watches the show can attest), it is often the case that the audience will know the answer to a question even when an "expert" does not.[5] The trick on the show, therefore, is not just having good general knowledge, but knowing when to use which lifeline, the other two being "phone a friend" (where you can call your own expert) and "fifty/fifty" (which eliminates two wrong answers). Don't some members of the audience get the answer wrong? Yes, but as long as the group is large enough (and the errors are random) these will be smoothed out.

This simple observation on the power of aggregated knowledge has big implications for how to find the truth. It suggests that despite the sort of individual reasoning errors we saw in Chapter 2, there are mechanisms that we can embrace to try to overcome these and nonetheless use human reason to arrive at true knowledge. One mechanism is simply the power of the group itself. As Sunstein notes, there is something to the "wisdom of crowds"; the aggregation of human knowledge is usually more reliable than any given member of a group. But another possible mechanism is something that normally, though not always, happens within a group and that is openness to new ideas and the critique of old ones. Here we are not talking, of course, about anything like "ask the audience," for, on the show (and in real-life polls), individuals are not allowed to talk to one another. But what might happen if they do?

Recall here Mercier and Sperber's mention of the "freakish" individuals who were able to critique their own ideas and overcome their own erroneous cognitive tendencies? This is rare. Most of us need a group to do this. But if we are open to the ideas of others, and use their feedback to sharpen our own ideas, we can improve our ability to find the truth, despite our individual cognitive limitations. Mercier and Sperber themselves noted an experiment where the members of a group were able to solve a logic puzzle that no individual member of the group could solve. This is best understood as a synergistic effect, where it is not a mere aggregation of the group's knowledge that improves accuracy (surely a poll wouldn't have worked), but the interaction between members of the group itself.

Of course neither effect is guaranteed. Both the aggregation and synergistic effects of a group's search for knowledge can be undermined by various factors. As Sunstein notes, groups can fail if they are too hierarchical and there is too much deference to authority. Pressure to conform can easily quash the beneficial effect of the wisdom of crowds.[6] For a group to work, individuals must have the freedom to offer their own views and to make and receive criticism from others. If there is "group think," it just won't work to aggregate the opinions of the members of a group, because they will all think the same, usually out of deference to the group's leader. In the US military, for instance, "ask the audience" might well become "ask the General." If there is deference to authority, synergistic effects are threatened. If people regard criticism not as helpful, but rather as a negative result that undermines the team, they will be afraid to say what they know, even if they are pretty sure that the leaders of the group are wrong. In such situations, groups may indeed amplify the foibles of individual reasoning and truth will suffer.

An example of just this effect was explored earlier in this book, when we examined how NASA's culture of conformity and pressure to discount risk may have contributed to the explosion of the space shuttle *Challenger*.[7] But this is nothing new. After the disastrous Bay of Pigs invasion of Cuba, President Kennedy lamented that all of his generals had given him the same advice to invade, one after another, even though they later expressed private disagreement. The following year, during the Cuban missile crisis, Kennedy designated his brother Robert, the attorney general, to play "devil's advocate" in every meeting, so that he could break up facile consensus.[8] Sometimes leaders (and the rest of us) live in what Sunstein calls an "information cocoon," where we listen only to like-minded people or hear information that is favorable to our point of view.⁹ When this happens, the consequences for the discovery of truth are dire:

> As a result. ... groups often fall prey to a series of problems. They do not correct but instead amplify individual errors. They emphasize information held by all or most at the expense of information held by a few or one. They fall victim to bandwagon or cascade effects. They end up in a more extreme position in line with the predeliberation tendencies of their members.¹⁰

But there is a way to overcome this. One of the best, in fact, was instituted in that most hierarchical of groups: the US military. Before he was supreme military commander of the US wars in Iraq and Afghanistan (and later director of the CIA), General David Petraeus was at the forefront of a new paradigm in military education, which emphasized that soldiers must be taught not only how to fight but also how to think. Before going to the Middle East, Petraeus (who has a PhD in international relations from Princeton University), was one of a group of military leaders who came up with an innovative pilot program for the education of military officers that was instituted at Fort Leavenworth, Kansas. Concerned about the problem of "group think" that is so easily absorbed in the hierarchical and team-oriented atmosphere of military units, Petraeus advocated for what he called a "designated skeptic" in every outfit; someone whose job it was to question others' decisions, who could not be criticized for pointing out a flaw in strategy or failing to go along with the group's plan. The ability to be flexible in one's thinking and to seek out the truth in ambiguous situations, Petraeus argued, are key to success both on and off the battlefield. According to Petraeus, "the truth is not found in any one school of thought, and arguably it's found in discussion among them. This is a flexibility of mind that really helps you when you are in ambiguous, tough situations."¹¹

Of course, even with such safeguards in place, a group can still fail to discover the truth or even outperform its individual members. Recall the problem of needing to guarantee that the individuals in a group would know enough to get to the 51 percent level? When this is violated it can lead to something that Sunstein calls the "dark side" of the Condorcet Jury Theorem, which is that groups can amplify not just truth but falsehood. When individuals in a group are *less* than 50 percent likely to have the right answer, the statistical magic of the group dynamic will converge on *falsehood* rather than truth.¹²

In such situations, we should instead seek out information from experts. For instance, when one is dealing with technical topics, if we care about reaching truth it probably should *not* be open to everyone to offer an opinion. Yet the Condorcet Jury logic works for experts too; groups of experts (who presumably have a greater than 51 percent chance of getting the right answer) outperform individual experts. Of course, there is always the problem of how to determine *when* one needs an expert in the first place (not to mention how to determine who is an expert). One needs to think in advance about whether the problem at issue is something that a layperson would be in a position to know ("How many US Presidents have there been?") or not ("What is the best way to stop O-ring leakage during a space shuttle launch?"). It is easy to see how "ask the audience" wouldn't be helpful—and may even be counterproductive—in the latter situation.[13]

The general principle here seems to be the same whether one is talking about groups of individuals or groups of experts: a group will probably converge on the truth faster than its individual members. But there is still a further question, which is whether an *interactive* group (what Sunstein calls a "deliberative group") will generally outperform the aggregate knowledge of a group that is non-interactive. Sunstein reviews three possible reasons that it *might*:

> (1) In groups, someone will know the answer. ("Truth wins.")
> (2) In groups, knowledge is aggregated: the whole is equal to the sum of its parts. (Even if there is no interaction, a group will still do better than an individual, due to the "ask the audience" effect.)
> (3) In groups, there are potential synergistic effects: the whole is *more* than the sum of its parts. (We learn from one another and make our ideas better.)[14]

But there are no guarantees. In fact, there is ample room for pessimism. Due to all of the problems of deference to authority and undue influence that we have already seen, a deliberative group may magnify error rather than truth. Unless certain conditions are met, one cannot conclude that an interactive group will do any better than an aggregate of group knowledge that was taken before deliberations began, and in fact it may do worse. First, the true belief must have some initial support, to prevent the "cascade effect" of the first person who speaks influencing all of the others to accept an erroneous view (especially if that person is an authority figure). Second, the belief at issue must have a demonstrably correct answer, that everyone in the group can understand once it has been discovered (this is sometimes called the "eureka effect").[15]

It is intriguing to note that the latter observation fits perfectly with Mercier and Sperber's earlier example, where a group solved a logic problem only after talking about it. On their own none of the subjects could do it, but once they worked together they could. Why? Mercier and Sperber dismiss Sunstein's "smartest person in the room" hypothesis (though they too seem fond of the phrase "truth wins") for good reason: none of the subjects individually could solve the puzzle. They would probably also dismiss the "aggregate knowledge" hypothesis, because the solution that the group arrived at was definitely more than just the average (wrong) answer of the group. So was it due to synergistic effects? Likely yes, but note that this may only be because this example meets both of Sunstein's criteria for synergistic effects to trump aggregate ones: there was apparently no "leader" in the group to defer to and, since it was a logic puzzle, there must have been a eureka effect once it was solved. As Sunstein notes, when these conditions are met, "a deliberating group will converge on the truth, and outperform statistical groups."[16]

But now things are quite complicated! It is an aggravation of reading Sunstein's book that he often says something in one place, then appears to take it back in another. On page 55 he writes "some of the time, deliberation will create a process of synergy or learning, spurring creativity and producing an outcome that is far better than a mere aggregation of preexisting knowledge. In fact, groups sometimes do outperform their best members, in a way that suggests that synergy is involved." By the time we get to page 84, however, he says this: "In a key study, deliberating groups would have lost *nothing* in terms of accuracy if they had simply averaged the judgments of the people involved—a clear finding that deliberation may not improve on the judgments of statistical groups." Okay, so which is it? Could both be true? Of course the answer is yes. By using strategic qualifiers such as "sometimes" and "may" the case is covered both ways. So what are we to conclude about the prospects for relying on group knowledge to help us to discover the truth?

There are three key claims to keep track of:

(1) That groups outperform individuals.
(2) That experts outperform laypeople.
(3) That interactive (deliberative) groups outperform aggregates.

The limiting conditions that Sunstein has applied throughout his analysis here make their pay-off. (1) Do groups outperform individuals? Yes, if we use majority rule and the members of the group are at least 51 percent likely to know the right answer. (2) Is expert opinion more reliable than that of laypeople? Yes, if one is talking about technical subjects, where the experts are at least 51 percent likely to know the right answer, but the general public is not. (3) But now we come to the biggest question, which goes to the heart of why groups outperform individuals in the first place: is this due to the wisdom-of-crowds effect, where group knowledge is merely aggregated, or is it due to some sort of synergistic effect, where interactions between the members of the group improve the group's overall knowledge? Either, of course, could explain why groups outperform individuals, but what we really want to know is *whether interactive groups outperform non-interactive ones*.

It is at this point that Sunstein throws a pot of cold water on any enthusiasm that may have built up for the potential benefits of synergy. He writes, "unfortunately, there is no clear evidence that deliberating groups eliminate the effects of [individual] heuristics and biases. ... In fact, individual errors are not merely replicated but are actually amplified in group decisions. ... "[17] Then he makes it worse:

> Unfortunately, there is no systematic evidence that deliberating groups do well by any ... baseline ... (1) it cannot be shown that deliberating groups generally arrive at the truth. As we shall see, the truth is likely to win only

> when the correct view has a lot of support within the group [and] the correct answer, once announced, is clearly right, and appears clearly right to everyone. (2) Much of the time, deliberating groups do quite poorly at aggregating the information that their members have. ... Relevant knowledge is often ignored or downplayed. ... (3) Deliberating groups sometimes outperform statistical groups, but sometimes the opposite is the case. When individuals show a strong bias or a clear tendency toward error, deliberating groups often show a greater bias and hence a greater tendency toward error. ... In tasks where the right answer cannot easily be shown to be correct, groups tend to be *more* biased than individuals.[18]

Is there any hope? Actually, there is quite a lot. Despite the problems that Sunstein identifies here and in the rest of his book regarding the potentially truth-killing effects of caving in to social pressure to conform, relying on those who have spoken before us or those who are in authority to be right, failing to elicit hidden knowledge that others in the group may be reluctant to share, and polarization or hardening of one's views once we have found that they are shared by others, these are all problems that can be remedied by attending to a series of "best practices" in group dynamics that Sunstein outlines at the end of his book. Of course, where one is merely aggregating group opinion, some of the problems above melt away; if we do not know what others think, how can we be influenced negatively by them? But if one is hoping to encourage more interactive groups in order to capitalize on the synergistic effect, aren't there some remedies we can try? Yes, and the hopeful news is that these are potentially high reward, for *if* we can meet the conditions to make an interactive group successful, it has the potential to be the best of all possible ways to arrive at the truth.

In a chapter entitled "Implications and Reforms," Sunstein makes the following series of recommendations, all of which are consistent with a general principle of openness: "*Groups should take firm steps to increase the likelihood that people will disclose what they know.*"[19]

(1) Groups should regard "dissent as an obligation."
(2) Critical thinking should be prized.
(3) Group success should be rewarded.
(4) Whistleblowers should be celebrated.
(5) Leaders of groups should indicate their "willingness and even desire to hear information that is held by one or a few members [who] might otherwise receive little or no attention."[20]
(6) Initial opinions should be stated anonymously.
(7) Devil's advocates should be encouraged.

The problem with groups, Sunstein seems to be saying, is not that they do not possess the relevant information to arrive at truth, but that the group is sometimes structured so that this information never sees the light of day. All of the above recommendations, therefore, seem basically consistent with the idea that *it is the open and free exchange of ideas that occurs in a group that is most valuable in its search for truth.* The aggregation of group knowledge is important, but if a group is structured in the right way, the result of interaction between the members has the potential to be even *more* valuable in the search for truth.

Have we perhaps here arrived at a general theory of how to respect truth? The first principle is to be open to new ideas; to offer and to accept criticism of one's own views and to critique others' as well. One must make all efforts not to live in an information cocoon. The second principle is that the best way for *this* to happen is in a group setting, where ideas are shared and information can flow freely. Can these two principles be reduced to a single slogan? *The best way to respect truth is to pursue the free and open exchange of ideas in a group setting, preferably of knowledgeable people, where one's ideas can be shared and critiqued.*

Conversely, the times when people are most likely to *miss* the truth is when they are not open to new ideas, either because they do not share their views with anyone else (they live in an information cocoon) or because they think that truth is determined by authority (they either bully or defer to others).

In the remainder of this chapter, I will discuss several of the most promising routes to the discovery of truth that seem consonant with this principle: (1) science, (2) philosophy and logic, (3) the democratic flow of information through the Internet, *Wikipedia*, and social media.

Science

What can one say about science that has not already been said? Throughout this book, I have offered the idea that science is perhaps the best way of respecting truth, because it has a built in mechanism for eliminating bias and providing for the correction of error. If one pursues a sophisticated understanding of science (rather than the caricature of "scientific method" that one finds in textbooks) one sees that the standard of insistence on empirical evidence, peer review, and the replication of experiments provides a tonic to disrespect. The distinguishing characteristic of science is not just reliance on empirical evidence, but openness to revision in those theories that are offered to *explain* that evidence. Science is an open process, where results are shared and theories are freely criticized. And the only goal is to make one's explanations better: to get them closer to the truth. As such, science proves to be the opposite of ideology, which disrespects truth by trying to substitute wish-fulfillment for facts. In science, we suffer when we try to fool ourselves into thinking that something is true when it is not. This is why there is no role for ideology in science. It is also why there is no such thing as left-wing science or right-wing science. As we learned from the example of Freeman Dyson, science has no heretics. The "group" may be crucial for the vetting of scientific ideas but, except for cases of fraud, there should be no excommunication.

Here once again it is fruitful to circle back to Mercier and Sperber. I trust that by now it is clear that I am deeply skeptical of their incredible claim that reason evolved not because it helps us to discover the truth (which would be directly valuable in our struggle for survival), but instead because it makes us better debaters (which would somehow improve our social and reproductive success, whether or not our arguments were true). But they make one important claim near the end of their paper that provides a key confirmation of Sunstein's analysis, while offering a link to science: the notion that truth is most readily arrived at in groups and that this is perhaps what explains the tremendous success of science.

> [R]easoning is responsible for some of the greatest achievements of human thought in the epistemic and moral domains. This is undeniably true, but the achievements involved are all collective and result from interactions over many generations. ... The whole scientific enterprise has always been structured around groups, from the Lincean Academy down to the Large Hadron Collider. ... [I]n group settings, reasoning biases can become a positive force and contribute to a kind of division of cognitive labor. ... By anticipating objections, one may even be able to recognize flaws in one's own hypotheses and go on to revise them.[21]

Mercier and Sperber, of course, are not the first to note that science thrives by critiquing ideas, thus eliciting knowledge that might otherwise be unavailable if it were not for the clash of ideas in an open forum. But are they correct in their claim that the primary reason science is so good at this is because research is done in groups?

We have already said a good deal about the open character of science, but perhaps it is now appropriate to say a bit more about how this is facilitated by it being a public process. As Mercier and Sperber have pointed out, a good deal of science these days is done in groups. Groups, as we have seen, can be an important part of collecting wisdom and arriving at truth, either through the aggregation of individual knowledge or the sharpening of ideas through deliberation. In the search for truth, groups often outperform even the wisest individuals. But does this mean that it is the group itself that explains scientific success? Even if we believe that "groups beat individuals," it is time to ask whether it is the group itself—or the fact that groups are an excellent way of making science an open process—that explains scientific success.

As we learned from Sunstein, groups can have problems and it matters a good deal how they are structured. If a group is too hierarchical or has no mechanism to elicit the small but crucial bits of information that may be held by its fringe members, it will not likely allow one to "anticipat[e] objections [or] recognize flaws in one's own hypotheses and go on to revise them." Fortunately, science *does* have such a mechanism in place, through the democratic nature of peer review and the reward system of being hailed for finding a flaw in someone else's theory. I submit that it is not, therefore, so much the fact that scientific work is done in *groups* as the fact that it is done in *public* that encourages the dissent, criticism, and revision that is the hallmark of science.

It is also important to note that while Mercier and Sperber are correct to note that these days, unlike in the not-too-distant past, a good deal of science *is* "big science" (like the Large Hadron Collider), this could hardly be the distinguishing feature of what makes science an open process, for if it were then what to say about the value of those scientific theories put forward by solo practitioners such as Newton, Darwin, and Einstein in science's storied past? Working in groups is one way of exposing scientific hypotheses to public scrutiny. But there are others. Even if one is working alone, before a scientific hypothesis can be accepted as true, it still must be vetted by the larger scientific community, so that it can be scrutinized for error. Also, it is a central canon of good scientific work that one's data should be shared, so that others can try to replicate one's findings before they are accepted as true. *This* is what makes science open; not the fact that scientists these days often work in groups. No matter their source, scientific ideas are always subject to public scrutiny before they can be accepted as true. Sunstein, Mercier, and Sperber are all right that groups can be an effective way of overcoming individual bias, thus facilitating respect for truth. But they must be used in the right way. It is not just the fact that science is a community effort but that it is an *open and critical* community effort that makes it effective.

Knowing this, is it now possible to try to identify further "sources of hope" for respecting truth by trying to grow science in those remaining areas of human ignorance, by creating a culture of openness and critique? Surely one fruitful area for such growth might be the social sciences, where we still have a comparatively shallow understanding of human behavior, contradicting theories, inconsistent use of empirical methods, lack of a culture of data sharing and the replication of experiments, and widespread infection with ideology.[22] Here I return to an earlier idea: that there should be no clear division between the methods of natural and social science, insofar as both are intended to discover the truth about their respective (empirical) subject matter by studying the causal relations within it. I am happy to report that there has been some progress along these lines in recent years, yet there remains some unfortunate (mostly ideological) controversy, even within social science itself. A stubborn few continue to resist the idea that we can have a science of human behavior, because they are afraid of the results that it might turn up and the potential consequences for human autonomy. Others cloak their objections in the language of concern about the particular methodological challenges of studying human behavior, even though these are easily refuted.[23] Good work nonetheless continues to be done (one such example—Roland Fryer's work on education—will be discussed in the next chapter). But, if we are committed to the idea that there is truth to be discovered, not just about nature but also about *human* nature, we cannot just wait for such work to be done. As we've seen through the creationist attacks on Darwin's theory of evolution and the political attacks on global warming, even the best scientific work must be defended. And certainly one must try to create an environment of respect for truth if we expect the scientific process to flourish. If we want to see more credible theories in the social sciences then we must commit ourselves to creating a culture of respect for truth *in the social sciences* even as we defend that culture from the ideological zealots who would attack it in the natural sciences.

It is easy to stand up for science when all we have to do is talk about the past victories of Galileo and Darwin. But under today's assault on science—from the right and from the left—one has to be prepared to defend not only the achievements of the past, but also those of evolutionary psychology, behavioral economics, and even behavioral genetics as well. Those fields may turn up no good results or someday dissolve in a puff of methodological smoke, but unless one is willing to say that they have a right to make their hypotheses and have them tested by the same rigorous public procedures that are used throughout science, one has no business calling oneself an advocate of science who respects the procedures that lead to truth. If science is one of the best ways of respecting truth, it must be championed wherever we may use it, even when it turns up truths that make us uncomfortable. That is the risk of openness.

Philosophy and Logic

Although science may be an exemplar for how to respect truth, it is not the only way to do so, which is fortunate since not all truths are empirical. What can one say about those areas of inquiry where one cannot rely on data or experiment, but there is still truth to be had?

It is sometimes lamented by philosophers that what makes philosophy so difficult is that they are left by attrition with all of the hardest problems. At one time psychology, medicine, and even physics were all part of philosophy, before they proved subject to empirical methods. But when a field becomes ripe for scientific investigation, it goes out on its own and takes the empirical topics with it, leaving philosophy to ponder the mystifying leftovers: What is causation? How can I know what is ethical? Is a scientific theory valuable only if it reduces to some more basic theory?

There may be no good proof procedures (or concrete evidence) to answer these questions, but at the very least one can make sure that one's thinking is consistent and does not violate the norms of good reasoning. Cognitive bias and wishful thinking are as much of a threat to philosophical truth as they are to scientific truth, and it is important to have some method to combat them. Enter logic.

Logic is largely known in the academy these days by the buzz word "critical thinking," which college deans love to talk about, even if they cannot always define it. But the backbone of this is surely the good old-fashioned topic of symbolic logic, that scares the hell out of legions of students, due to its stringently clear standards for good reasoning. It may seem funny to admit that logicians themselves are not so often concerned with "truth" as they are with "validity," but it is nonetheless true that one of the best ways to respect truth is to make sure that you are not making a logical mistake in reasoning.

Examples of bad logic abound in everyday life. The politician who attacks a "slippery slope" argument when it is used to defend late-term abortion, who then turns around and uses an identical argument against banning assault weapons. The TV commentator who does not understand the difference between saying "all socialists are liberals" and "all liberals are socialists." But perhaps the most distressing examples come from scientists themselves, who sometimes base an entire research program on a logical misunderstanding. Remember Mahzarin Banaji's confusion when saying "racists' ears don't get hot"? The point here wasn't that if you are a racist you don't care how you do on the IAT, it's that if you are *not* a racist you *do* care, and this might in turn affect your performance.

Logic demonstrates respect for truth by adhering to widely held community standards for what constitutes good reasoning and what does not. There are proof procedures to check what one says. There are methods for adjudicating disputes, even when they are not empirical. Do these take place in groups? Sometimes. But just as in science, the point is not where one is when one has the "eureka" moment of solving a logical puzzle or finding a logical flaw in someone's argument. It is that, like science, logic is based on an undisputed public set of rules and procedures by which others may critique and reject our work.

Another important contribution that philosophy can make to the search for truth is championing the role of doubt. Doubt, it is sometimes thought by laypeople, is just the opposite of knowledge. It is when one cannot reach the truth due to uncertainty. But this is a misunderstanding of what it means to doubt, borne of failure to appreciate Socrates's wisdom that the enemy of knowledge is often not falsehood or even ignorance, but false belief. When one is skeptical, that is when one will examine one's beliefs more closely, try to find a flaw and root out any error. Uncertainty is not an enemy of truth; it is often the best means of finding it.

Perhaps the best example of the powerful role of doubt goes back to Descartes, who sought wisdom by questioning each of his beliefs one by one, until he was left with something so foundational that he could not doubt it. Of course, one may quarrel with the result of Descartes's search (and many have), but the *method* seems fruitful. In order to find truth, one must first clear the field of any falsehoods, superstitions, and lies that one has told oneself, to prepare the way for truth.

But isn't this precisely what the "skeptics" on climate change take themselves to be doing, when they argue that scientific knowledge is too uncertain to justify the conclusion that global warming is occurring as a result of human activity? While it is true that doubt can play an important role in the discovery of truth for both empirical and non-empirical topics, it is important to understand that when one is dealing with scientific evidence there will *always* be a degree of uncertainty *even when one has found the truth*. Science is not logic. There is no empirical proof of validity that just cannot be quarreled with. Instead, science must rely on the preponderance of evidence, which is the best indicator of the direction of truth. Does this mean that science can never make a mistake? Of course not. A deductively valid syllogism in logic is valid for all time. But in science, we understand that knowledge evolves. Through the critique that scientists make of one another's theories, even good theories may be revised so that they are closer to the truth. Thus does the Ptolemaic theory of the heavens get replaced by the Copernican, which is further revised over the centuries by Kepler, Galileo, and Newton, until our understanding is finally revolutionized by Einstein. The problem with scientific knowledge is that we never know when we have heard the last word. And, technically speaking, any theory—no matter how promising the empirical evidence—could prove to be wrong in the long run.

But this does not mean that doubt should be exploited by those who would use it to stand in the way of scientific progress. It is one thing to have actual doubts about the truth of a scientific theory, based on some anomaly that it cannot explain or prediction that it did not get quite right.[24] And the answer in this case is to try to come up with a better theory. It is quite another thing to counsel blanket rejection of a scientific theory that one hopes is not true, based merely on commitment to a competing ideology, for which there is no evidence. Doubt, when it is used in the right spirit, can be an effective tool in the search for truth. But when it is misused as a shield for one's prejudices, doubt can make a mockery of the search for truth.

Unlike ideology, true philosophical skepticism is respectful of the search for truth.

The Internet, *Wikipedia*, and Social Media

In the modern age, there are many possible examples that one could pursue to make the point about how new media enable the sort of open exchange of information that has the best chance of discovering truth. In his book *Infotopia*, Sunstein talks about prediction markets, open source software, blogs, and wikis as methods that demonstrate the powerful effects of aggregation and synergy. The Internet, of course, is the source that makes all of this possible and it is easy to appreciate its beneficial effect of eliciting hidden information and allowing many eyes to scrutinize it. One might think of the Internet as the biggest "ask the audience" lifeline that has ever been invented.

But there is a downside. For even as the Internet democratizes the flow of information that enables "many minds to produce knowledge" it also suffers from the removal of gatekeepers who can vet that information, so that misunderstandings—and worse—can proliferate. Recall the problems that can occur when the mainstream media decides to present two sides to every story, no matter how ludicrous one might be? The Internet has that problem on steroids.

Naomi Oreskes and Erik M. Conway write:

> With the rise of radio, television, and now the Internet, it sometimes seems that anyone can have their opinion heard, quoted, and repeated, whether it is true or false, sensible or ridiculous, fair-minded or malicious. The Internet has created an information hall of mirrors, where any claim, no matter how preposterous, can be multiplied indefinitely. And on the Internet disinformation never dies. "Electronic barbarism" one commentator has called it—an environment that is all sail and no anchor. Pluralism run amok.[25]

It is a terrible cliche to say that the Internet "cuts two ways," but it does. Falsehood as well as truth can be digitally disseminated at lightning speed. So what can we do about it?

The problems with the Internet are well known. In fact, they are so widely known that one might suspect that it would be all but impossible to have an honest exchange of information in a public forum, which capitalizes on the wisdom-of-crowds effect to produce new information, without being swamped by a tidal wave of disinformation. But that would be wrong. Below I will examine two final "sources of hope" that, like science, may capitalize on the virtues of openness and interaction in working toward the identification and dissemination of truth: *Wikipedia* and social media.

Although it is far from perfect, *Wikipedia* is one of the greatest successes of crowd sourcing that has ever been created. Since its founding in 2001, *Wikipedia* has been expanding at a furious rate, in hopes of reaching its goal "to distribute a free encyclopedia to every single person on the planet in their own language." Until recently, *Wikipedia*'s growth had been exponential. Up until 2007, Wikipedians were adding 2,200 new articles every day; the English language version hit 2 million articles in 2007, then 3 million in August 2009.[26] At present, it is the largest compilation of knowledge ever created. Indeed, some would say that *Wikipedia*'s success is part of what put the print edition of *Encyclopedia Britannica* out of business in 2012.

Unlike traditional encyclopedias, however, *Wikipedia* is based entirely on volunteer effort and was created by thousands of users who are free to create articles and add and correct information with no process of peer review or vetting by experts. Capitalizing on the wisdom-of-crowds effect—and a spirit of good will—*Wikipedia* succeeded even in the face of dire predictions that a knowledge source based on volunteers would be rife with errors and held hostage to those with an agenda. What actually happened, however, is that the many eyes looking at each entry soon sniffed out error and bias, resulting in a knowledge source that is astonishingly reliable, for what it is.

Sunstein comments:

> It is an understatement to say that Wikipedia generally works. In terms of sheer volume, it dwarfs the *Encyclopedia Britannica*. The number of articles is

extraordinary. True, the quality does not always match the quantity; you can easily find articles that are thin or amateurish or that contain significant omissions and errors. But for the most part, the quality tends to be high as well.[27]

As with science, one might attribute Wikipedia's success to the idea that mass scrutiny of errors in an open forum is a powerful way to create knowledge, and may even be the best way to reach toward truth.

Are there problems with *Wikipedia*? Certainly. Not only are there errors in some of the articles—due to ignorance—but there is also the problem of hackers (sometimes called "wreckers") or partisans, who deliberately try to sabotage articles for sport or self-benefit. In one of the most famous cases, an entry on the journalist John Seigenthaler claimed (for four months in 2005) that he had been involved in the assassination of both John and Robert Kennedy.[28] For the most part, such errors or hacks are dealt with by the "many-eyes" method, but as this example demonstrates, problems can still slip through. Because of this, *Wikipedia* has over the years instituted some measure of quality control, such as flagging material that seems biased or controversial, moving matters of opinion to discussion pages, putting new edits on a "recent changes" page that is reviewed by many people before being added, and imposing a layer of editorial control on articles about living people.[29] Although *Wikipedia* is shaped significantly by the approximately 1,000 editors who are most active on the site, it still relies heavily on the millions of daily users to point out and correct error. This is to say that the main weapon *Wikipedia* has against error is that there are more people who are rooting for and working toward its success than those who abuse it. As it says on the site "we assume that the world is full of reasonable people and that collectively they can arrive eventually at a reasonable conclusion, despite the worst efforts of a very few wreckers."[30] As Sunstein himself comments, "Wikipedia works because those who know the truth, or something close to it, are usually more numerous and more committed than those who believe in a falsehood."[31]

Openness works. Groups beat individuals. Truth wins.

Naturally, there are lingering criticisms. First, some have claimed that *Wikipedia* itself is biased. Indeed a rival site "*Conservapedia*" has been created to challenge what it claims is liberal bias in a number of articles on *Wikipedia*. In a 2012 study Greenstein and Zhu examined the use of traditionally "democratic" and "republican" phrases and found some bias, especially in the articles written in early years. Over time, however, *Wikipedia* has mitigated this bias, through the addition of counterbalancing articles.[32] A more stinging criticism, perhaps, is that over time *Wikipedia* has gotten more bureaucratic and its cadre of primary editors have begun to institute more stringent quality controls, which has scared off new participants. Indeed, some have claimed that this is why *Wikipedia*'s growth has flattened in recent years, as new volunteers become fed up with too much editorial control.[33] Others, however, have said that this simply reflects the long-expected natural limit to growth as *Wikipedia* has neared its goal of creating an article on every topic. And, even if increased editorial control *has* been responsible for some limits, one might argue that this is much needed and expected in any institution that has gained a certain amount of credibility. Science, after all, is also a largely democratic process, but it does not proceed without layers of review by experts to assure a level of quality control. Even science, after all, is expected to police itself for fraud.

And as *Wikipedia* gains more credibility over time, it is not surprising that, like science, it would be subject to hijack by those who wish to advance their own ideological agenda. Many eyes may be sufficient to fend off isolated hackers and charlatans, but what should one do when there is a relentless campaign to control what the public might read about a religion? In 2009, *Wikipedia* barred online edits from computer addresses that were "owned or operated by the Church of Scientology or its associates." Should they be blamed for defending themselves? Just as science suffers at the hands of those who wish to exploit its open process in service of their own ideological agenda, so *Wikipedia* may be exploited. Merely to give up and let the charlatans destroy what a collective has built is not required by openness nor is it wise. Sometimes defending oneself is a legitimate way of respecting truth.

The rise of social media and its relationship to truth is an enormous topic that could itself fill an entire book. Like *Wikipedia*, social media provide ample opportunities for crowd sourcing and sharing information, but they also enable the spread of disinformation as well. As with so many things on the Internet, it really does cut both ways. Now, however, I would like to focus on whether, despite their potential drawbacks, social media sites such as Twitter, Facebook, and YouTube might provide another "source of hope" for respecting truth in coming years. Indeed, it has arguably already begun.

In the 2011 "Arab Spring" uprisings in Egypt and Tunisia, social media played a crucial role. Given the widespread saturation of social media in those two countries they were "fertile ground for an Internet-enabled uprising."[34] According to Madeline Storck:

> 94% of Tunisians get their news from social media tools, as do 88% of Egyptians. Both countries also relied the least on state-sponsored media for their information (at 40% and 36% of people in Tunisia and Egypt respectively). Equally noteworthy, in Egypt there are now more users of Facebook than there are subscribers to newspapers.[35]

Given this, when the uprisings started, government attempts at censorship were no match for the "truth" that was being shared moment by moment on millions of smart phones. Pictures of demonstrations and violence were capable of being shared with the world in real time, thwarting lies propagated through newspapers and television that were controlled by the government. As one anonymous

Egyptian activist put it: "We use Facebook to schedule the protests, Twitter to coordinate, and YouTube to tell the world."[36]

Some have disputed the idea that social media "caused" the Arab revolution, claiming that revolutions happened before there was social media, so how could they have been that important?[37] But this seems a bit like claiming that wars were fought before the atomic bomb, so how could this have explained the Japanese surrender in 1945? Of course, such claims are impossible to test one way or the other; a revolution cannot be rerun without smart phones to see how it might have come out. Even so, it is obvious that even if the role of social media in *causing* the Arab Spring uprisings has been overblown, they did in fact play an important role in getting the news out to a world that might otherwise have been forced to rely on less immediate sources.

By now this is a familiar story. The openness and widespread availability of social media enables the sort of information dissemination that is crucial to keep from living in an information cocoon that is so destructive of learning the truth. Yes, social media can also be used to spread lies and disinformation. (In an attempt to get ahead of the protestors, at one point the Mubarak regime ordered mobile service providers to send text messages rallying his supporters).[38] But, just as with *Wikipedia*'s response to "wreckers" or scientists' reaction to those who present fraudulent research, there are ways to dampen such effects, if there are more people who respect truth than those who wish to subvert it.

And the reach of social media will likely grow in future years. As President Bill Clinton noted in a recent article outlining "The Case for Optimism" in the world, "phones mean freedom. ... only 4% of households in Africa have Internet access, but more than 50% have cell phones."[39] As more and more of the world's population is able to access sources like *Wikipedia*, Twitter, Facebook, and *You-Tube* on their smart phones, what more opportunities might we have for sharing knowledge openly, capitalizing on the benefits of crowd sourcing and the democratic flow of information, in the interests of respecting truth?

Conclusion

There are surely further topics that could be covered in search of more sources of hope to fight against disrespect for truth, but the general principles by now are clear. Community scrutiny is the best way to combat error, ideology, and disinformation, because mistakes are less likely to remain unchallenged when they are made in public. Sometimes one must rely on expert knowledge or overt rules to accomplish this; other times a YouTube video of a burning car is enough. Those who would disrespect truth may be legion, but just as we have seen at the individual level, we can *choose* those cognitive habits and procedures that lead to truth, and be reinforced in this choice by the community of truth-seekers around us. The barriers to truth are within our power to overcome. For in an open forum—with many eyes watching—falsehood is no match for inquiry, and lies are no match for a group of committed individuals who just want to know the truth.

Notes

1 Of course, perhaps one reason for this is that we have largely the same brains as our ancestors and suffer from the same cognitive biases. But we can *train* ourselves to improve at recognizing and overcoming bias. For more here see Kahneman's *Thinking Fast and Slow*.
2 Cass Sunstein, *Infotopia: How Many Minds Produce Knowledge* (Oxford: Oxford University Press, 2006).
3 Ibid., 10.
4 Ibid., 26.
5 Ibid., 32.
6 Sunstein outlines two routes for this: (1) "informational influences," where members think "I must be wrong since these other people seem so sure" and (2) "social pressures" where they think "I know I'm right, but I'd better keep my mouth shut" (ibid., 14).
7 Unfortunately, some seventeen years later there was another disaster when the space shuttle *Columbia* broke apart upon re-entry and some of the same communication and cultural criticisms were made about NASA.
8 Sunstein, *Infotopia*, 211.
9 Ibid., 9.
10 Ibid., 14.
11 Julian Barnes, "An open mind for a new army," *US News and World Report*, October 31, 2005.
12 Sunstein, *Infotopia*, 28.
13 Also, there is of course the problem of what to do when there is no way to know if even the *experts* are likely to be right. (The example of string theory comes to mind.)
14 Ibid., 52–55.
15 Ibid., 63.
16 Ibid., 63.
17 Ibid., 78.
18 Ibid., 57–58.
19 Ibid., 201 (emphasis in original).
20 Ibid., 207.
21 Mercier and Sperber, "Why Do Humans Reason? Arguments for an Argumentative Theory," *Behavioral and Brain Sciences* 34, no. 2 (2011): 57–111, at 72–73.
22 Is there, perhaps, a linkage between these sins, such as refusing to share data, and bias or even outright fraud in one's results? In a fascinating review of this question entitled "Fraud, Disclosure, and Degrees of Freedom in Science," Robert Trivers explores several studies in psychology which show that a shockingly high percentage of psychologists did not share their data when asked to, even though they publish in journals that require this. In one study a 67 percent non-compliance rate was followed up by analysis of whether those papers were more likely to commit statistical errors. They were, and 96 percent of the mistakes were in the scientists' favor; *Psychology Today*, May 10, 2012, <http://psychologytoday.com/blog/the-folly-fools/201205/fraud-disclosure-and-degrees-freedom-in-science>.
23 Bent Flyvbjerg, *Making Social Science Matter: Why Social Inquiry Fails and How It Can Succeed Again* (Cambridge: Cambridge University Press, 2001).
24 For more on the idea that science proceeds by revolutions based on just such empirical minutae, see Thomas Kuhn's *The Structure of Scientific Revolutions* (Chicago: University of Chicago Press, 1962).

25 Naomi Oreskes and Erik M. Conway, *Merchants of Doubt: How a Handful of Scientists Obscured the Truth on Issues from Tobacco Smoke to Global Warming* (New York: Bloomsbury Press, 2010), 240–41.
26 Farhad Manjoo, "Where Wikipedia ends," *Time*, September 28, 2009, 50.
27 Sunstein, *Infotopia*, 151.
28 Ibid., 156.
29 Manjoo, "Where Wikipedia ends," 50.
30 Quoted from Sunstein, *Infotopia*, 153.
31 Ibid., 154.
32 S. Greenstein and F. Zhu, "Is Wikipedia Biased?" *American Economic Review* (May 2012).
33 Manjoo, "Where Wikipedia ends," 51.
34 Colin Delany, "How social media accelerated Tunisia's revolution: An inside view," *Huffington Post*, February 10, 2011.
35 "The Role of Social Media in Political Mobilisation: A Case Study of the January 2011 Egyptian Uprising," MA dissertation, University of St. Andrews, December 2011, pp. 5–6.
36 Ibid., 4.
37 Peter Beaumont, "The truth about Twitter, Facebook, and the uprisings in the Arab world," *Guardian* (London), February 24, 2011.
38 Ibid., 5.
39 *Time*, October 1, 2012.

7

A MORE REASONABLE WORLD

Better Living Through Empirical Social Science

> When people look back at our time, they will be amazed at one thing more than
> any other: that we know more about ourselves now than people did in the past,
> but that very little of it has been put into effect.
>
> Doris Lessing, "When in the Future They Look Back at Us"

In this book, I have argued that although truth may be an elusive goal, we cannot
do without it. It defines who we are and our hopes for the future. It is our
lodestar. Despite the problems and biases that are built into us—or cynically
embraced by those who decide that ideology is more important than reality—few
have given up on the idea of truth. Although we may sometimes treat it brutally,
most of us have a deep-seated commitment to the idea that truth will always be
out there waiting for us, when we are finally ready to embrace it.

But what would the world look like if we took more seriously the idea that
respecting truth should matter *right now*—that although we are not exactly
"wired" to discover truth, we can nonetheless choose to pursue it and use this
knowledge to make the world a better place? Winston Churchill once observed
that "men occasionally stumble over the truth, but most of them pick themselves
up and hurry off as if nothing ever happened." But what if we did a better job of
giving truth the respect it deserves?

Some might argue that this would be a disaster: that the reason we do not
more frequently face the truth is that we do not want to. But the pertinent
question here is not whether facing the truth would make us uncomfortable, but
whether there might be benefits that would outweigh the costs. Below I will
make two proposals for how we might begin to reap the benefits of respecting
truth: first by allowing science to have a more prominent role in influencing
public policy and second by committing ourselves more fully to the pursuit of
empirical social science.

Science and Public Policy

In his 2009 Inaugural Address, President Obama said words that were music to the ears of the nation's scientists: "we will restore science to its rightful place." After eight years of contending with the Bush administration's distortion and manipulation of scientific results to fit its ideological agenda on topics such as stem cells, global warming, and birth control, a new attitude seemed to be emerging. Under President George W. Bush, things had gotten so bad that in 2004, the Union of Concerned Scientists took out full page ads in some of the nation's leading newspapers in which they accused the Bush administration of interference, censorship, and manipulation of scientific results.[1] Ironically, after George W. Bush's *father* had elevated the president's "science advisor" to a cabinet-level post, the younger Bush became notorious for kicking his science advisor out of the White House, making him take up residence in an office down the street.

When Obama took office, things improved somewhat, but there is still too much political influence on policy decisions in which science should have a more determinative role. Although Obama has in John Holdren a well-respected science advisor (indeed a whole Office of Science and Technology Policy), a good deal of policy that comes out of Washington these days is still influenced by members of Congress who have the same benighted view of science that Bush did. Indeed, since the Office of Technology Assessment was dissolved in 1995, *Congress has had no formal mechanism for receiving objective scientific advice.* And, even if Obama continues to say the right things in his speeches, some have criticized him for excessive capitulation to those who disrespect the truth about global warming. Where was the issue of global warming, for instance, on the campaign trail in 2012? Why did Obama open up new territory off the northern coast of Alaska to oil drilling? Why has he offered so much support to shale gas drilling throughout the continental United States? And when is he going to make a decision about the Keystone XL Pipeline?

This is not just a matter of Obama becoming jaded by the politics of Washington; he has always been a political animal. Indeed, at times he has even seemed willing to disrespect science when it suited him. Consider the following statement, taken from a campaign rally in April 2008:

> We've just seen a skyrocketing autism rate. Some people are suspicious that it's connected to the vaccines. … The science right now is inconclusive, but we have to research it.

Remember that this was *four years* after Wakefield's study had been debunked and anyone who was paying attention (and not running for office) should have known better. By December 2008, safely after the election, Obama could afford more high rhetoric:

Today, more than ever before, science holds the key to our survival as a planet and our security and prosperity as a nation. It's time we once again put science at the top of our agenda and worked to restore America's place as the world leader in science and technology. ... [But] science isn't just about providing resources—it's about protecting free and open inquiry. It's about ensuring that facts and evidence are never twisted or obscured by politics or ideology. It's about listening to what our scientists have to say, even when it's inconvenient—especially when it's inconvenient. Because the highest purpose of science is the search for knowledge, truth and a greater understanding of the world around us. That will be my goal as President of the United States.

Welcome as this was, one regrets that the practical effect of this high-flying commitment has not made more of a difference in his presidency. This is not to argue that Obama has done nothing for science or even that he has not done a good deal more than most Presidents. In 2009, Obama lifted the Bush administration's limits on federal funding for stem-cell research. Despite his focus on increasing fossil-fuel energy production, he has also made a solid commitment to the exploration of renewable energy sources. Obama also established long-overdue increased fuel-efficiency standards for new cars and trucks. And he has made a genuine commitment to increasing funding for both basic scientific research and the training of science educators.[2]

Just after inauguration for his second term, Obama announced a proposal to use federal funds for a Brain Activity Map, which may open the door to new therapies for brain diseases in much the same way that the Human Genome Project paved the way for new genetic therapies. These are encouraging developments. Yet what is most needed, perhaps, is a President with the political courage to engage in a full-on frontal assault on the ignorant anti-science views of so many members of Congress, who are holding up federal efforts to combat global warming. Is there really a more pressing scientific commitment during Obama's presidency than to fight against something that may threaten our very existence on this planet? Yes, Obama has instituted a few policies that have advanced the cause of science. But has he really done much to challenge the endemic disrespect for truth that stands behind most of the anti-science ideology in Washington?

Of course, there is also the problem that a good deal of policy in Washington these days falls within the domain not just of natural science but of social science. Immigration, guns, capital punishment—not to mention taxes and job creation—all have deep roots in empirical problems that have been studied by social scientists for decades. Yet (unless it agrees with their ideology) this research is routinely ignored at every level of government. One could argue, of course, that we need better social science before it can be more influential. But, as I hope to show in the next section, there is already some very good social scientific research out there and perhaps it might be the job of a newly created *social science advisor* to help the President (and Congress) pick and choose among social scientific research to find good empirical work that might serve as the foundation for better social policy.[3]

It is unfortunately true that a good deal of social science today is unreliable, due to its infection by political ideology. Even in universities, in some fields there is no clear line between "research" and political advocacy. As such, can one blame politicians in Washington for refusing to rely on the conclusions of social scientists? Actually yes, for this is just the kind of lazy thinking engaged in by those who rationalize their own ideological views by dismissing *everything* as ideological.

As the pro–death penalty Governor of Massachusetts, Mitt Romney had this to say when confronted by a journalist with the fact that there was little evidence to support the view that the death penalty deters crime:

> Studies can show whatever you want them to show. Punishment has an impact on action, and the idea that a more severe punishment would have an impact on action is obvious to even a schoolchild. There's absolutely no question but that the death penalty would reduce a certain number of heinous crimes.[4]

Thus is intuition substituted for empirical study on some of the most important public policy issues throughout our government. And there is a lesson here for social theorists on the left, who may think that the best way to fight against right-wing ideology is with left-wing ideology. Does advocacy research really work? Does it help the people that it is meant most to help? One might argue that what the poor need most in this country is not advocacy rooted in high theory about racism and oppression, but *good empirical data* that will reveal the truth about wealth inequality and ineffective educational policy, which disproportionately affect the poor. What better to combat a wrong ideology than facts? Thus on the subjects of guns, immigration, welfare, affirmative action, housing, education, and a host of other topics, perhaps the best way to make political progress is first to understand that these are *empirical* topics, on which it is possible to gather data that might help to create a more enlightened public policy. Science, of course, cannot tell us what our values should be. But neither should intuition substitute for scientific study. When a topic is empirical, policy is best made in an environment in which we have first faced the truth.

Better Social Science

I have already begun to outline the benefits of a more rigorous understanding of human behavior. Despite our current struggles, it was respect for truth that brought the natural sciences into the modern era, as it did much later for medicine. And it is my conviction that the same could be true right now for the study of human behavior, if only we heed the lessons from natural science.

Some already have.

Roland Fryer is something of a wunderkind in economics. After a youth marked by poverty, racism, and brushes with the law, Fryer says that he finally got serious about school when he started college, accepting an athletic scholarship, then electing not to play in favor of devoting himself to the study of the powerful mathematical tools that would later enable him to study problems like inequality, race, and educational policy that had such an effect on his own life. After graduate school, the bidding war for his talents began, landing Fryer at the prestigious Society of Fellows at Harvard University and later a professorship in the Economics Department there, where he earned tenure at thirty.

Since then, Fryer's research has been nothing short of courageous, using the mathematical techniques of economics to study social problems that other economists seem afraid to touch.

> I take stubborn old questions of racial inequality that have been around for decades and decades and try to use simple mathematics to be able to answer those questions. ... It's a way of taking politics, taking emotion, taking anecdotes out of the study of racial inequality.[5]

And the questions are hot ones: Is black culture a cause or a consequence of racial inequality? Can crack cocaine be blamed for the nationwide decline in black health and economic outcomes in the late 1980s and early 90s? Is color-sighted affirmative action more efficient than color-blind affirmative action? Are black youth faring worse than whites in school because of the social stigma of "acting white"?[6]

As if merely asking these questions were not incendiary enough, Fryer's approach to them is completely empirical. He takes no hypotheses off the table:

> I want to have an honest discussion about race in a time and a place where I don't think we can. ... Blacks and whites are both to blame. As soon as you say something like, "Well, could the black-white test-score gap be genetics?" everybody gets tensed up. But why shouldn't that be on the table?[7]

Attracted to the explanatory power of economics, he decided to use this to study race.

> We learned all these powerful math tools that were very deep, very insightful, and were being used to solve ... silly problems [like corn growth]. ... At the same time you'd look on TV and see people literally yelling at each other about affirmative action, bringing up anecdotal stories of one white guy who lost his house and his wife and his kids. The whole

debate could be turned by bringing in some horrible travesty. And I thought, here's the exact way that these tools should be used.[8]

So what has Fryer found? In one result he found that there *was* such a thing as a stigma for "acting white" but that it could not explain the entire black-white achievement gap, for the simple reason that it could not account for why students in all-black schools still weren't performing well.

In more recent work, Fryer has delved deeper into educational policy, studying whether cash incentives might work to keep kids in school and what might be learned from a rigorous empirical analysis of high-performing charter schools. With sparse data behind some of the more sweeping education proposals in recent years, education seems a ripe area for scientific inquiry. Here Fryer has learned that, in contrast to conventional wisdom, it is not class size or spending per pupil that makes a difference in educational outcome, but instead factors like giving frequent feedback to teachers, using data on individual students to guide their instruction, using tutors, increasing instructional time, and maintaining high expectations.[9] After instituting these reforms in some school districts, the results have been stunning. "In just one year, kids in one of their schools went from 40 percent proficient in math on a standardized test to 85 percent proficient; high school seniors were 50 percent more likely to enroll in a four year college."[10]

Could this example of empirical analysis of a stubborn social problem provide inspiration for work in other fields, where one hopes to replace anecdote and intuition with scientific rigor in order to make better public policy? When one starts to look, examples are everywhere.

April Zeoli's work at Michigan State University has found that public health tracking methods for disease can be used to predict where homicides are most likely to occur in an urban area. Using medical geography to identify homicide "hot spots," researchers hope to enable law enforcement to predict, and therefore possibly prevent, murder. As a corollary of her work, Zeoli has studied some communities in Newark, NJ, that—despite being surrounded by violence—had no homicide clusters over the twenty-six-year period of her study. "If we could discover why some of those communities are resistant," Zeoli said, "we could work on increasing the resistance of our communities that are more susceptible to homicide."[11]

In other work, James Greiner, a law professor at Harvard, decided to use scientific techniques to study another hot-button topic with a political dimension: whether the use of free legal services had an impact on whether a client won his or her case. With a limited budget for legal aid, shouldn't we know which clients were most likely to benefit from such help? But how to study this?

For Greiner, the solution is one that has already revolutionized other fields, most notably medicine. He is part of a budding movement that wants to introduce randomized experiments and put hard numbers to what have traditionally been treated as unquantifiable social problems. In medicine, he and his allies point out, such tests have revealed that once-common treatments—hormone replacement therapy, for instance—were not only ineffective but harmful. "The mission," Greiner said, "is to make law more evidence-based, more rational and scientific."[12]

The preliminary results, done with those clients who were seeking unemployment benefits with the assistance of Harvard's Legal Aid Bureau (HLAB), turned up the surprising result that they were no more likely to win their case than those who had not used HLAB's help. This, of course, caused controversy and the HLAB team quickly distanced itself from Greiner's research and criticized his methodology. His experiments are ongoing, however, with more results to come on divorce, social security disability claims, and federal prisoners who make civil rights complaints.

None of this proves, of course, that all social science needs to do is study something mathematically, and the truth will emerge. It is not that easy in natural science, so why should it be in social science? But the commitment to rigorous empirical analysis is nonetheless the first step toward scientific rigor and an essential part of respecting truth. Surely there will be criticisms of empirical social science, and some of the results will be controversial. But this is as it should be in science. As long as the criticisms and controversies are over *empirical* matters, so that they can be settled by further inquiry rather than degenerating into ideological disputes, all is well. As in natural science, we must understand that even the most rigorous studies will be attacked. When they are attacked not because we are afraid of what they show, but in the interest of trying to replicate their findings and push for better methodology, we will have made progress toward respecting truth.

Conclusion

Truth is neither wired into us, nor are we built always to recognize it when we see it. Truth does not come to us by intuition or by instinct. But we can still *choose* truth, if we want it to be a part of our lives. Truth is valuable not only for its survival value, but for the benefit that it can bring in building better lives for ourselves and our fellow human beings. Evolution is a slow process, which seems ill-suited to the survival of entire populations that may be wiped out by isolated irrationalities involving nuclear weapons, the failure to control pollution, or the outbreak of disease. Instead of relying on our intuition and cognitive reflexes (which are the product of evolution in a less global environment), we have to start thinking not just about our individual survival, but about the good of everyone on this planet. And to do that we have to learn to embrace and respect truth.

As we have seen throughout this book, there are certain strategies that facilitate the search for truth. Working in groups. Embracing openness. Creating an environment in which we can feel free to share our ideas and critique the ideas of others. Some of the best ways of doing this have already been discovered by science, but perhaps there are others as well. But even if the routes to truth are not new, our commitment to them has to be reaffirmed in the face of constant threat by the ideologies and wishful thinking that are often more tempting than truth.

How to deal with those who continue to resist? The best way is to stand up to them and expose their resistance and irrationality for what it is. President Harry Truman was famous for saying, "I don't give 'em hell, I tell 'em the truth and they think it's hell." Critique is valuable, not just for finding truth, but in defending it. We must not be afraid to confront falsehood. Breaking through the bubble of our cognitive limitations and lazy intuitions is tailor-made for science, and it is important that we continue to embrace this, especially when truth is in peril.

Science is fragile and easily attacked by those who are threatened by its conclusions. But progress in human civilization has always been marked by openness to truth. The sort of group openness and critique of ideas that is used in science seems particularly beneficial. But as we've seen, groups can be dangerous too. Groups can help us to converge on the truth, but they can also have a dark side, which is that if a group has bad information it can become an echo chamber for falsehood and may even harden the opinions of those who are mistaken into thinking that they are right.[13] Saddam Hussein attacked us on 9/11. Obama wasn't born in the USA. Global warming is a hoax. Ideology fueled by wishful thinking needs scant evidence to catch fire and incinerate truth.

Information cocoons are dangerous as well, both for individuals and for the group. When we stop getting information from outside sources (or from our interactions with the world), where is the check on our wildest suppositions? When we think that we already know the truth and don't need to investigate any more, that is when truth is most in danger. Socrates taught us long ago that ignorance and error are not nearly as dangerous as the hubris of false knowledge. Whether we are liberal or conservative, no ideology has all of the right answers. The truth is rarely revealed to us in a blinding insight so much as a result of hard thought, critique, and openness to new ideas.

If we want to respect truth, the best way is to break out of our certainties. We should open ourselves to new sources of information and be prepared to critique what we most desperately want to believe. The media can help by exposing liars; universities can help by training us to be better critical thinkers.[14] And, although we've seen that groups can help, we must use them in the right way. There should be no deference to authority and no pressure to silence oneself. Groups work best when there is a true democracy of ideas. Indeed the real insight here is that we must practice openness even *within* groups for them to be effective. We saw in Chapter 3 that individuals suffer from cognitive biases, but we have learned since then that groups can suffer from biases too. Perhaps the analogy to "confirmation bias" at the individual level is "informational influence" at the group level. And perhaps the analogy to "motivated reasoning" at the individual level is "social pressure" at the group level.

So we need to practice openness in our thinking at the individual level (perhaps some are born with it and others can learn it through critical thinking) by trying to overcome our inborn cognitive biases and embracing the search for truth. But we also need to work more at the group level not to rely on others to correct our individual foibles and push to create an environment where we don't defer to experts and silence our criticisms.

Whether it is in a group or as an individual, with science or with some other method, the important thing is that we do not expect truth to come easily or to be congenial, but that we push ourselves to look for it anyway, because we know that it matters. However we get there, the message is the same: there is no method that will substitute for admitting that you do not already know everything and being willing to consider new evidence and entertain new ideas, even if they conflict with what you already believe. Sometimes these new ideas will be wrong, of course, but so might our old ideas too, and we will never learn this unless we are willing to push the limits of what we think we know.

Science has an important role to play in all this, but we must not misunderstand it. There is no recipe that inevitably leads to truth. Indeed what is most distinctive about science is probably not its so-called method, but the open attitude that scientists take toward new evidence and the revision of old theories. If there is a lesson that we can learn from science in the search for truth it is probably this: method is important, but attitude is crucial.

And an open attitude is perhaps the best way of all to respect truth.

Notes

1 See Chris Mooney, *The Republican War on Science* (New York: Basic Books, 2005).
2 "Obama's science report card," *Scientist*, October 1, 2012.
3 It is encouraging that, as discussed earlier in this book, Obama has already introduced some new initiatives, based on Thaler and Sunstein's work from behavioral economics. One might hope for more along these lines, if he had a social science advisor to steer him in the right direction.
4 Karen Olsson, "Death wish," *Boston Globe Magazine*, January 1, 2006, p. 20.
5 Beth Potier, "Applying math to racial issues," *Harvard Gazette*, August 25, 2005.
6 Ibid.
7 Stephen J. Dubner, "Toward a unified theory of Black America," *New York Times*, March 20, 2005.
8 Ibid.
9 Gareth Cook, "Education's coconut cake problem," *Boston Globe*, December 18, 2011.
10 Ibid.
11 "Homicide spreads like infectious disease," press release, Michigan State University, November 29, 2012.
12 Leon Neyfakh, "What we don't know about America's legal safety net," *Boston Globe*, December 23, 2012.

13 Cass Sunstein, *Infotopia: How Many Minds Produce Knowledge* (Oxford: Oxford University Press, 2006), 55.

14 One study recently showed that for a vast percentage of students, critical reasoning skills actually *deteriorate* during college! See Richard Arum and Josipa Roksa, *Academically Adrift: Limited Learning on College Campuses* (Chicago: University of Chicago Press, 2011). See also Sara Rimer, "Study: Many college students not learning to think critically," *McClatchy DC News* [*Hechinger Report*, January 18, 2011], <www.mcclatchydc.com/2011/01/18/106949/study-many-college-students-not.html>.

SELECTED BIBLIOGRAPHY

Ariely, Dan. *Predictably Irrational: The Hidden Forces That Shape Our Decisions.* New York: HarperCollins, 2008.

Banaji, Mahzarin and Anthony Greenwald. *Blindspot: Hidden Biases of Good People.* New York: Delacorte Press, 2013.

Benson, Ophelia and Jeremy Stangroom. *Why Truth Matters.* London: Continuum, 2006.

Blackburn, Simon. *Truth: A Guide.* Oxford: Oxford University Press, 2005.

Boghossian, Paul. *Fear of Knowledge.* Oxford: Oxford University Press, 2006.

Buller, David. *Adapting Minds: Evolutionary Psychology and the Persistent Quest for Human Nature.* Cambridge: MIT Press, 2005.

Dawkins, Richard. *The God Delusion.* New York: Houghton Mifflin, 2006.

——*Climbing Mount Improbable.* New York: Norton, 1997.

Flyvbjerg, Bent. *Making Social Science Matter: Why Social Inquiry Fails and How It Can Succeed Again.* Cambridge: Cambridge University Press, 2001.

Frankfurt, Harry. *On Truth.* New York: Knopf, 2006.

Gaffron, Hans. *Resistance to Knowledge.* San Diego: Salk Institute for Biological Studies, 1970.

Gladwell, Malcolm. *Blink: The Science of Thinking without Thinking.* New York: Little, Brown, 2005.

Gore, Al. *The Assault on Reason.* New York: Penguin, 2007.

Graves, Joseph. *The Race Myth: Why We Pretend Race Exists in America.* New York: Dutton, 2004.

Gross, Paul and Norman Levitt. *Higher Superstition: The Academic Left and Its Quarrels with Science.* Baltimore: Johns Hopkins University Press, 1994.

Gross, Paul, Norman Levitt, and Martin W. Lewis, eds. *The Flight from Science and Reason.* New York: New York Academy of Sciences, 1996.

Hansen, James. *Storms of My Grandchildren.* New York: Bloomsbury, 2009.

Harris, Sam. *Letter to a Christian Nation.* New York: Vintage, 2008.

——*The End of Faith: Religion, Terror, and the Future of Reason.* New York: Norton, 2004.

Henderson, Bobby. *The Gospel of the Flying Spaghetti Monster.* New York: Villard Books, 2006.

Hitchens, Christopher. *god is not Great: How Religion Poisons Everything.* New York: Twelve, 2007.

Hoggan, James and Richard Littlemore. *Climate Cover-Up: The Crusade to Deny Global Warming.* Vancouver: Greystone Books, 2009.

Huffington, Arianna. *Right Is Wrong*. New York: Knopf, 2008.

Iyengar, Sheena. *The Art of Choosing*. New York: Twelve, 2010.

Jacoby, Susan. *The Age of American Unreason*. New York: Pantheon, 2008.

Kahneman, Daniel. *Thinking, Fast and Slow*. New York: Farrar, Straus and Giroux, 2011.

Kahneman, Daniel and Amos Tversky, eds. *Judgment under Uncertainty: Heuristics and Biases*. Cambridge: Cambridge University Press, 1982.

Kamin, Leon, R. C. Lewontin, and Steven Rose. *Not in Our Genes: Biology, Ideology, and Human Nature*. New York: Pantheon, 1984.

Koertge, Noretta, ed. *A House Built on Sand: Exposing Postmodernist Myths about Science*. New York: Oxford University Press, 2000.

Kuhn, Thomas. *The Structure of Scientific Revolutions*. Chicago: University of Chicago Press, 1962.

Levitt, Steven and Stephen Dubner. *Freakonomics: A Rogue Economist Explores the Hidden Side of Everything*. New York: HarperCollins, 2005.

Lynch, Michael. *In Praise of Reason*. Cambridge: MIT Press, 2012.

———*True to Life: Why Truth Matters*. Cambridge: MIT Press, 2004.

McIntyre, Lee. *Dark Ages: The Case for a Science of Human Behavior*. Cambridge: MIT Press, 2006.

———*Laws and Explanation in the Social Sciences: Defending a Science of Human Behavior*. Boulder, CO: Westview Press, 1996.

Mercier, Hugo and Dan Sperber. "Why Do Humans Reason? Arguments for an Argumentative Theory." *Behavioral and Brain Sciences* 34, no. 2 (2011): 57–111.

Mooney, Chris. *The Republican Brain: The Science of Why They Deny Science—and Reality*. Hoboken, NJ: John Wiley & Sons, 2012.

———*The Republican War on Science*. New York: Basic Books, 2005.

Norman, Andrew. "Why We Reason: Intention-Alignment and the Genesis of Human Rationality" (unpublished manuscript).

Oreskes, Naomi and Erik M. Conway. *Merchants of Doubt: How a Handful of Scientists Obscured the Truth on Issues from Tobacco Smoke to Global Warming*. New York: Bloomsbury Press, 2010.

Park, Robert. *Superstition: Belief in the Age of Science*. Princeton: Princeton University Press, 2008.

Parnia, Sam. *Erasing Death: The Science That Is Rewriting the Boundaries between Life and Death*. New York: HarperCollins, 2013.

Pigliucci, Massimo. *Nonsense on Stilts: How to Tell Science from Bunk*. Chicago: University of Chicago Press, 2010.

Pinker, Steven. *The Blank Slate: The Modern Denial of Human Nature*. New York: Viking, 2002.

Popper, Karl. *Conjectures and Refutations*. London: Routledge, 2002.

———*The Logic of Scientific Discovery*. New York: Harper Torchbooks, 1959.

Rosenberg, Alexander. *The Atheist's Guide to Reality: Enjoying Life without Illusions*. New York: Norton, 2011.

Ruse, Michael. *But Is It Science? The Philosophical Question in the Creation/Evolution Controversy*. Amherst, NY: Prometheus Books, 1996.

Sagan, Carl. *The Demon Haunted World: Science as a Candle in the Dark*. New York: Random House, 1995.

Shermer, Michael. *The Believing Brain*. New York: Times Books, 2011.

Specter, Michael. *Denialism: How Irrational Thinking Hinders Scientific Progress, Harms the Planet, and Threatens Our Lives*. New York: Penguin, 2009.

Sunstein, Cass. *Infotopia: How Many Minds Produce Knowledge*. Oxford: Oxford University Press, 2006.

Thaler, Richard and Cass Sunstein. *Nudge: Improving Decisions about Health, Wealth, and Happiness*. New Haven: Yale University Press, 2008.

Trivers, Robert. *The Folly of Fools: The Logic of Deceit and Self-Deception in Human Life*. New York: Basic Books, 2011.

Wilson, Edward. *On Human Nature*. Cambridge: Harvard University Press, 1978.

Wright, Robert. *The Moral Animal: Why We Are the Way We Are: The New Science of Evolutionary Psychology*. New York: Vintage, 1995.

INDEX